FOUR CENTURIES OF WITCH BELIEFS

FOUR CENTURIES OF WITCH BELIEFS
With special reference to the Great Rebellion

R. TREVOR DAVIES

Volume 2

LONDON AND NEW YORK

First published in 1947

This edition first published in 2011
by Routledge
2 Park Square, Milton Park, Abingdon, Oxfordshire OX14 4RN

Simultaneously published in the USA and Canada
by Routledge
711 Third Avenue, New York, NY 10017

First issued in paperback 2016

Routledge is an imprint of the Taylor & Francis Group, an informa business

© Methuen & Co 1947

British Library Cataloguing in Publication Data
A catalogue record for this book is available from the British Library

ISBN 13: 978-1-138-97459-3 (pbk)
ISBN 13: 978-0-415-60419-2 (hbk)

Publisher's Note
The publisher has gone to great lengths to ensure the quality of this reprint but
points out that some imperfections in the original copies may be apparent.

Disclaimer
The publisher has made every effort to trace copyright holders and would
welcome correspondence from those they have been unable to trace.

FOUR CENTURIES OF WITCH-BELIEFS

With special reference to the Great Rebellion

by

R. TREVOR DAVIES

METHUEN & CO. LTD. LONDON
36 Essex Street, Strand, W.C.2

First published in 1947

CATALOGUE No. 3967/U

THIS BOOK IS PRODUCED IN
COMPLETE CONFORMITY WITH THE
AUTHORIZED ECONOMY STANDARDS

PREFACE

THE OBJECT of this volume, as its title implies, is twofold.

It seeks, in the first place, to trace the development and decay of witch-belief in England since the accession of Elizabeth. In so doing it gives especial consideration to the views of the more important writers who either supported or opposed such beliefs; and a special feature is the inclusion of substantial passages from their works. Though such quotations tend sometimes to break the continuity of the discussion, they have two more than compensating advantages. An operative passage in the writer's *ipsissima verba* usually conveys a truer and more vivid notion of his attitude than the best of mere summaries or paraphrases could achieve. Moreover, many of the books quoted are of such exceeding rarity that they can be consulted only in a few of the world's largest libraries. Thus the volume incidentally supplies something that has long been wanting—a brief spicilegium of writers on witchcraft for England such as was supplied for medieval Europe by J. Hansen's excellently assembled *Quellen und Untersuchungen zur Geschichte des Hexenwahns*.

The second and lesser purpose is to throw light upon an obscure area in one of the most important episodes of our national history, viz., the function of witch-beliefs—if indeed they exercised any such function—in provoking that hostility to the earlier Stuarts, which culminated in the Great Rebellion and the establishment of the Commonwealth and Protectorate. Though the writer cannot pretend to have arrived at any hard-and-fast solution of the problem, he has at least done something that is long overdue in calling attention to the existence of such a problem. For where among modern historians of the seventeenth century is even the faintest inkling of it to be found?

The question whether there is, or ever has been, such a thing as genuine witchcraft does not fall within the scope of this book. The writer assumes that the particular witchcraft here considered was pure delusion and superstition. Whether all witchcraft has always been so is a moot point upon which he adventures no opinion: nor is he qualified to do so.

Another question which has been so ably investigated by Miss M. Murray and other writers he also ignores— viz., whether witches were members of a pre-Christian religious body that has survived underground since the Dark Ages.

The researches and discoveries of the past twenty years have produced an unexampled wealth of new information. They have rendered obsolete large portions of even comparatively modern books on English witchcraft. They have made hay of the facile conclusions of such standard historical works as touch upon the subject. They call for a new book. Hence the present attempt to provide one. The bibliography, including as it does the more pertinent Continental, Scottish, and American publications, is somewhat larger than might be expected in a volume of this small compass.

R. TREVOR DAVIES

101 Iffley Road, Oxford
    Jan. 1946

CONTENTS

vii

CHAPTER V

THE ATTEMPTS OF JAMES I AND CHARLES I TO EXTINGUISH WITCH-MANIA (1618-42)

CHAPTER VIII

THE SECOND PERIOD OF THE GREAT WITCH SCARE: 1642–9

CHAPTER IX

OLIVER CROMWELL AND WITCHCRAFT

CHAPTER I

THE GROWTH OF WITCH-MANIA IN EUROPE AT THE END OF THE MIDDLE AGES

§ I. TO READ history backwards and see the issues of the present reproduced in the struggles of the past is a temptation that historians have seldom overcome. In the Victorian Age they saw the Great Rebellion as a rising of Russellite or Gladstonian liberals in defence of democratic institutions, individual liberty, and the rule of law, or as an effort of the Victorian nonconformist conscience to secure the disestablishment of the Church of England. In the early twentieth century historians stole Marxist thunder to denounce the Civil War as a rising of the *bourgeoisie* under the banner of economic individualism against the benevolent collectivism of the Stuarts. At the same time Roman Catholic writers painted the Rebellion as a rising of the grandsons of those who had plundered the Church at the Reformation, in order to guarantee their threatened inheritance by making the country safe for protestantism. In more recent times historians have viewed the Civil War as the transference of power from a weak and irresolute monarchy to a fascist dictatorship.

All these presentations of the history of the Great Rebellion contain much that is valuable—if only as a mental stimulus—and many fragments of truth. But they are, one and all, fundamentally unscientific; because they fail to take account of all the available facts. Facts that have few points of contact with the movements of the historian's day are virtually ignored. They are never allowed to cast their light upon the obscure complex of motives that led men to overthrow the historic monarchy and to become victims of the strongest military despotism this country has ever endured. Of these obscured facts the most important is that the middle of the seventeenth century witnessed the climax of a period of witch-terror the like of which has never been known in this country either before or since. Had this great terror any part in shaping the history of the fall of Charles I and the rise of Cromwell?

One of the objects of the following pages is an attempt to

answer this question. The attempt must begin by tracing the flood of English witch-mania to its source, which was situated upon the continent of Europe.

§ 2. The evolutionary historian would expect to find witch terror at its maximum during the Dark Ages and to perceive a weakening of its influence as the dawn of the so-called Renaissance drew near. Such an expectation suffers swift disappointment.[1] The men of the Early Middle Ages, who had inherited the witch-beliefs of the Græco-Roman World and of the Barbarian invaders, were surprisingly little disturbed by their grim legacy. The Church, as a rule, tended to encourage scepticism about the more sensational claims of superstition. Thus, for example, belief in the Witches Sabbath was denounced as early as the tenth century by the so-called *Canon Episcopi*,[2] which was adopted by the canonists and given enormous authority by being embodied in the successive collections of Regino, Ivo, Gratian, and others. Its scepticism is so striking as to justify a short quotation.

> Some wicked women [it declares] reverting to Satan, and seduced by the illusions and phantasms of demons, believe and profess that they ride at night with Diana on certain beasts with an innumerable multitude of women, passing over immense distances, obeying her commands as their mistress, and evoked by her on certain nights.   It were well if they alone perished in their infidelity and did not draw so many along with them.   For innumerable multitudes, deceived by this false opinion, believe all this to be true, and thus relapse into pagan errors.   Therefore priests everywhere should preach that they know this to be false, and that such phantasms are sent by the Evil Spirit, who deludes them in dreams.   Who is there who is not led out of himself in dreams, seeing much in sleeping that he never saw waking ?   And who is such a fool that he believes that to happen to the body which is only done in the spirit ?   It is to be taught that he who believes such things has lost his faith, and that he who has not the true faith is not of God, but of the Devil.[3]

Scepticism about witchcraft was further strengthened by the conviction that the Devil was powerless to harm the true Christian.

---

[1] E. B. Tylor, *Primitive Culture* (4th ed., London, 1903), vol. i, p. 138, ' The prevailing belief in witchcraft that sat like a nightmare on public opinion from the thirteenth to the seventeenth centuries, so far from being itself a product of mediævalism, was a revival from the remote days of primæval history '.

[2] This was supposed by Gratian and others to have been a canon of the Council of Ancyra of A.D. 314.   It is first found in a work of Regino, Abbot of Prum, who died in 915.   It may be part of an old Frankish capitulary.

[3] J. Hansen, *Quellen und Untersuchungen zur Geschichte des Hexenwahns* (Bonn, 1901), pp. 38 sqq.

It was firmly believed [wrote Lecky [1]] that the arch-fiend was for ever hovering about the Christian; but it was also believed, that the sign of the cross, or a few drops of holy water, or the name of Mary, could put him to an immediate and ignominious flight. The lives of the saints were crowded with his devices, but they represented him as uniformly vanquished, humbled, and contemned. . . . The Gospel of St. John suspended around the neck, a rosary, a relic of Christ or of a saint, any one of a thousand talismans that were distributed among the faithful, sufficed to baffle the utmost efforts of diabolical malice.

Such an attitude accounts for the comparative mildness of the earlier Middle Ages in dealing with accusations of witchcraft. The great law codes of the period, the so-called *Établissements* of St. Louis, the Assizes of Jerusalem and of Antioch, the *Kayser Recht*, and the *Sachsische Weichbuild* in all their abundance of minute provisions make no mention of witchcraft. The *Siete Partidas* of Castille (*circa* 1260),[2] which does mention it, regards it as a thing to be punished or rewarded according as it is used for evil or for good.

With the weakening of religious belief and the underground growth of heresy at the end of the period of the Crusades, witch-belief advanced with rapid strides. The scepticism of the ecclesiastical authorities with regard to the more extravagant items of witch-belief was rapidly overcome by the ingenuity of famous schoolmen. Some of the best brains in Europe made out a plausible case for the supposition that witches really did fly through the air to their Sabbats, and really could do many other marvels that the earlier generations had believed impossible. But the greatest responsibility for the rising terror of witches lies at the door of the Inquisition. This body in the middle of the thirteenth century decided that witchcraft involved a pact with the Devil and was, consequently, heresy.[2] The resulting witch-trials supported witch-belief with all the immense authority and prestige of the Inquisition. At the same time the vast volume of

[1] W. E. H. Lecky, *Rationalism in Europe*, 1901 ed., vol. i, pp. 38–9. Augusti, *Dogmengeschichte*, p. 320. ' It is somewhat remarkable that the devil of the middle ages seems to have lost much of his terror and hideousness, and to play rather the part of a cunning impostor and merry fellow . . . more like a faun who excites laughter rather than fear.'

[2] H. C. Lea, *Materials toward a History of Witchcraft*, vol. i, pp. 199 sqq. (University of Pennsylvania Press, Philadelphia, 1939.)

G. F. Black, *A Calendar of Cases of Witchcraft in Scotland* (New York, 1938), p. 5, ' The Eastern Church continued to look upon witchcraft much in the same light as the superstition had been viewed in the West in the earlier centuries and consequently never developed a witch-mania '.

confessions, which it was so successful in extorting from suspects, provided an ever-increasing store of material for enlarging and elaborating the theory of witchcraft and for spreading the terror of demons all over Christendom. The famous Bull of Pope Innocent VIII, *Summis desiderantes affectibus* (5th December 1484), did much to intensify the terror.

> Many persons of both sexes [it declares], unmindful of their own salvation and straying from the Catholic Faith, have abandoned themselves to devils, *incubi* and *succubi*, and by their incantations, spells, conjurations, and other accursed charms and crafts, enormities and horrid offences have slain unborn infants and the unborn offspring of cattle, have blasted the produce of the earth . . . nay, men and women, beasts of burden . . . vineyards . . . wheat and other cereals; these wretches furthermore afflict and torment men and women . . . with terrible and piteous pains . . . over and above this they blasphemously renounce the Faith which is theirs by the Sacrament of Baptism, and at the instigation of the Enemy of Mankind do not shrink from committing and perpetrating the foulest.abominations and filthiest excesses. . . .

Such an utterance [1] from the Holy Father was calculated to remove all doubts as to the truth of the most extravagant claims of witch-hunters; and the *Malleus Maleficarum*, published shortly afterwards (1487) by the Dominican inquisitors appointed by the Pope, provided a complete guide, theoretical as well as practical, for the discovery, examination, torture, trial, and execution of witches. It was reprinted more than a dozen times within half a century of its publication and exercised a potent influence on Roman Catholic and Protestant alike for more than two centuries. As suspects might be tried either by the secular or by the ecclesiastical courts, the net was spread as widely as possible; and the method of trial made conviction fearfully easy. Moreover, every conviction added its quota to the terror, so that the appetite for witch-killing was one which grew with what it fed upon. The terrible penalty of being burnt alive—a penalty quite frequently inflicted upon young children—served to rivet public attention upon witchcraft, and so still more to intensify the terror. Thus Europe at the end of the fifteenth century entered upon a period of frenzy which endured for nearly two centuries. The total number of witches burnt during this period cannot be estimated, as only a minute proportion of the trials and executions are recorded in any extant documents. It is nonethe-

---

[1] Hansen, op. cit., pp. 25–7.

less certain that many tens, if not hundreds, of thousands died at the stake.

§ 3. It might have been supposed that the outbreak of the Protestant Revolution would act as a check on witch-hunting. In fact it had the contrary effect. The Protestant Reformers were even more zealous witch-hunters than the Roman Catholics themselves. The century after the Schism seems to have witnessed far more witch-killings than the century before it.[1]

The emphatic belief in witchcraft of Luther[2] and Melanchthon[3] is well known. Henry Bullinger, whose house at Zürich was the refuge of so many English Protestants during the reign of Mary Tudor, argued that all who dabbled in sorcery, however good their motives, should be put to death.

> Imperial law decreed [he wrote] that they must be put to death. Therefore let those men consider what they are doing who dispute against these laws and decide that witches who deal only with dreams and hallucinations should not be burnt or put to death; however mistaken the papist writers may have been in their doctrines, they nevertheless condemned all arts and enjoined on the ministers of the Church to expel from the Church all who meddled with them.[4]

The Zwinglian theologian Thomas Erastus in his *Disputatio de Lamiis seu Strigibus* (Basle, 1577) is equally credulous and severe.

§ 4. The most zealous of all Protestant persuasions, Calvinism, excelled all others in its zeal against witchcraft. Peter Martyr (Vermigli), who acted as Divinity Professor at Oxford during the reign of Edward VI, was a voluminous writer on the subject of alliances between witches and the Devil, of *incubi* and *succubi*, and of infernal compacts.[5] Calvin[6] himself and his followers in Geneva were conspicuous beyond all others, even in this age, for their zeal in witch-killing. A Protestant writing in the last quarter

---

[1] J. Diefenbach, *Der Hexenwahn vor und nach der Glaubensspaltung in Deutschland*, pp. 288 sqq. (Mainz, 1886). Some of Diefenbach's conclusions were contested by G. Längin, *Religion und Hexenprozesse* (Leipsig, 1888).

[2] Soldan and Heppe, *Geschichte der Hexenprozesse*, 3rd ed., by Max Bauer, vol. i, p. 422 (Munich, 1911); H. C. Lea, *Materials towards a History of Witchcraft*, vol. i, pp. 416 sqq. (Philadelphia, 1939).

[3] K. Hartfelder, 'Der Aberglaube Ph. Melanchthons' in *Histor. Taschenbuch*, pp. 252 sqq.; H. C. Lea, op. cit., vol. i, p. 423.

[4] *Theatrum de Veneficiis*, pp. 304, 305. From the pamphlet *In Acta Apostolorum Commentarii*, lib. vi, in cap. 19 (Tiguri, 1535).

[5] Peter Martyr, *Loci Communes*, pp. 30 sqq.; *De Maleficiis* (Tiguri, 1580).

[6] H. C. Lea, op. cit., vol. i, pp. 428–30.

B

of the sixteenth century expresses the view that 'although we both wish to and must punish and root out spirits and sorcerers in accordance with God's stern command, nevertheless it is not considered wise by all people to proceed against them so extravagantly as was done under Calvin in Switzerland '.[1]   The special fear of the Genevans was witches' unguents, which were held responsible for the frequent pestilences that wasted their city.   One outbreak of pestilence was dying down when on 22nd January 1545 the *bailli* of Thonon announced that a certain Bernard Dallinges, who had been arrested, had confessed to having joined with a certain Dunant alias Lentille to cover with ointment the foot of a man who had been hanged and by Satan's malice to rub with it the bolts of doors in order to spread the pestilence.[2] Lentille was at once arrested, taken to Thonon to be confronted with Dallinges, brought back to Geneva, and put to the torture. He endured two twists of the rope without confessing.   He was then put to the torture of the *strappado*, under which he lost so much blood that he died (17th February 1545).   His body was ordered to be dragged through the city to Plainpalais, and there to be burnt.

Meanwhile the Captains of the Quarters were instructed to watch for the plague-spreaders (*semeurs de peste*); and a considerable number of men and women were arrested and charged with having made a formal pact with the Devil and with having, under the Devil's orders, formed an association to devote the city to destruction by plague.   On 7th March two women were executed for making a contract with the Devil, and an order was made twelve days later[3] that in view of the great harm done by these persons in Geneva the men should have their flesh torn off with pincers before being put to death, and that the women should have their right hands cut off before being burnt at the stake

---

[1] *Kurzes Traktätlein von Zauberei.*   The date and place of publication of this work are unknown.   But it is shown by internal evidence to have been written after 1573.   See J. Janssen, *History of the German People*, Eng. trans, vol. xvi, p. 505 (London, 1910).

[2] Amadée Roget, *Histoire du Peuple de Genève depuis la Reforme jusqu'a l'Escalade*, vol. ii, p. 154 (Geneva, 1873).   On this method of spreading pestilence, see Henri Boguet, *Discours des Sorciers*, p. 71 (Lyons, 1608), and C. L'Estrange Ewen, *Witchcraft and Demonianism*, p. 79 (London, 1933).

[3] Registres du Conseil, 19th March 1545, ' *Vu les grands maux que telles gens ont faits dans Genève, ordonné que les hommes soient tenaillés par la ville et après condamnés à mort, ainsi qu'on verra par conseil, et que les femmes aient la main droit coupée au Molard et soient menées de là à Plainpalais pour y être brulées, et que de jour en jour et, d'heure en heure soit procédé à la formation de leur procès.*'   See Sigmund Riezler, *Geschichte der Hexenprozesse in Bayern*, p. 143 (Stuttgart, 1896).

at Plainpalais, and that the accusations and trials should continue from day to day and hour to hour. On the day when this order was issued Calvin presented himself before the Council with the request that the prisoners' death-agonies should not be excessively prolonged, with the result that the executioner was ordered to be diligent in the cutting off of hands and in seeing that death followed without delay. Calvin had been very active in all the proceedings, and had personally laid information against sorcerers as heretics ' in order that beings of this type might be wiped out'. In a letter [1] to Myconius he gave a calm and business-like account of the terrible proceedings (27th March, 1545):—

Here [he wrote] God is trying us sorely. A conspiracy of men and women has been discovered, who for the space of three years have spread the plague through the city, by what sorceries [2] I know not (*nescio quibus veneficiis*). Fifteen women have already been burnt. Some of the men have been punished even more severely. Some have committed suicide in prison. Twenty-five are still in custody. Notwithstanding the conspirators do not cease to smear the locks of doors with their ointments. Behold the perils that beset us. Hitherto God has preserved our household uninjured however frequently it has been assailed.

In a letter addressed to Farel on the 25th April he wrote about the hospital official René, who had confessed to having caused the deaths of five persons, while his wife had killed eighteen. Calvin adds that this couple went to execution gaily after giving striking signs of repentance and conversion.

Meanwhile the witch-persecution went on gaining in intensity. It had been decided on 19th March to imprison all poor people of bad reputation in order to find out whether there were any plague-spreaders among them. Some of those detained would not confess under torture even after several twists of the rope; and, as they were under strong suspicion, it was decided to wring the truth out of them by some more terrible tortures. On 21st March three more women were executed. On the 25th Council were informed that two prisoners who were under the deepest suspicion of having been in league with the Devil would not confess in spite

---

[1] *Ioannis Calvini Opera quae Supersunt Omnia*, ed. Baum, Cunitz, Reuss, vol. xii, p. 55, Epist. 627.

[2] H. Y. Reyburn, *John Calvin* (London, 1914), p. 129, translates ' by what means I know not '. He thus misses the allusion to witchcraft. *Veneficium* was one of the commonest Latin words for witchcraft or sorcery. See Du Cange, *Glossarium*, vol. ix, p. 160, and Forcellini's *Lexicon*. It is used in the Vulgate in II(IV) Kings ix. 22 of Jezebel's witchcrafts, in Hebrew *Kĕshaphim*, and in Galatians v. 20, where it stands for the Greek φαρμαχεία.

of all the tortures that had been applied. Some advocated walling them up, and others suggested drowning them. It was consequently decided ' to consult the doctors upon the best means of proceeding against such wicked people '. As a result of the consultation it was decided that the prisoners should be walled up until they had confessed the truth.[1]   On 26th March four more were executed ; and on the 28th the hospital barber and a grave-digger were decapitated. With the execution of one François Boulat on 16th May after particularly excruciating tortures, a total of thirty-one persons had been put to death in the space of three months.[2]   A number of women against whom evidence was insufficient were banished for ever from the Republic. As late as the month of August 1545 Council ordered that information should be taken against the wife of a certain Antoine de Rovera, surnamed *Sept-Diables*, on suspicion of her connivance with the pest spreaders.

During these trials the judges listened with the utmost credulity to evidence that the witches had kissed, in token of homage, the posterior of a black dog named Marguet, who was the Devil in disguise, and who had provided them with the magic unguents for the spreading of the pestilence.[3]   Geneva came to be regarded as the city that occupied a leading position in the sphere of witch-persecution. By some it was regarded as the source whence witches had spread to other lands.[4]   Others regarded Geneva as the highest authority on methods of witch-hunting; and the magistrates of Lyons, Valais, several Swiss cantons, and various parts of Savoy wrote to consult the Council on the treatment of their own witches. Other outbursts of witch-mania in Geneva in 1566, 1568, and 1615 added to its reputation, so much so that allusions are to be found to it in books published in many parts of Europe, such as the *Démonomanie* (bk. iv, cap. iv) of Jean Bodin (1580), the *Scaligerana* of the famous classical scholar, J. J. Scaliger, and the *De Prestigiis* of Wier. Geneva was far-famed also as the source of many of the most famous books on witch-

---

[1] Registres du Conseil 2nd April 1545, ' *Ordonné qu'ils soient murés et ne soient ôtés de là jusqu'à ce qu'ils aient confessé la verité, autrement finiront leurs jours à tel tourment*'.

[2] Spon, *Histoire de Genève*, vol. ii, p. 44 (Geneva, 1730); F. W. Kamp-schulte, *Johann Calvin, seine Kirche und sein Staat in Genf*, vol. i, p. 428 (Leipzig, 1869).

[3] J. B. G. Galiffe, *Genève Historique et Archæologique*, p. 139 (Geneva, 1872).

[4] Michael Roset, *Les Chroniques de Genève*, ed. H. Fazy (Geneva, 1894), pp. 306–8.

craft, such as Lambert Daneau's *De Veneficiis* (1564), the French translation of Lavater's *De Spectris* (1571), and François Perreauld's *Démonologie* (1653), which included the story of the demon of Mâcon so often quoted by English writers. Even in the eighteenth century the witch-beliefs of Geneva had not died out.[1]

The city of Basle, in which Calvin finished the first draft of his *Institutio*, and in which many English Protestants sought refuge during the reign of Mary Tudor, witnessed some of the most amazing witch-trials on record during the years 1530, 1532, 1546, and 1550. In this last year a woman was sentenced to be burnt as a consequence of her confession that she had kept 'a live female gnome' and had visited the Venusberg in company with her husband. 'The maddest things were put on record with the blindest credulity and with a calmness and objectivity appropriate to the most ordinary crimes.'[2]

Theodore Beza, who succeeded Calvin at Geneva, shared his master's attitude towards witchcraft to the full. He even accused the Parliament of Paris of slackness in proceeding against witches[3] in spite of the enormous numbers who perished at the hands of that tribunal.[4]

§ 5 (*a*) The witch-terror of the fathers of Calvinism in its earliest homes probably had a considerable influence upon Calvinist posterity for many generations. But there were other and more fundamental reasons for the Calvinist fear of witchcraft. In the first place, it should be remembered that Calvinism, of all religious persuasions, faced sin and the power of the Devil most squarely as tremendous realities. Calvin's *Institutio* taught that the Fall of Man was an act by which his inmost nature was completely corrupted and his original righteousness changed into absolute depravity, so that no man in his natural condition is capable of the performance of any deed that is not evil.[5]

---

[1] J. B. G. Galiffe, op. cit., supplement, p. 15.
[2] Fr. Fischer, *Die Basler Hexenprozesse in dem 16ten und 17ten Jahrhundert* (Basle, 1840).
[3] Soldan and Heppe, *Hexenprozesse*, ed. Max Bauer (Munich, 1911), vol. i, p. 420.
[4] On the almost daily executions of witches ordered by the Parliament of Paris, see L. Daneau, *De Veneficis, quos olim Sortilegos, nunc autem Vulgo Sortiarios Vocant* (Colonia Agrippinæ, 1575). The first edition was published in French at Geneva in 1564. Daneau, who was a Calvinist himself, urges that the utmost vigour should be put into the work of destroying witches.
[5] Calvin, *Institutio*, ii, I, ss, p. 79 (ed. Geneva, 1559 fol.). '*Non aliter intepretari licet quod dicitur, nos in Adam mortuos esse, quam quod ipse peccando non sibi tantum cladem ac ruinam ascivit, sed naturam quoque nostram in simile præipitavit exitium,*' &c.

All of us, therefore, descending from an impure seed [wrote Calvin (*Institutio*, bk. ii, cap. 1)] come into the world tainted with the contagion of sin. Nay, before we behold the light of sun we are in God's sight defiled and polluted . . . even infants bringing their condemnation with them from their mother's womb, suffer not from another's but from their own defect . . . their whole nature is, as it were, a seed-bed of sin, and therefore cannot but be odious and abominable to God.

The natural man, being completely bad, would be altogether at one with the Devil, and, consequently, easily capable of those pacts with demons that figured so largely in witch-trials.

(*b*) Secondly, the Calvinist took his stand on the verbal inspiration of the Scripture.[1] He was compelled by the very nature of his position to set up an infallible Bible as a counter-blast to the claims of an infallible Roman Church; and the Bible literally interpreted text by text without regard to historical background or historical criticism of its documents seemed quite decisive on the subject of witchcraft in general and on many of the current accusations against witches in particular. The command ' Thou shalt not suffer a witch to live ' (Exodus xxii. 18) seemed in these circumstances to settle the matter once for all, as did the fuller specification of diabolical practices enumerated in Deuteronomy (xviii. 10–11). Sceptics about the power allowed to the Devil and his servants in this world could be silenced by the story of the Witch of Endor (I Samuel xxviii.) and the permission given by God to Satan to afflict Job (Job i, 7–12). Where the Old Testament failed, the New made up the deficiency with its records of demoniac possession and magic arts. ' The devil ', wrote Calvin (*Institutio*, bk i. cap. 14), ' is said to have undisputed possession of this world until he is dispossessed by Christ . . . the wicked are properly regarded as the children of Satan, from having degenerated into his image.'

(*c*) Yet another reason for the Calvinists' especial concern about magic and witchcraft was the influence of the Jews, who

---

[1] *Institutio*, I, 8, also *The Genevan Liturgy* of 1542, *Formula Baptismi administrandi*; J. B. Kidd, *Documents of the Continental Reformation*, p. 624 (Oxford, 1911).

' *Spondetis igitur vos daturos operam, ut omni hac disciplina instruatur, ac generatim omnibus his, quae scriptis divinis continentur, id est, tum veteri tum novo Testamento : ut ea amplectatur et audiat tanquam verbum sermonemque Dei certissimum, coelitus demissum.*'

Lutheran divines held equally definite views about verbal inspiration. Some went so far as to teach that all the vowel points in the Hebrew Bible were inspired. E. G. Gerhard, *Loc. Theol.*, i. c, 14, 15, Quaest. i, 272.

had long been the supreme masters of the forbidden sciences.[1] The Calvinists' devotion to the Old Testament led them to the study of the Hebrew Language, which was difficult to acquire except from Jews. Also the study of Hebrew brought them into touch with the Talmud, Targums, Zohar, and other Jewish writings [2] in which good and evil spirits and magic practices abound. Thus—to give one typical example out of a multitude—the Talmud (*Pesachim* 111a) warns the reader:

> If two women are sitting at the cross-roads, each one side of the pathway, with their faces turned towards one another, it is certain they are engaged in witchcraft. What is the remedy? If there is another way, let him take it; if not and there is somebody else with him, they should hold each other's hand and pass through; but in the event of there being nobody with him, he should exclaim, ' Agrath, Azlath, Usya, and Belusya [the names of demons] have already been killed by arrows '.

It will be remembered that Menasseh ben Israel, with whom Oliver Cromwell negotiated the return of the Jews to England, was the author of a Hebrew book in which witch-beliefs in their most extravagant form were strongly affirmed.[3]

(*d*) Moreover, the form of government most congenial to Calvinism would probably be favourable to witch-hunting. The Genevan theocracy made the State a department of the Church, and the Church was ordered, in theory at least, according to the votes of every church-member. The will of the common people was therefore strongly felt in a Calvinist State. Hence the demand of the more ignorant sections of the populace for witch-killings would be likely to remain effective—as it was in Calvinist

---

[1] Janssen, *History of the German People at the End of the Middle Ages*, vol. xvi, p. 507 (Eng. trans., London, 1910).
Grillot de Givry, *Witchcraft, Magic, and Alchemy*, pp. 206 sqq. (Eng. trans. London, 1931).
H. C. Lea, *Materials towards a History of Witchcraft*, vol. i, pp. 10 sqq. (Philadelphia, 1939).

[2] A. Cohen, *Everyman's Talmud*, pp. 276 sqq. (London, 1932); Soldan-Heppe, *Geschichte der Hexenprozesse*, ed. Max Bauer, vol. i, pp. 414–15 (Munich, 1911); Meiners, *Histor. Vergleichnung der Sitten des Mittelalters*, vol. iii, pp. 279 sqq.; *The Targum of Palestine* on Exodus I, vii, 11, Numbers xx, 22 &c.; J. A. Eisenmenger, *Entdektes Judenthum* (Konigsberg, 1711), contains a wealth of information, which is not, however, completely reliable.

[3] Menasseh ben Israel's book was written in unpointed Hebrew and printed at Amsterdam in 1651. It contains a summary in Latin, in which it is called *Libri Quattuor de Immortalitate Animæ*. Bk. iii, cc. 14–29 is filled with the most extravagant witch-beliefs, including *incubi* and *succubi* and changes into the shape of various animals. On the negotiations with Oliver Cromwell, see Lucien Wolf, *Menasseh Ben Israel's Mission to Oliver Cromwell* (London, 1901).

Scotland and New England—long after a spirit of scepticism had possessed the more educated classes.

(e) Finally, it should be noticed that the cradle of Calvinism lay in those regions of Switzerland and south-eastern France where the Oriental dualism of the Manichaeans, Paulicians, Cathari, and Albigenses had been widespread amongst the people ever since the early Middle Ages, and merely driven underground by the ruthless efforts of the Inquisition. These dualistic systems regarded the Devil as the ruler of the material world,[1] and developed an elaborate system of demonology singularly suitable for the elaboration of witch-beliefs. Their doctrine that all matter was evil, and all pleasure on a material plane sinful, gave them a sufficient superficial resemblance to Calvinism to make coalescence possible, and in the course of it to intensify the Calvinist belief in demonology and witchcraft.

§ 6. In view of these circumstances it is not surprising to find that, as the spiritual empire of Geneva enlarged its borders, witch-mania found new worlds to conquer. Nor is it surprising that the last defenders of witch-belief were mostly men in the Calvinist tradition such as Richard Baxter—one of the lesser heroes of Macaulay's *History of England*—who as late as 1691 attempted, in his *Certainty of the World of Spirits*, to use the recent outburst of witch-terror in New England to revive similar terrors in this country.[2] About the same time Balthasar Bekker, who had questioned the more sensational phenomena of witchcraft in *The Enchanted World* (*De Betoverde Weereld*), was expelled from the ministry of the Dutch Reformed (Calvinist) Church (7th August 1692), excluded from communion, and never again admitted.[3] As late as 1722 a woman was burnt for witchcraft in Calvinist Scotland, and in 1736 'the divines of the Associated Presbytery' passed a resolution declaring their belief in witchcraft and deploring the scepticism that was general in their day.

[1] H. C. Lea, *History of the Inquisition in the Middle Ages*, vol. i, pp. 89 sqq. (New York, 1906).
[2] The life of Baxter in the *Dictionary of National Biography* and that by F. J. Powicke (London, 1924) make no allusion to this important book or, indeed, to Baxter's important place in the history of witch-beliefs.
[3] W. P. C. Knuttel, *Balthasar Bekker*, p. 315 (The Hague, 1906).

CHAPTER II

THE INTRODUCTION OF CONTINENTAL WITCH-BELIEFS INTO ENGLAND, 1558–88

§ 1. THE INSULATION of England from continental storms was never more strikingly exemplified than in the matter of witch-mania. While the smoke of holocausts of women, old and young, darkened skies beyond the Channel, England went on her way unperturbed. It is true, of course, that this country, like everyone else in the world, was not without its primitive belief in magic arts, to which so many references are made in the works of Chaucer and Gower. Laws against witchcraft—some severe and some curiously mild—had been issued occasionally ever since the early Anglo-Saxon period.[1] Occasionally, too—especially in the fifteenth century—it was found convenient to dispose of a political opponent such as the Duchess of Gloucester (1441), the Duchess of Bedford (1478), or Jane Shore [2] by means of a charge of witch-craft or magic. Such practices as the injuring of images with the object of causing analogous injuries to the persons represented, soothsaying, fortune-telling, the concocting of love-potions, and such like were far from uncommon. But they aroused com-paratively little interest or fear. The few charges of witchcraft that came before the secular courts were often treated with con-spicuous leniency. The great English authorities on law, Glan-ville, Bracton, the Fleta, and Britton, are silent on this subject.[3] So also is Edward I in the minute instructions given to the sheriffs in the Statute of Ruddlan (1283). The medieval laws of Scot-land preserve a similar silence.

Though an Act (33 Hen. VIII, c. 8, 1542) was passed against ' conjuracions and wichecraftes and sorcery and enchantments ' during the Catholic reaction towards the end of Henry VIII's reign, it was of little or no consequence. It is doubtful whether

---

[1] C. L'Estrange Ewen, *Witch-Hunting and Witch Trials*, pp. 1 sqq. (London, 1929); Kittredge, *Witchcraft in Old and New England*, pp. 38 sqq. (Cambridge, Massachusetts, 1929).
[2] More, *Rycharde the Thirde*, ed. Lumly, p. 47.
[3] Lea, *Inquisition in the Middle Ages*, vol. iii, p. 427 (New York, 1888).

it was ever put into force against witches.[1] Also it is directed partly against those who were digging up crosses in the name of the reformed religion; and it adopts a somewhat sceptical tone in its enumeration of some of the current beliefs of those who ' have made or caused to be made dyvers images and pictures . . . and giving faith and credit to such fantasticall practices have digged up and pulled down an infinite number of crosses within this Realme, and taken upon them to declare where things lost or stolen be become'. Moreover, when this Act was annulled (1547), in company with a batch of others, there is not the slightest evidence that its repeal aroused either opposition or misgiving.[2]

Cranmer in one of his articles of visitations[3] of 1549 ordered his clergy to seek for ' any that use charms, sorcery, enchantments, witchcrafts, soothsaying or any like craft invented by the Devil '. But the article was given little prominence. It is chiefly interesting as the first spark from the continental conflagration to blow over to England. For Cranmer had spent considerable periods in Germany (1530–33), where he had married his second wife, a niece of the protestant reformer Osiander of Nuremberg. He can, therefore, hardly have failed to come into contact with the witch-hunters who were at that very time burning suspects by the hundred.

Yet there is little trace anywhere in England at this time of a coherent theory of witchcraft such as had been elaborated by schoolmen and inquisitors in the later Middle Ages and published in the *Malleus Maleficarum*. Still less was there any elaborate system for the detection of witchcraft or any insistence upon the existence of pacts with the Devil. Neither was there any carefully planned method of questioning the accused such as the *Malleus* recommended. The beliefs that witches attended the Sabbat and that they could change their form were also absent. The country as a whole regarded witchcraft with profound indifference, and

---

[1] W. Notestein, *A History of Witchcraft in England from 1558 to 1718*, p. 11, ft. n. (Washington, 1911); C. L'Estrange Ewen, *Witch-Hunting and Witch Trials*, p. 11 (London, 1929).

[2] Ewen, *Witchcraft and Demonianism*, p. 45 (London, 1933).
Lecky, *Rationalism*, p. 111, ft. n. 1 (2nd ed., London, 1865).

[3] With the accession of Elizabeth such articles of visitations became customary. See F. Hutchinson, *Historical Essay Concerning Witchcraft* (London, 1718), p. 181, ' Are not our good *women* deliver'd with as much Ease and Safety now, as they were in 1559, when it was put into the Articles of Visitations, that they should enquire, *Whether any Sorcerers hurt the Women in the time of Travel ?* '

attributed charms and fortune-telling to kindly spirits of the air, elementals or fairies, rather than to satanic agencies.

§ 2 (a) It is not till the accession of Elizabeth that the history of witch-mania in England begins. From that date onwards events moved rapidly towards a witch-terror of the continental type. A Bill against witchcraft was drafted and passed by the House of Commons [1] in the very first year of Elizabeth's reign. Its failure to become law was due to a dissolution of Parliament (May 1559) before it reached the House of Lords. With the meeting of a new Parliament (1563) it soon made its way to the Statute Book (5 Eliz., c. 16). The essential provision of this important Act [2] was that those ' who shall use practice or exercise any Witchecrafte Enchantment Charme or Sorcerie whereby any person shall happen to be killed or destroyed . . . their Councellors and Aidours . . . shall suffer paynes of Dethe as a Felon or Felons '. Witchcraft which caused lesser pains than death was to be punished with one year's imprisonment and four appearances in the pillory. Considering the Draconian tendency of the penal code of the time the Act is conspicuously mild. It did little more than inflict the death penalty on those who were regarded as guilty of murder. It does not make witchcraft a capital offence on the ground, usually taken on the Continent, that it always involves a pact with the Devil. Nevertheless it was this Act which marked the opening of the floodgates to a deluge of terror and cruelty that did not subside for more than a century.

How is this sudden rise of witch-mania in an England that had formerly cared so little about witchcraft to be explained?

There is little doubt that the answer lies in the religious history of the period. Many Protestants, both clerical and lay, had fled the country after the accession of Mary Tudor.[3] They had sought refuge amongst their co-religionists in Geneva, Basle, Zürich, Strassbourg, and other cities where witch-burnings were taking place on a most extensive scale in the midst of unimaginable popular terror. Here they had every opportunity for witnessing

---

[1] *Journal of the House of Commons*, vol. i, pp. 57–60.

[2] *Statutes of the Realm*, vol. iv, pt. i, p. 446. An Act of 1581 (23 Eliz., c. II) enacts ' that if any person . . . shall by setting or erecting any figure or by casting of nativities or by calculation or by any prophesying, witchcraft, conjurations . . . seek to know . . . how long her Majesty shall live . . . that then every such offence shall be felony. . . .'

[3] C. H. Garrett, *The Marian Exiles* (Cambridge, 1938), gives a census of 472 exiles. See also W. H. Frere, *The English Church in the Reigns of Elizabeth and James I*, p. 8.

the trials and the burnings and for discussing the theory and practice of witchcraft with the most eminent Zwinglian and Calvinist theologians. They became deeply convinced of the fearful reality of the power of the Devil and of those who had so basely renounced God and sold themselves to work iniquity. They, consequently, returned to England with the accession of Elizabeth prepared to introduce continental witch-mania full-grown.[1]

(*b*) Prominent among the returned exiles was John Jewel (1522–71), who had fled (1555) first to Frankfurt-on-Maine, one of the most noted centres of witch-mania. Thence he proceeded to Strassbourg on the invitation of Peter Martyr, whose views have been mentioned in the preceding chapter. From Strassbourg he accompanied Peter Martyr to witch-ridden Zürich (July 1556), where he stayed till his return to England (1559). Jewel was almost immediately made Bishop of Salisbury and one of Elizabeth's most trusted advisers. He ' began his episcopate with decided leanings to Calvinism, and hoped that the Elizabethan Church would develope in a Calvinistic direction '.[2] The effect of his long sojourn amongst continental witch-hunters showed itself in a famous sermon which he preached before the Queen on an unknown date between November 1559 and March 1560. In the midst of a totally unrelated argument he abruptly turns aside to urge upon Elizabeth the gravity of the witch-problem. ' It is ', he contended, ' the horrible using of your subjects ' that compelled him to broach the matter.

---

[1] G. L. Kittredge, *Witchcraft in Old and New England*, p. 250 (Harvard Univ. Press, 1929), opposes the view that the returned exiles ' introduced foreign ideas on witchcraft into their native country '. Professor C. R. Adair (*Eng. Hist. Rev.*, October 1932, pp. 673 sqq.) supports him in this view. See, however, the reply by Professor G. L. Burr in *American Historical Review* for July 1929, p. 815. It should be noticed especially that in 1582 Brian Darcy, an Essex J.P., expressly connected witch-hunting with the immigrants from abroad. ' There is a man of great cunning and knowledge, come over lately unto our Queen's Majesty ', he is reported to have said, ' which hath advertised her what a company and number of witches be within England.'

On this point see C. L'E. Ewen, *Witchcraft and Demonianism*, pp. 47, 157 (London, 1933).

The whole of Prof. Kittredge's fine scholarly volume is coloured by its purpose of defending the witch-persecutors of Salem, New England, at the end of the seventeenth century. With this purpose in view he exerts himself to the utmost to deny any connexion between Puritanism and witch-beliefs, and is involved in a good deal of special pleading, to which reference will be made in later chapters. It should be remembered that Professor Kittredge's book was printed before the publication of the many discoveries of Ewen, which have rendered obsolete so many conclusions of earlier writers.

[2] *Dictionary of National Biography*, vol. x, p. 817, *sub* ' Jewel '.

This kind of people (I mean witches and sorcerers) within the last few years are marvellously increased within your grace's realm. These eyes have seen the most evident and manifest marks of their wickedness. Your grace's subjects pine away even unto death, their colour fadeth, their flesh rotteth, their speech is benumbed, their senses are bereft. Wherefore your poor subjects' most humble petition to your highness is, that the laws touching such malefactors may be put in due execution.[1]

Jewel's absorption in the subject is further revealed in a letter to Peter Martyr (2nd November 1559) written shortly after a visit to the West of England. 'The number of witches', he assures his friend, 'had everywhere become enormous.'[2]

Jewel's great influence at Court, his learning, energy, and brilliance as a controversialist would suggest the surmise that he was largely responsible for the statute against witchcraft. Such a surmise is confirmed by Strype,[3] who says that Jewel's sermon 'I make no doubt was the occasion of bringing in a Bill in the next Parliament, for making Enchantments and Witchcraft Felony'.

(c) The influence of other returned exiles is probably to be traced in those regions where the witch-mania grew most acute. The total number of indictments for witchcraft unearthed by modern research for the reign of Elizabeth is 535 and the number of executions at least eighty-two. These figures are, of course, only a small fraction of the total number actually indicted or executed. The great majority have left no record.[4] The most noticeable feature of the available figures is the enormous proportion that goes to Essex and Middlesex. Essex had 303 indictments and at least fifty-three executions. At the same time Middlesex had seventeen indictments and at least three executions. The recorded total for these two counties is thus between 60 and 70 per cent. of the total for the whole kingdom. What is the explanation? The most obvious one is that the two counties made up the diocese of London, and to this the Bishop appointed was

[1] *The Works of Jewel*, vol. ii, pp. 1025-34, ed. for Parker Society (Cambridge, 1845-50).

[2] 'Magarum et veneficarum numerus ubique in immensum excreverat.' *Zürich Letters*, vol. 1, p. 44, ed. Parker Society (Cambridge, 1842).

[3] Strype, *Annals of the Reformation*, vol. i, pp. 7, 8 (London, 1709). Richard Baxter in his *Certainty of the World of Spirits* (1691) also stresses the importance of the passage quoted from Jewel's sermon.

[4] The calculations that follow are based mainly upon C. L'E. Ewen, *Witch-Hunting and Witch Trials* (London, 1929), and *Witchcraft and Demonianism* (London, 1933).

Edmund Grindal, who had lived in exile amongst the witch-hunting Calvinists of Strassbourg, Speier, and Frankfort. That he had learned his lesson well is shown by a letter (17th April 1561) he wrote to Sir William Cecil, the Queen's Secretary, enclosing a confession of 'magic and Conjuration' made by a certain priest named John Coxe *alias* Devon.[1] Grindal begged the Council to appoint 'some extraordinary punishment for example. My Lord Chief Justice sayeth the temporal law will not meddle with them. Our ecclesiastical punishment is too slender for so grievous offences.' As the statute against witchcraft had not yet been passed, Cecil in reply made some historical investigations as to the penalties that had formerly been inflicted. So rare, however, had accusations of this kind been hitherto that the only precedent he could find was the case of a Southwark magician as far back as the year 1371. Kent, largely in the diocese of Canterbury, to which Grindal was translated in 1576, had forty-eight recorded indictments and at least seven executions of witches during the reign.

The counties of Norfolk and Suffolk had between them fourteen recorded indictments and at least five executions—one of them the burning alive of one Margaret Read [2] at King's Lynn in 1590. These two shires formed the diocese of John Parkhurst, who had spent his exile amongst the witch-hunters of Zürich. The counties of Surrey, Sussex, and Hertford, which border on the regions already mentioned, had between them 125 recorded indictments and at least seven executions. Jewel's diocese of Salisbury, which then consisted of Wilts and Berks, showed little sign of witch-mania except in the easterly part of Berks, where four women of Windsor were accused of witchcraft and hanged (1579) at Abingdon.[3] This lack of witch-mania in these regions is partly perhaps to be explained by the fact that Jewel soon repented of his Calvinism. 'A little experience brought him into

---

[1] *Calendar of State Papers, Domestic,* 1547–80, ed. R. Lemon, pp. 173 sqq. (London, 1856). John Coxe is not to be confused with Francis Coxe, who was summoned before the Privy Council on a charge of sorcery and, having been severely punished, made a public confession of his 'employment of certayne sinistral and divelysh arts' at the Pillory in Cheapside on the 25th June, 1561.

[2] B. Mackerell, *History and Antiquities of King's Lynn,* p. 231 (1738).

[3] *A Rehearsall both straung and true, of hainous and horrible actes committed by Elizabeth Stile, Alias Rockingham, Mother Dutten, Mother Deuell, Mother Margaret, Fower notorious Witches, apprehended in Winsore in the Countie of Barks, and at Abbington arraigned, condemned and executed on the 26 daye of Februarie laste Anno 1579.* Imprinted at London . . .

harmony with the Anglican system.'[1] His *Apologia pro Ecclesia Anglicana*, published in 1562, shows a very definite retreat from the extreme Calvinist position. Also, Jewel died young, and was succeeded (1571) by Edmund Guest, who was neither a returned exile nor a Calvinist.

(d) Apart from the counties mentioned and a few others bordering upon them, the rest of England had either no recorded witch-trials, or at most a negligibly small number of them. It thus appears that witch-mania during the reign of Elizabeth was confined almost entirely to the south-east part of England. Such geographical limitations suggest the view that the influence of the returned exiles was by no means the only cause of the growth of witch-belief. The south-east of England was at this time the part most highly developed industrially and commercially. Consequently economic as well as geographical reasons brought it into the closest communication with the Continent. Also Calvinism, with its worldly asceticism and its toleration of usury, would be likely to spread most readily in an industrial and commercial community. These circumstances almost as much as the influence of the returned exiles help to explain the intensity of witch-mania in the south-east.

The gradual growth of witch-terror after the return of the exiles may be traced in the numbers of accused and convicted at the assizes of the Home Circuit, since these have been brought to light by modern research.[2] It must, however, be remembered that witches were brought before many other courts, both lay and ecclesiastical, besides the Assizes. Thus, for example, one witch is recorded as having been condemned and executed by the town court of Faversham (Joan Cason in 1586). Again, some Oxfordshire suspects were brought before the Archdeacon's Court (1593[3]). Nevertheless the records of the Home Circuit may be taken as an indication of the state of public opinion. For the first decade of Elizabeth's reign (1558–67) they show twenty-four indictments for witchcraft and four witches hanged. In the next

[1] *Dict. of Nat. Biog.*, vol. x, p. 816, *sub nomine*.

[2] C. L'E. Ewen, *Witch-Hunting and Witch Trials*, p. 99 (London, 1929).

[3] *Victoria County History of Oxfordshire*, vol. ii, pp. 40, 41 (London, 1907), article by H. E. Salter. 'As regards witchcraft, for instance, two women of Long Combe presented on that charge in 1593, deny that "they did ever commit any witchcraft, neither have they any such skyll, neither hath the Devil tempted them to that ".' (MS Top. Oxon, c. 56. 1.)

On the case of Joan Cason of Faversham see Ewen, *Witchcraft and Demonianism*, p. 164.

decade (1568–77) the figures were eighty-eight indicted and sixteen hanged. They had risen in the next period (1578–87) to 147 indictments and nineteen hangings. During the next (1588–97) the figures were 156 and eighteen. The steadiness of the rise both in the indictments and the hangings is unmistakable.

It is, at first sight, difficult to account for the rapid spread of continental witch-beliefs during the forty years after the return of the Protestant exiles. For these exiles numbered much fewer than 500, all told. How could so small a number exercise so potent an influence?

(i) The answer to this riddle lies partly in the fact that witch-craft was from the beginning associated with Roman Catholicism. Thus, for example, Edmund Grindal in the case already mentioned of Coxe *alias* Devon, the priest, associated 'mass matters' with ' magic and conjuration '. [1] Again, it was widely believed that the followers of Mary Queen of Scots were using witchcraft for the destruction of the Anglican Queen.

> There were some already of the Popish faction [wrote Strype [2]] contriving mischief against the Queen, by setting up the Scotch Queen's title . . . by dealing with some conjurors to cast their Figures to calculate the Queen's Life, and the Duration of her Government and the like. The knowledge of this coming to the Queen and her Council, it was ordered at Council November the 22nd (1558) that Anthony Fortesque, who had been Comptroller of the Cardinal (Pole) should be apprehended . . . Sir John Mason had the Bodies of two more charged with the same accusation, viz., Kele and Prestal . . . one named Thirkel a Taylor, was now also in hold for conjuring about the Matters aforesaid. . . . And Richard Parleben was another of these conjurors taken up. . . . Thus early did this excellent Lady's enemies . . . continue their devices of mischief against her . . . when she had been scarcely possessed of her Crown.

Another curious example of the supposed connexion between Roman Catholicism and witchcraft comes in 1572, when the Earl of Shrewsbury, who was in charge of Mary Queen of Scots, employed two spies to find out a ' Nest of conjuring Mass-mongers '. [3] Again, the stir in London was immense when three waxen

---

[1] *Calendar of State Papers, Domestic*, 1547–80, ed. R. Lemon, pp. 173 sqq. (London, 1856) ; Ludwig Lavater's, *De Spectris* (Zurich, 1569), published in an English translation (London, 1572), stresses at great length the connexion between Roman Catholicism and witchcraft.

[2] Strype, *Annals of the Reformation*, vol. i (London, 1709). Thomas Ady, *A Candle in the Dark*, pp. 95 sqq. (London, 1655), pointed out that in Roman Catholic countries witchcraft was associated with Protestantism.

[3] Strype, *Annals*, vol. ii, p. 181.

figures were discovered in the house of a **Roman Catholic priest** at Islington (1578) and assumed to represent the Queen, Burleigh, and Leicester.[1] Even an outbreak of jail-fever at the Oxford Assizes of 1579 was attributed to the witchcraft of a bookseller named Ronald Jenks who was a ' Popish Recusant '.[2]

The frequent association of witchcraft and Roman Catholicism did not escape Reginald Scot. ' One such sort as are said to be witches ', he remarks,[3] ' are women which be commonly old . . . poor, sullen, superstitious, and Papists. . . .'

It is noteworthy that such a connexion was also suspected in contemporary Denmark.[4] The suspicion was partly due to the conduct of the Roman Catholics themselves. They were quick to notice that the growth of witch-terror would give them a chance to use their ritual for the exorcism of those possessed by evil spirits, and thus to avail themselves of a powerful means of propaganda. There were instances, too, of Catholics even training children to feign diabolical possession in order to display their powers of exorcism or to involve their opponents in a charge of witchcraft. The most famous instance of this was the case of ' the Boy of Bilson ', whose story will be discussed in a later chapter.

The supposed ' papistry ' of witches caused the terror to spread over the country in pace with the growing patriotic dislike of Rome. As the menace of Spain and the House of Guise grew large it became increasingly difficult for a patriot to be other than a Reformationist and, as such, a believer that his religious and political enemies were in league with the Devil. Thus the rapid spread of Reformationism in the middle years of the reign of Elizabeth was accompanied by an equally rapid spread of continental witch-beliefs.

[1] M. Casaubon, *Traité de la Credulité*, p. 93; Stowe, *Annales of England*, p. 1171 (London, 1592).

[2] Fuller, *Church History of Britain*, bk. ix, Cent. XVI; Stowe, *Chronicle*, p. 1165 (London, 1592).

[3] *Discoverie of Witchcraft* (London, 1584).

[4] Soldan and Heppe, *Geschichte der Hexenprozesse*, ed. Max Bauer (Munich, 1911), vol. i, p. 537, ' In seinen (i.e. Bishop Peter Palladius's) Augen gehörten auch alle jene zu Hexen, die sich noch katholischer Segnungen und Gebete bedienten '. Sometimes the contrary occurred, and Roman Catholics accused Protestants of witchcraft—e.g., in Scotland, ' when Knox at the age of sixty married Margaret Stewart, daughter of Andrew, Lord Ochiltree, then only in her fifteenth year. This unnatural marriage of May and December gave Catholics occasion to ascribe to Knox the knowledge and use of the magic art.' G. F. Black, *A Calendar of Cases of Witchcraft in Scotland*, p. 11 (New York, 1938).

C

(ii) A hardly less potent cause of the relentless advance of continental witch-beliefs was the hold which these beliefs took upon the wealthy and educated classes. Views held strongly by the uppermost strata of society are almost certain to seep gradually down to those at the bottom of the social structure. So it was with the new doctrines of witchcraft.

It has often been assumed that such a superstition would find most welcome among the ignorant peasantry and would be regarded with more scepticism by the upper classes. The available evidence shows fairly decisively that this assumption is exactly the reverse of the truth. The poor had, it is true, their superstitions in abundance. But continental witch-belief was not regarded as a vulgar superstition. Far from that, it was taken as an exact science based on the accurate observations of able and enlightened men and built upon the reasoning of generations of famous scholars. The continental witch-beliefs were held by those in leading positions—by Elizabeth and James I, two of the most learned monarchs in our history; by statesmen and men of wide experience such as Burleigh and Raleigh, by great landed magnates like Sir Henry Cromwell and the Earl of Rutland, and, as will be shown in a later chapter, by the authorities of the University of Cambridge. Judges and dramatists, theologians and medical men combined to emphasize the seriousness of witchcraft.[1] The poor, on the other hand, treated the new doctrines about witches with indifference and scepticism. Their attitude is well portrayed in an example given by Reginald Scott.[2] This greatest of the witch-hunters' enemies describes how Simon Davie, a simple husbandman, with whom he was acquainted, found his wife, Ade, in a fit of the deepest depression. On his attempting to comfort her she begged him most earnestly for forgiveness, declaring that she had grievously offended both God and him.

[1] The Act against witchcraft of 1604 was redrafted by a committee of the House of Lords consisting, amongst others, of the Earl of Northumberland, the Earl of Derby, the Earl of Northampton, and the Bishop of Lincoln. The Committee acted with the advice of the Chief Justice of Common Pleas (Anderson), the Chief Baron of the Exchequer (Sir William Peryam), two justices of the King's Bench (Sir Christopher Yelverton and Sir David Williams), Serjeant Croke, the Attorney-General (Sir Edward Coke), and Sir John Tindall, an ecclesiastical lawyer. Among the Commons Committee which considered the Bill was Henry Montague, afterwards Chief Justice of the King's Bench (1616) and Earl of Manchester (1626).
[2] Reginald Scot, *Discoverie of Witchcraft* (London, 1584), bk. iii, ch. x.

Her poor husband being abashed at this her behaviour, comforted her as he could; asking her the cause of her trouble and greefe; who told him that she had, contrary to God's law, and to the offence of all good Christians, to the injury of him, and specially to the losse of her own soul, bargained and given her soul to the devill, to be delivered unto him within a short space. Wherefore her husband answered, saying, ' Wife, be of good cheer, this thy bargain is void and of none effect; for thou hast sold that which is none of thine to sell: sith it belongeth to Christ, who hath bought it, and dearly paid for it, even with his blood, which is shed upon the crosse; so as the devil hath no interest in thee.' After this with like submission, teares, and penitence, she said unto him, ' Oh, husband, I have yet committed another fault, and done you more injury; for I have bewitched you and four children.' ' Be content,' quoth he, ' by the grace of God, Jesus can unwitch us; for none evil can happen to them that fear God.'

§ 3 (a) Such homespun apathy towards continental witch-beliefs was bound in the long run to give ground before the influence of the more educated classes. For their influence was exercised not merely by word and example, but by a number of books emanating from scholars of the first magnitude in many parts of Europe. For nearly three centuries the outlook of the ordinary Englishman was moulded by *The Acts and Monuments* (1563) of John Foxe, known affectionately as *Foxe's Martyrs*. This weighty work, which passed through four editions during the author's lifetime, was commonly to be found beside the Bible in parish churches. Indeed, a copy of the second edition of 1570 was ordered by Convocation to be placed in every collegiate church in the kingdom; and few households which possessed any books at all were without a copy. The author, who had spent the reign of Mary amongst the witch-hunters of Strassbourg, Frankfort, and Basle, did not fail to make his book a powerful defence of the dominant superstition and an impressive warning against the wiles of witches.

In writing of Gerbert (Pope Sylvester II), perhaps the greatest scientist of the early Middle Ages, this is his conclusion.

This Sylvester was a sorcerer,[1] who after the manner of those who work by familiars, as they call them, and by conjuration, compacted with the devil to be made pope; and so he was, through the operation of Satan, according to his request, which thing, some historians say, he did greatly repent before his death; but for a more ample declaration hereof, I will bring in the words of Johannes Stella a

---

[1] John Foxe, *Acts and Monuments*, ed. Josiah Pratt, 8 vols. (London, 1877), vol. ii, pp. 95 sqq., 120 sqq., vol. iii, p. 131, vol. iv, p. 656, vol. v, p. 129, &c.

Venetian, translated from Latin into English, concerning the said Sylvester, to the intent that our enchanters and sorcerers now-a-days, of whom there be too many in England, may the better, through his example, be admonished. . . . Thus much out of Johannes Stella concerning Sylvester, by whom our sorcerers and enchanters, or magicians, may learn to beware of the deceitful operations of Satan, who in the end deceiveth and frustrateth all them that have to do with him, as the end of all such doth declare commonly, who use the like art or trade. The Lord and God of all Mercy . . . dissolve the works of Satan, and preserve the hearts of our nobles, and all other Englishmen, from such infection! Amen!

Here, as elsewhere, it should be noticed that Foxe insists on the continental doctrine that all witchcraft involves a pact with Satan.

He writes in a similar strain about Hildebrand (Pope Gregory VII), and concludes with the story of two servants who consulted a ' Satanical book ' of his and were, consequently, able to raise devils—much to their own embarrassment. Coming to more recent times, he narrates on the authority of Edmund Grindal (1519–83), Bishop of London, and afterwards Archbishop of Canterbury, the story of a reformer of Henry VIII's time.

For as the plague was sore at Cambridge, and amongst others a certain priest, called Sir Henry Conjuror, lay sore sick of the said plague, Master Stafford, hearing thereof, and seeing the horrible danger that his soul was in, was so moved in conscience to help the dangerous case of the priest, that he neglecting his own bodily-death, to recover the other from eternal damnation, came unto him, exhorted him and so laboured him, that he would not leave him before he had converted him, and saw his conjuring books burnt before his face. This being done, Master Stafford went home, and immediately sickened, and, shortly after, most Christianly deceased.

Later he records how William Tyndale (1490–1536), the translator of the Bible, was invited to a supper at which a certain juggler undertook ' through his diabolical enchantments of art magical ' to ' fetch all kinds of viands and wines from any place they would, and set them before them '. In Tyndale's presence, however, ' all his enchantments were void. He was compelled openly to confess that there was some man present at supper who disturbed and letted all his doings.' These and such-like passages read and re-read many times all over England could hardly fail to instil into the simple folk a terror of witchcraft and a readiness to attribute even the sleight of hand of the travelling showman to a dread compact with the Devil.

(b) One of the greatest landmarks in the history of witch-mania was the publication at Paris in 1580 of *De la Démonomanie des Sorciers*. A Latin version was printed at Basle the following year; and new and enlarged editions of the original appeared at Paris in 1587, at Antwerp and Lyons in 1593, at Paris again in 1598, and, finally, at Rouen in 1604. The author of this voluminous work, Jean Bodin (1530–96), commanded the attention of the civilized world by reason of his eminence as a philosopher, jurist, economist, publicist, and classical scholar. Among his many great achievements in so many fields was the first clear enunciation of the quantity theory of money, which revolutionized the science of economics. He visited England in the train of the Duke of Alençon, the ' frog ' who came to woo Elizabeth (1581). His writings were, moreover, especially acceptable in England, owing to his advocacy of complete toleration for French Calvinists and other dissidents in Roman Catholic countries. The *Démonomanie* was, consequently, read with the utmost avidity by educated men in England either in the Latin or the French, as the many copies that still exist in this country show. What made this large exposition of witchcraft especially impressive was the fact that so many of the witches he describes had actually been brought before him in his judicial capacity.

In his preface Bodin states that he was led to write this book by the case of a woman named Jean Harvilliers, who had been accused of witchcraft (April 1578). After first denying her guilt, she afterwards confessed that her mother had devoted her to the Devil when she was twelve years old, and that she had continued to have intimate relations with him till she was about fifty. He used to come to her booted and spurred and wearing dark clothes—a tall gentleman wearing a sword. Her mother had been burnt as a witch thirty years before, and she herself had been scourged. She was now arrested for spreading powder which caused a passer-by, for whom it was not intended, to sicken and die. After being condemned to the stake she made an alarming confession about flying to the Sabbat, worshipping Beelzebub, and many other wonders, all of which Bodin accepts as true. He goes on to attack those who are sceptical about such confessions, asserting that those who deny the existence of witchcraft are almost always witches themselves—an assertion which he supports with many examples. His purpose, he declares, is to inspire judges with greater zeal in the punishment of witches. He therefore paints a harrowing picture of the disasters that have followed upon the leniency of the courts in the trial of witches. In a well-stated argument he shows how little we know of natural and physical laws, and hence the absurdity of refusing to believe the facts of sorcery because we cannot explain them.

The book which follows consists of more than four hundred pages of terrifying stories of witchcraft, most of them more or less contemporary. Among the more recent cases was that of a lawyer in Paris in 1571 who confessed to entering into a contract with the Devil signed in his own blood. Four witches at Poitiers in 1564 had confessed that they had been thrice to the Sabbat at a certain cross-roads, where innumerable witches gathered. The meeting was presided over by a huge black goat, around whom they danced, after each of them bearing a candle had, one by one, kissed him under the tail. The goat was then consumed by fire, and his ashes furnished a powder which had been spread later on for the destruction of people and cattle. At the end of the proceedings the Devil dismissed them, saying in a terrible voice, ' Revenge yourselves or die ' ! President Salvert, who tried the witches, told Bodin that more than a hundred years before, as the records showed, witches had been condemned for meeting at the same rendez-vous. At Geneva, where dancing was especially hateful, a girl had recently been burnt for receiving from the Devil an iron rod which caused everyone whom she touched with it to dance.

Perhaps the most notable feature of Bodin's work is the cento of examples of witches changing into the shapes of various animals—particularly werewolves. Lycanthropy, he considers, is a result of eating human flesh;[1] and he connects it with the old pagan worship of Jupiter on Mount Lycaeus. One of his most recent examples of a werewolf was Gilles Garnier of Lyons, who was condemned (17th January 1573) by the Parlement of Dol to be burnt. According to his confession, which was substantiated by other evidence, he had killed a girl in the neighbouring forest of La Serre on the Feast of St. Michael. On this occasion he had the feet, paws, and teeth of a wolf, and he devoured the

---

[1] *Démonomanie*, Antwerp ed. of 1593, p. 205 : ' Et s'il faut rendre quelque raison pourquoy principalement les hommes sont plutost tournez en loups et asnes qu'en autres bestes, la raison m'a semblé que les premiers qu'on voit avoir changé de forme en Loup, mangeoyent la chaire humaine en sacrifiant a Jupiter, qui s'appeloit pour ceste cause *Lycaeus*, comme qui diroit Louuet. Aussi voit-on que celuy qui fut executé a Dole, qui changeoit d'homme en loup, & ceux de Savoye confesseront avoir mangé plusieurs enfants. Et par un juste jugement de Dieu il permet, qu'ils perdent la figure humaine, & qu'ilz soyent loups comme ilz meritent '.

flesh of the girl's arms and carried some of it home to his wife. A month later, again in the shape of a wolf, he had killed a girl, and would have eaten her had he not been driven off. Fifteen days later he strayed from home and ate a boy of ten in a neighbouring vineyard.

From the adventures of the French juggler Triscalain he draws the conclusion that witches must never on any account be pardoned. For the death of Charles IX was probably the result of his ill-judged mercy to this witch, who entertained him with stories of the Sabbat and such-like. Had he ordered Triscalain and others like him to be burnt, God would probably have granted him a longer life. For he was in perfect health when he entertained the sorcerer, but died shortly afterwards. Elsewhere Bodin argues that no penalty for witchcraft can be too harsh.[1] Even burning to death by a slow fire was an insufficient penalty for witchcraft, since it does not last more than half an hour or an hour. As for torture, witches care little for it, and are often able to escape death by its means. Bodin's own practice was to torture children and delicate persons,[2] but not the old and hardened. The judge who does not send a convicted witch to the stake should himself be put to death.[3] A person accused of witchcraft should never be acquitted unless the falsity of the accusation has been more obvious than the Sun.[4] In any consideration of this book of horrors it is

---

[1] *Démonomanie*, Antwerp, ed. 1593, p. 365, ' Or si'l y eut oncques moyen d'appaiser l'ire de Dieu d'obtenir sa benediction . . . c'est de chastier à toute rigeur les sorciers : combien que le mot de Rigeur est mal pris, attendu que il n'a peine si cruelle qui puest suffire à punir les meschancetez des sorciers '.

[2] *Démonomanie*, ed. 1593, ' Toutesfois je serai toujours d'avis, si c'est une jeune fille, un jeune enfant, ou une femme delicate, ou quelque mignart, si'l a presumptions violents, qu'on presente les uns a la question avec terreur, & qu'on y applique les autres : & non pas, les vielles sorcieres endurcies & opiniastres en leur meschancete '.

[3] Op. cit., p. 384. ' Et si'l est ainsi que le Iuge est coulpable, & doit suffrir la peine de leze Maieste qui a remis ou diminué la peine de leze Maieste comme dit la loy : combien plus est coulpable de Iuge qui remet ou diminue la peine de celui qui est coulpable de leze Maieste Divine ? . . . Autant peut on dire de ceux qui envoyent absoultes les sorcieres (encores qu'elles soient convaincues) & disent pour toute excuse qu'ils ne peuvent croire ce qu'on en dit, qu'ils meritaient la mort. Car c'est revoquer en doute la loy de Dieu & toutes les loix humaines. . . .'

[4] Op. cit., p. 401. ' Aussi ceux-là qui font evader les sorciers, ou qui non font punition à toute rigeur, se peuvent assurer qu'ils seront abandonnez de Dieu à la mercy des sorciers. Et la pays qui les endurera, sera battu de pestes, famines & guerres, et ceux qui en feront la vengeance seront benits de Dieu feront cesser sa fureur. C'est pourquoi celuy qui est attaint & accuse d'estre sorcier, ne doibt iamais estre envoyé absoubs à pur & à plein, si la calomnie de l'accusateur ou delateur n'est plus claire que le soleil.'

difficult to keep in mind the immense and lasting prestige of the author. Yet it is necessary to do so in order to appreciate the immensity and long endurance of the book's influence. Bodin was described by the sceptical Montaigne as the highest literary genius of his time, and by Bayle as the ablest writer of sixteenth-century France.

(c) A few years before Bodin's book had become known in England a powerful incitement to witch-persecution arrived from Geneva, in which city was published *Les Sorciers, dialogue très utile et très necessaire pour ce temps* in 1564. So great was the demand for it that it was reprinted in 1574, 1577, and 1579. A Latin version appeared at Cologne in 1575, and an English version made from the Latin appeared later the same year, with the following portentous title: *A Dialogue of Witches, in foretime named Lot-tellers, and now commonly called Sorcerers. Wherein is declared breefly and effectually, whatsoever may be required, touching that argument. A treatise very profitable, by reason of the diverse and sundry opinions of men in this question, and right necessary for Judges to understand, which sit upon life or death.* The author, Lambert Daneau (1530–95), was one of the best-known Calvinist theologians in Europe. He became (1572) Professor of Theology at Geneva, where he was granted citizenship. Later he occupied the chair of Theology at Leyden, where he commended himself to the English by his whole-hearted support of the claims of the Earl of Leicester to the sovereignty of the Netherlands. His reputation stood high for his scriptural commentaries and his polemical works against Roman Catholics and Lutherans—numbering in all fifty-five. That a book on witchcraft from such a pen should enjoy immense prestige among Elizabethan Englishmen was only to be expected; and the literary dependence of later English works shows that the expectation was abundantly fulfilled.

The *Dialogue* was occasioned by the execution of ' almost an infinite number' of witches in Paris—an event which gave rise to much discussion about the reality of sorcery. Daneau's object was to remove all doubts by pure argument instead of the recitation of examples of the doings of witches. The increase of their activities in modern times he explains by the increasing wicked-ness of mankind, which increased Satan's power to win souls from God—by Divine permission, which is given or withheld on grounds which it is beyond our power to understand. One of the most ominous features of Daneau's book is the stress he lays on ' witches' marks '—a subject which occupied so large a place in the evidence at later witch-trials in this country.

> This much I dare affirm to you [he writes] (Ch. IV), that there is no sorcerer but he maketh a league and covenant with the Divel, and voweth himself unto him. In confirmation of which vowing he receeaveth in his body some note or marke made and imprinted by Satan in some parte, which he always beareth aboute him, some under theyr eye liddes, others betwene their buttockes, some in the roofe of their mouth, and in other places where it may be hid and concealed from us. Although some be of opinion, that all sorcorers are not privily pricked and marked by Satan, but onely these of whose constancie towards him he standeth in doubt, and those of whom he doubeth not, are left unmarked: yet I may say this certenly and truly, that there is none of them upon whom he doth not set some note or token of his power and prerogative over them: which to thintent the judges and such as are let in aucthoritie of life and death, and to enquire of such matters, may the better perceave, let them specially provide, that when any of them shall be convented before them, to poulle and shave where occasion shall serve all the body over, least haply the marke may lurke under the heare in any place.

Daneau describes the Sabbat and the witches flying thither on a staff; and rejects any theory of illusion on the ground that an infinite number of confessions prove beyond doubt the bodily presence of the witches at the Sabbat.

> He (the Devil) promiseth that himself will convey them thither, that are so weak that they cannot travaile of themselves: which many times he doth by means of a staffe or rod, which he delivereth to them, or promiseth to do it by force of a certain oynt-ment which he will geve them . . . when they meete together he appeareth visibly unto them in sundrie fourmes . . . sometimes . . . with the shape of a man, sometime like a most filthie bucke goate, and sometimes in other licknesses.

The book concludes with an exhortation to the pitiless extirpation of witches and a condemnation of judges who for any reason suffer them to live.

> I marvel therefore [he writes] (Bk. V) that at this present there be some Iudges so parciall, or rather so unfreendly to all mankynde, that they be affearde, or rather wil not ryd away out of the worlde, such horrible and cruell beastes, as Sorcerers bee, and punish them when they come into their handes . . . they declare by this fond-nesse of their owne mynde, howe much they contemne God, and are great and manifest despisers of his honour and glory, whose mortall and sworne enemies when they have founde, and taken: yet do they let them goe and suffer them to live.

All right-thinking men from of old agree that witches deserve the severest penalties. They should be condemned without wasting time on vain and curious questions. There should be no appeals or other devices by which some of them may be enabled to escape their doom.

(*d*) Such uncompromising opinions coming from so notable a writer must have contributed much to the confirmation of educated opinion in England. A less direct but no less potent stimulus to witch-mania was a volume published in 1572 under the title *Of Ghostes and Spirites walking by nyght.* The German original was published at Zürich in 1569. So immediate and widespread was its popularity that a Latin translation appeared the following year; a French translation was published in Geneva and Paris in 1571; and in various languages the book went through more than sixteen editions during the course of a century. The author, Lewes Lavater (1527–86), a son-in-law of Bullinger, was among the most famous of the second generation of Calvinist theologians and a voluminous writer of Biblical commentaries. He reached the high position of Chief Pastor (1585) of the Calvinist Church of Zürich. The main argument of his book is that, after making the fullest allowance for ocular illusion, hallucination, and jugglers' tricks, there can be no doubt that genuine ghosts do really appear. All literature, sacred and profane, as well as an abundance of experiences among men now living, put this beyond all possible doubt.

> To al the premisses before handled [he writes] (Bk. I, ch. xvi) this also is to be added, which no man can deny, but the many honest & credible persons . . . which have and do affirm that they have sometimes in the day, & sometimes in the nyght seen and hard spirits. Some man walketh alone in his house, & behold a spirit apeereth in his sight, yea & sometimes the dogs also perceve them, & fal down at their masters fete, & wil by no means depart from them, for they are sore afraid themselves too. Some man goeth to bed and laieth him down to rest, and by and by there is something pinching him, or pulleth off the clothes: sometimes it sitteth on him, or lyeth down in bed with him: and many times it walketh up and down the Chamber . . . Many use at this day to serch and sifte every corner of the house before they go to bed that they may sleep more soundly: & yet nevertheless, they heare some scrying out, and making a lamentable noise &c.

He goes on to argue that it is not the dead who are seen as ghosts, since the dead go either to Heaven or to Hell, whence there is no return, there being no such place as Purgatory. It

was not the true Samuel that appeared to the Witch of Endor
(Bk. II, cap. vii, viii). Ghosts are devils (Bk. II, cap. vii).

> But it is no difficult matter for the devil to appeare in divers
> shapes, not only of those which are alive, but also of dead menne
> . . . yea, and (which is a lesse matter) in the fourme of beastes and
> birdes &c. as to appear in the likenesse of a Black Dog, or a Horsse,
> an Owle, and also to bring incredible things to passe. . . .

The power of the Devil is for Lavater proved by the fact of
witchcraft. He quotes (Bk. II, cap. xvii) from the Chronicles
of Johannes Tritenhemius (Trithemius)

> in the yeare of our Lorde 970 . . . one named Baianus was
> thoroughly seen in the Art of Necromancie, and thereby wrought
> many myracles. He chaunged himselfe into a Wolfe so often as he
> list, or into the likenesse of any other beaste, or in such sort that he
> could not be discerned of any man. . . . There are also coniurers
> founde even at this day, who bragge of themselves that they can so
> by enchauntments saddle an horse, that in a fewe houres they wil
> dispatch a very long iourney. God at last wil chasten these men with
> deserved punishment. What strange things are reported of one
> *Faustus* a German, which he did in these our dayes by enchaunt-
> ments? . . . Hagges, witches and Inchaunters are sayde to hurt
> men and cattell, if they do but touch them or stroake them, they do
> horrible things whereof there are whole bookes extant. . . . Magi-
> tians, iugglers, inchanters and Necromanciers, are no others than
> servants of the Diuel : you do not thinke their mayster reserveth some
> cunning to him self ?

(*e*) During the period between the accession of Elizabeth and
the destruction of the Spanish Armada the writings of Foxe, Bodin,
Daneau, and Lavater did much to deepen the witch-terror in
England. Others, such as Ralph Holingshed, whose *Chronicles
of England, Scotland, and Ireland*, with their many witch-stories, were
first published in 1577, provided a substantial quota to the same
effect. So also did a considerable pamphlet literature. For few
sensational witch-trials went by without resulting in some rapidly
printed pages recording the more ghastly details elicited by the
court. Many of these are no longer extant. Others, such as
A True and Iust Recorde of all the Witches taken at St Oses (London,
1582), survive to suggest to a modern reader the measure of the
panic they must have caused amongst a credulous reading public
of the later sixteenth century.

CHAPTER III

THE FIRST PERIOD OF THE GREAT WITCH-SCARE,
1588–1618

§ 1. THE COMING of the Spanish Armada has been regarded from many points of view as a turning-point in English history. It marks the date when England was finally relieved from the long-standing peril of the Habsburg–Guise alliance. It probably marks the date, too, when the mass of the English people, after halting long between two opinions, decided, in its access of patriotism at the defeat of the hated Spaniard, that its religion should be of a non-Papal type. These and other changes associated with the coming of the Armada are probably not unconnected with the fact that the year 1588 marks the beginning of a period, more than a quarter of a century long, in which a great witch-scare, with the fullest encouragement of the Government, seized upon a considerable part of England and rapidly encroached on those regions which had hitherto been insensitive to continental demonology. In order to understand this period it is necessary to consider a series of events which were at the same time both results of the prevailing witch-scare and also causes of its increase.

§ 2 (a) The first of these in order of time, and little less than first in order of importance, is the trial of the Witches of Warboys. This astonishing, though not untypical, case has been recorded with a wealth of curious detail of especial interest to the student of folk-lore. Here it is necessary to deal with it only in the barest outline.

Warboys is situated some six or seven miles north-east of Huntingdon. Here in November 1589 Robert Throckmorton, who had recently come to live in the largest house in the village, was much troubled about the health of his five daughters. Joan, the eldest daughter, aged about ten, as well as her sisters, used to fall into strange fits. They more than once accused an old village woman, Mrs. Alice Samuel, of having bewitched them, by means of a familiar spirit who took the form of a chicken. Dr.

Barrow,[1] a well-known Cambridge physician, who was called in to treat the girls, attributed their fits to diabolical agencies, adding significantly that he had ' some experience of the malice of witches '.   On hearing of the troubles of the Throckmorton household, Susan, Lady Cromwell, the second wife of Sir Henry Cromwell,[2] a grandfather of the Lord Protector, came from Ramsey on a visit of sympathy (September 1590).   She sent for Mrs. Samuel, and noticed that the old woman's arrival seemed to make the condition of the children obviously worse.   She consequently took the old woman aside and taxed her with witchcraft.   This charge Mrs. Samuel indignantly denied.   At the same time she refused to be examined by a certain Doctor of Divinity named Hall, who was waiting in another room.   Lady Cromwell, who was evidently *au fait* with the technique of witch-hunting, thereupon removed the old woman's knitted cap and cut off a lock of her hair.   This she handed to Mrs. Throckmorton together with the hairlace, telling her quietly to burn them.   Old Mrs. Samuel was quick to recognize the significance of these proceedings, and said as she left the house, ' Madam, why do you use me thus ?   I never did you any harm, *as yet.*'

That night Lady Cromwell suffered from terrible dreams of old Mother Samuel and her cat.   Her cries awakened her daughter-in-law, Mrs. Oliver Cromwell, who was sleeping in the same bed.   This dream proved to be the beginning of a long and fatal illness.   A year and a quarter later Lady Cromwell died (July 1592).

Meanwhile Mrs. Samuel, curiously enough, came to stay for some time at the Throckmortons' house.   During her stay she became seriously ill, and confessed that she was a witch.   Dr. Dorrington,[3] the rector of Warboys, was summoned.   So edified was he by the old woman's penitence that he made it the subject of his sermon next day, which was Sunday and Christmas Eve

---

[1] Possibly Philip Barrow, who was licensed as a physician (1572) and a surgeon (1559) by the University of Cambridge. His book *Method of Physicke, containing the Causes, Signs and Cures of Inward Diseases in Man's Body from head to foot* (London 1590) reached its fifth edition in 1617.

[2] Sir Walter Scott in his *Demonology and Witchcraft* calls him, by an obvious slip of the pen, Sir *Samuel* Cromwell. This slip, which originated with Hutchinson, has been copied by many later writers : E. G. M. Summers, *The Geography of Witchcraft*, p. 127 (London, 1927). It has done much to conceal the identity of the grandfather of the Lord Protector.

[3] Dorrington was a Fellow of St. Catherine's College, Cambridge, 1558; B.D. Queen's College, Cambridge, 1565, and D.D. 1575.

(1592). His eloquence brought profuse tears of penitence from Mrs. Samuel, who was by this time well enough to take her place in the congregation. Next day she returned to her own home and, possibly under the influence of her husband John and her daughter Agnes, completely recanted her confession. Throckmorton and Dr. Dorrington now took counsel together and decided on the arrest of the old woman and her daughter, who were accordingly sent to be examined before the Bishop [1] of Lincoln (William Wickham) at Buckden the day after Christmas. Mrs. Samuel was by now thoroughly frightened and ready to confess anything.

Her revelations about her dun chicken were so alarming that three days later she was examined again, before the Bishop of Lincoln and two Justices of the Peace, Francis Cromwell and Richard Tryce. This time she made a further confession, with the result that she and her daughter were consigned to Huntingdon Jail to await the Assizes.

Agnes was, however, brought back to Warboys on bail for purposes of experiment. It was soon discovered that the children would immediately recover from a fit on Agnes's repeating the formula, ' Even as I am a witch and consented to the death of Lady Cromwell, so I charge thee, spirit, to depart and let her be well.' Old John Samuel, who happened to call when these experiments were going on, was himself put to the same test. On his repeating the formula, one of the children, who had fallen into a fit as soon as he entered the room, recovered immediately. He, too, was consequently charged with witchcraft and sent to prison to await his trial.

When the Judge [2] arrived for the Assizes, the eldest of the Throckmorton children and Agnes Samuel were taken to ' The Crown ', where he lodged, for further experiments. It was found that when the Judge or anyone except Agnes repeated the formula. the result was negative; also that when Agnes repeated the formula in the negative the result was also negative. But when she repeated the formula in its original (positive) form the child at once recovered from her fit.

[1] William Wickham (1539–95) was a Fellow of King's College, Cambridge, a chaplain to the Queen, and a friend of Burghley and Grindal. He preached at the funeral of Mary Queen of Scots, and was translated to the See of Winchester shortly before his death.

[2] Edward Fenner, who was appointed a judge of the Court of King's Bench on 26th May 1590 and continued in office till his death on 23rd January 1611/12. He was a Puritan in his sympathies, and as J.P. for Surrey had shown a kindly attitude towards John Udall, a Puritan fanatic.

After a trial (5th April 1593) in which the evidence for the Crown lasted five hours, all three Samuels were found guilty of bewitching to death Lady Cromwell and of bewitching Joan and Jane Throckmorton and others. They were consequently hanged, and their naked bodies, the perquisite of the jailer, were afterwards displayed to an awed and curious crowd.

The Warboys affair is of considerable importance in the history of continental witch-beliefs in England, for at least four reasons.

(i) In the first place, it led to the endowment in perpetuity of propaganda in the town of Huntingdon. The property of the Samuels—estimated to be worth about forty pounds—went legally to Sir Henry Cromwell, who was lord of the manor of Warboys; and Sir Henry gave (according to one of the Corporation books) ' goods to forty pounds' value of the said goods to the said Corporation to pay Queen's College, Cambridge, for a sermon to be preached yearly upon Lady Day, by a Doctor or Bachelor of Divinity, that should preach and inveigh against the detestable practice sin and offence of witchcraft, enchantment, charm and sorcery; for which he should have forty shillings. . . .' As a result of this settlement a sermon on witchcraft was preached annually in All Saints' Church, Huntingdon, by a distinguished member of Queen's College, Cambridge.[1] It was not discontinued till 1814. Brayley, in his *Huntingdonshire*, published in 1808, wrote, ' May not this sermon have tended to encourage that strong belief in witches which is still current among the common people in this county . . . ? ' Huntingdonshire, as will be noticed later, became one of the most notable centres of witch-hunting in the seventeenth century and even later. The endowment of a sermon at Huntingdon foreshadows the foundation of those Puritan lecturerships up and down the country that were such an embarrassment to the earlier Stuarts. It will be pointed out in a later chapter that there is good reason to believe that one of the most prominent subjects in the discourses of these lecturers was the danger of witchcraft.[2]

---

[1] *Notes and Queries* for July 1879, pp. 70–71; M. Noble, *Memoirs of the Protectoral House of Cromwell*, pp. 22–6, 3rd ed. (London, 1787). Queen's was the college to which Dr. Dorrington, the rector of Warboys, belonged. It was also the college of Sir Henry Cromwell himself.

[2] At Nottingham in 1497 the Puritan John Darrel was made a preacher. ' His fame collected crowded congregations whom he entertained with tales of devils and possessions, which frightened the people till the servants were afraid to go into the cellar for beer without company.' *Athenae Cantabrigienses*, vol. ii, p. 381 (Cambridge, 1861). For Darrel's pretended exorcisms see below, Ch. v.

(ii) A second reason for the importance of the Warboys affair lies in the social consequence of so many of the persons involved in it.[1] Sir Henry Cromwell, often called the Golden Knight, was about the richest commoner in England. He and his family had inherited vast monastic estates from Richard Williams, a brother of Thomas Cromwell, Earl of Essex. Sir Henry's two sons, Sir Oliver and Henry, were members of Parliament ten years later, the one for the shire and the other for the borough of Huntingdon. Both of them were intimately concerned with the Throckmorton troubles. Henry had witnessed in person some of the fits of the Throckmorton girls in 1593 only a short time before the trial. As for Sir Oliver, it was his wife who had accompanied Lady Cromwell on her visit to the Throckmortons, and had been present at the interview with old Alice Samuel. She, too, it was who had been in bed with Lady Cromwell at the time of her terrible dream that had formed the prelude to her fatal illness. Both Henry and Sir Oliver could hardly fail to have been deeply affected by the mysterious death of their step-mother. Another member of this affluent family, Francis, a brother of Sir Henry, was one of the Justices of the Peace who examined Mrs. Samuel (29th December 1592) and committed her to prison.

Hardly inferior in consequence to the upstart family of Cromwell were the kinsmen of Robert Throckmorton. They existed in two powerful branches, one in Gloucestershire and the other in Warwickshire. A cousin, also named Robert Throckmorton, lived nearby at Brampton in Northamptonshire, and had often witnessed the girls' fits. Mrs. Throckmorton's brothers, Mr. (afterward Sir) Gilbert Pickering of Tichmarsh, John Pickering, and Henry Pickering,[2] were persons of more than local importance. That they also were deeply concerned about the matter is shown by their evidence at the Assizes.

(iii) A third reason for the importance of the Warboys affair, not unconnected with the second, is the immense use that was made of it in propaganda against those who still refused to believe all the continental doctrines about witchcraft.[3] The earliest extant account published is, probably, a black-letter

[1] G. L. Kittredge, *Witchcraft in Old and New England*, pp. 302 sqq. (Harvard Univ. Press, 1928), also *English Witchcraft and James I* (New York, 1912).

[2] Christ's College, Cambridge. B.A., 1586, M.A., 1590. Incorporated at Oxford 1593. Rector of Aldwincle, All Saints', Northamptonshire, 1597.

[3] *Notes and Queries*, 12th Series, vol. i, p. 283 (1916).

pamphlet of which only one copy—and that an imperfect one—survives. It has neither printer's name nor date. It is entitled ' *A true and particular observation of a notable piece of witchcraft, practised by John Samuel the Father, Alice Samuel the Mother and Alice Samuel the Daughter, of Warboise in the County of Huntingdon, Upon five Daughters of Robert Throckmorton of the same Towne and Countie, Esquire, and certain other, maid-servants to the number of twelve in the whole, all of them being in one house : November 1589* '. A fuller account was issued shortly afterwards in 1593, ' *The most strange and admirable discovery of the three Witches of Warboys* '. This was written by an eye-witness, possibly Dr. Dorrington, the rector of Warboys. Its entry in the Register of the Stationers' Hall seems to have been an event of some importance. For it is stated in an attached note that it was ' recommended for matter of truthe by Master Judge Ffenner under his handwrytinge showed in a court or assemblie holden this Daye according to the ordonnances of the company '. A further note states that ' The note under Mr. Justice Fenner's hand is layd up in the Warden's Cupboard '.

The same year the dread story was, apparently, put into the form of a song, so that it would gain the widest possible currency amongst the mass of the people. The song is no longer extant; but its publication is vouched for by an entry in the Register of the Stationers' Company for 4th December 1593: ' John Danter. Entred for his copie, &c. *A lamentable Songe of the Three Wyches of Warbos, and executed at Hunt* . . . vj d.'

Two more pamphlets were issued the same year ' to be sold in Paternoster Row, at the Signe of the Talbot '. From this time onward for the following quarter of a century the prolific literature of witchcraft made the utmost use of all the details of an episode that had the guarantee of so many persons of wealth and consequence.

(iv) A further reason for the importance of the Warboys affair as a means of spreading continental witch-beliefs was the part played by the University of Cambridge in the various incidents of the lengthy story. Both the physicians consulted by Robert Throckmorton—Dr. Barrow and Master Butler [1]—were resident members of the University, and the former's remark about ' having some knowledge of the malice of witches ' throws a ray of light upon the opinions of Cambridge dons at this time.

---

[1] William Butler (1535–1618) of Clare Hall is mentioned in Aubrey, *Brief Lives*, ed. Clark, vol. i, p. 138, as ' the greatest physitian of his time '.

D

The rector of Warboys, a brother-in-law of Throckmorton, was also a graduate of Cambridge. Yet another member of the same University was Henry Pickering, of Christ's College, one of Mrs. Throckmorton's brothers. He visited the Throckmortons in 1590, when their troubles were at their height, 'being then a Scholler of Cambridge', and took two other scholars to see the witch. His unwavering conviction that old Mother Samuel was a witch is shown by his furious warning that 'there was no way to prevent the judgements of God, but by her confession and repentance: which if she did not in time, he hoped one day to see her burned at the stake, and he himself would bring fire and wood and the children should blow the coals'. During most of the time when the Throckmorton children were suffering from their fits, William Perkins, the author of the *Discourse on the Damned Art of Witchcraft*, was a Fellow of Christ's College. His *Discourse* was published posthumously by a certain Thomas Pickering, possibly a relative of Mrs. Throckmorton, and certainly a Cambridge man. It should be noticed also that both Sir Henry Cromwell and his son, Sir Oliver, had studied at Cambridge.[1]

It was at Cambridge, too, that many of the most notable books on witchcraft were published at the University Press— amongst others the *Discourse* already mentioned and James Mason's *Anatomie of Sorcery* (1612). That the University authorities were not unaccustomed to consult white witches in their difficulties is shown by a curious passage in Richard Bernard's *Guide to Grandjurymen*.[2] Bernard contends that the showing of a suspected person in a glass was an 'undoubted marke of a Witch, as one Master *Edmunds* of Cambridge told me, who was one that for a time professed to help men to goods or money stolne, who was once by the heads of the University questioned, as he confessed to me . . . he said he might have made two hundred pound *per annum* of his skill'. Cambridge, which had become staunchly Calvinist under Elizabeth, was slow to abandon her convictions about witches even in the later seventeenth century, when some of her most famous sons, such as Henry More, insisted with the utmost energy upon the reality of witchcraft. The indirect influence of a great university upon popular opinion all

[1] G. L. Kitteredge, *English Witchcraft and James I*, p. 34 (New York, 1912).
[2] Published in London, 1627. Most orthodox witch-hunters regarded white witchcraft with the same abhorrence as black witchcraft, since it also involved a pact with the Devil.

over the country must have been enormous. The village sceptic could easily be reduced to silence by the observation that the great scholars of Cambridge were completely convinced about the powers of witches.[1]

(b) The influence of the Warboys affair in diffusing continental witch-beliefs can scarcely be overrated. Another influence that pulled strongly in the same direction was that of the judges— especially in their addresses to juries of simple countrymen, who would regard them with the utmost awe and reverence. One such address has come down to us from Sir Edmund Anderson (1530–1605)—a Calvinistic upholder of the Establishment, who had shown much energy in the suppression both of Brownists and of seminary priests. In trying Mary Glover (1602) he addressed the jury in words that made a profound impression throughout the country.

> The land [he said] is full of witches, they abound in all places, I have hanged five or six and twenty of them. There is no man here, can speak more of them than myself; few of them would confess it, some of them did; against whom the proofs were nothing so manifest, as against those that denied it. They have on their bodies divers strange marks, at which (as some of them have confessed) the Devil sucks their blood, for they have forsaken God, renounced their baptism, and vowed their service to the Devil: and so the sacrifice which they offer him is their blood. This woman hath the like marks on sundry places of her body, as you see testified under the hands of the women, that were appointed to search her. The Devil is a spirit of darkness, he deals closely and cunningly, you shall hardly find direct proofs in such a case, but by many presumptions and circumstances you may gather it. . . . Their malice is great, their practice devilish, and if we do not convict them, without their own confession or direct proof, where the presumptions are so great, and the circumstances so apparent, they will, in a short time overrun the whole land.[2]

If this is a fair sample—and it probably is—of a judge's address to a jury engaged in a witch trial, it is hardly surprising that the common people were so soon infected with the more sophisticated superstitions of their betters.

(c) (i) The year after Sir Edmund Anderson's speech the

---

[1] Atkinson and Clarke, *Cambridge* (1897), p. 93. 'At Cambridge in 1620, while the crusade against witchcraft was in full vigour, they had a separate place of confinement for this class of offender, called the Witches' Jail, which was separated by a partition from the felons' jail in the Jew's House given to the town in 1224 by Henry III.'

[2] C. L'Estrange Ewen, *Witchcraft and Demonianism*, pp. 127, 196–9 (London, 1933), from Sloane MS., 831, pp. 38–9.

accession of James I (1603) reinforced the English witch-hunters by the influx of crowds of Scots. The Northern kingdom, having been more completely subjugated by continental Calvinism, had suffered proportionately more from witch terror than England had hitherto done.[1] War against the infernal powers had been declared by an Act of Parliament of 1563—almost exactly contemporary with the Act of Elizabeth but far more severe (Mary 9). It forbad the use of 'witchcraftis, sorsarie, and negromancie . . . under pane of deid alsweill to be execute aganis the usar abusar as the seikar of the response or consultation'. It has been estimated that as many as 8,000 were burnt[2] for witchcraft in forty years; and the estimate, high as it is, is not altogether impossible. For the local magistrates were empowered not only to seek out, but to try and condemn to the stake those suspected of this most terrible of crimes. Moreover, the most excruciating tortures were used with the utmost freedom in order to obtain confessions; and the anonymous accusation of witches was encouraged.[3]

> A hollowe peece of wood or a chest is placed in the church [says Reginald Scot] into which anybodie may freely cast a little scroll of paper, wherein may be conteined the name of the witch, the time, place and fact etc. And the same chest being locked with three several locks, is opened every fifteenth daie by three inquisitors or officers appointed for that purpose; which keepe three several kaies. And thus the accuser need not be knowne, nor shamed with the reproach of slander or malice to his poore neighbour.

In such circumstances the numbers burnt by the inferior magistrates must have been enormous. They would also leave no record likely to survive. Many Scottish witch-burnings are known to have taken place only through some casual mention in a contemporary writer. Thus, for example, a stranger who

---

[1] Scotland in the Middle Ages was little troubled with witch-mania. G. F. Black, *A Calendar of Cases of Witchcraft in Scotland*, 1510–1727, p. 9: 'Previous to the passing of the Statute of June, 1563, there is but scant mention of witchcraft in Scotland' (New York, 1938). See also J. G. Dalyell, *Darker Superstitions of Scotland*, p. 618 (Edinburgh, 1834).

[2] *Acts of Parliament of Scotland*, vol. ii, p. 539.

Robert Steele, in *Social England*, vol. iv, p. 119 (ed. Traill and Mann, London, 1895), wrote: 'For forty years Scotland had been engaged in witch-hunting, with the result that 8,000 human beings are believed to have been burnt between 1560 and 1600. . . .' This is a high estimate, the total population of Scotland at the time being probably less than one million. See G. F. Black, op. cit., pp. 17, 18.

[3] R. Scot, *Discoverie*, bk. iii, ch. II, pp. 15–16 (London, 1584); cf. J. Bodin, *De Magorun Daemonomania*, p. 321 (Basle, 1581).

visited Scotland in 1644 remarks, ' I remember that I saw nine witches burnt at one time in Leith Links '.[1] Yet only one capital conviction for witchcraft appears in the records of the Supreme Court for the year in question.

James I himself is well known as a determined and experienced witch-hunter. The storms at sea which had accompanied his journey with his bride, Anne of Denmark, to Scotland (1589–90), and the subsequent confession of Dr. Fian—under terrible tortures—that he and others had raised the storms by throwing cats into the sea, drew his attention to the perils of the Black Art. He set out on a prolonged course of study of the whole subject from continental sources; and after seven years' research presented to the world his *Daemonologie* (1597), in which he argues with considerable shrewdness and erudition against those who sought to minimize belief in witchcraft. In the *Basilikon Doron*, addressed to Prince Henry, he mentions witchcraft among the ' horrible crymes that yee are bound in Conscience never to forgive '. Though James's credulity has often been grossly exaggerated,[2] his accession doubtless increased the impetus of the demand for more drastic legislation against witches.

(ii) The Bill introduced in the House of Lords in the first session of his first Parliament, when, after lengthy discussion, it became law, clothed the witch-hunter with well-nigh irresistible power. It supported with the highest authority in the realm the most extreme formulas of his grim creed. The Elizabethan Statute of 1563 had, in its main provision, been merely an extension of the law of murder, since it prescribed capital punishment mostly for those witches who had caused the death of others. The Jacobean Statute (1 Jas, c. 12, 1604), on the other hand, stresses the awful power of the Devil and the doctrine that all witchcraft, whether black or white, is the result of a contract with the Devil himself. Whether a witch had actually injured anyone was no longer the important question. The mere fact of a contract with the Devil

---

[1] Daylell, *Darker Superstitions of Scotland*, p. 670 (Edinburgh, 1834), quoted from Ramesay; ΕΛΜΙΝΘΟΛΟΓΙΑ, ch. 6, p. 71. It is highly probable that many witch executions both in England and Scotland have gone unrecorded owing to a strange reluctance of many writers to mentioning the subject of witchcraft. Thus, for example, Burnet in his *Life of Sir Matthew Hale* (1682) makes no mention of the witch trials at Bury St. Edmunds (1664) and the notable speech on that occasion for which Hale is chiefly remembered.

[2] On this exaggeration see G. L. Kittredge, *English Witchcraft and James I* (New York, 1912), also *Witchcraft in Old and New England*, pp. 276 sqq. (Cambridge, Mass., Harvard Univ. Press, 1929).

or of the keeping of imps was in itself sufficient to send a witch to the gallows.[1]

This statute—' An Act against Conjuration, Witchcrafte and dealing with evil and wicked Spirits '—was so potent in its influence during the subsequent century that some of its main provisions need to be quoted.

> If any person or persons . . . shall use practice or exercise any Invocation or Conjuration of any evil or wicked Spirit, or shall consult covenant with entertaine employ feede or rewarde any evil and wicked Spirit to or for any intent or purpose; or take any dead man or child out of his or her grave, or any other place where the dead body resteth, or the skin bone or any other part of any dead person, to be employed or used in any manner of Witchcrafte Sorcerie, Charm or Inchantment; or shall use practice or exercise any Witchcraft Inchantment or Sorcerie, whereby any person shall be killed destroyed wasted consumed pined or lamed in his or her body, or any part thereof; that then every such offender or offenders, theire Ayders Abettors and Counsellors, being of any of the saide offences dulie and lawfullie convicted and attainted, shall suffer pains of deathe as a Felon or Felons, and shall lose the priviledge and benefit of Cleargie or Sanctuarie.[2]

§ 3. It has been estimated by one writer that as many as 70,000 witches were put to death in England under the provisions of this statute.[3] Though this estimate is generally rejected by the most recent authorities, there is no doubt that the number hanged during the first twelve years of James I's reign was fearfully high, and that the great witch-terror had spread amongst all classes in an ever-widening area of the country. No longer was it confined to the south-eastern parts of England. It had spread across the country to Lancashire and the neighbouring West Riding of Yorkshire.

[1] It should not be forgotten, however, that the Elizabethan Statute fixed the death penalty for all who ' use, practice, or exercise invocations or conjurations of evil and wicked spirits to or for any intent or purpose ' without regard to the result of such invocations or conjurations. Kittredge, *Witchcraft in Old and New England*, p. 282 (Cambridge, Mass., 1929).

[2] Hutchinson, in his *Historical Essay concerning Witchcraft* (London, 1718), considers (p. 180) that the publication of the Authorized Version of Scripture contributed to the increase of witch-belief at this time. ' I must add, that the Translation of our *Bible* being made soon after, by King James's particular Desire hath made some Phrases that favour the vulgar Notions more than the Old Translation did. At that unhappy Time was brought in that gross Notion of a *Familiar Spirit*, tho' the *Hebrew* Word hath no Epithet at all, and should rather have been translated into some of those Words that signify a cheating Ventriloquist.'

[3] R. Steele in *Social England*, ed. H. D. Traill, vol. iv, p. 120 (London, 1903).

In Lancashire the efforts of Puritan preachers sent thither under Elizabeth had created a considerable Puritan nucleus in the midst of a Catholic population. The conditions were, consequently, extremely favourable to the rise of witch-terror. For the Puritans, here as ever, suspected Catholics of intimacy with the Prince of Darkness. So large grew the Puritan body in these parts that it was here that the protest against Sunday games was first heard, and during the Civil War Lancashire was the only county except Essex and Middlesex in which it was found possible to set up the Presbyterian system in its entirety. During the trials of the famous Lancashire witches in 1612 the fury of the mob could hardly have been surpassed in London or Essex. For example, on the acquittal of one of the accused—Mistress Redfern—it is said that such a furious shout of rage arose from the crowd that the court was intimidated into trying the unhappy woman all over again and, this time, finding her guilty and consigning her to the gallows.[1]

Any attempt to trace the rise of the great witch-scare would be incomplete if it failed to notice the influence of the Press. By an ordinance of the Star Chamber, Elizabeth had entrusted the censorship of the Press to the Archbishop of Canterbury and the Bishop of London. Hence, so long as the Puritan George Abbot (1562–1633) continued to act as Metropolitan a great stream of sensational popular pamphlets[2] and learned works issued from the Press, and not infrequently passed through several

---

[1] Notestein, *History of Witchcraft in England*, p. 127 (Washington, 1911); *Pott's Discovery of Witches in the County of Lancaster*, ed. James Crossley (Chetham Soc., 1845).

[2] Among the more notable pamphlets were the following:—

A true discourse. Declaring the Damnable life and death of one Stubbe Peeter, a most wicked Sorcerer, who in the likeness of a wolfe, committed many murders, continuing this diuelish practise 25 yeeres, killing and devouring Men, Woomen and Children . . . Trulye translated out of the high Dutch (London, 1590).

Newes from Scotland. Declaring the Damnable life and death of Dr Fian, a notable Sorcerer, who was burned at Edinbourough in January last 1591. Which Doctor was register to the Diuell. . . . (London, 1591).

Lamentable newes from Newgate, Barnet and Bragnford beinge the Indictment, Arraignment, Judgment and Execution of three wicked witches (London, 1595).

A Strange Report of Sixe other notorious witches, who by their diuelish practises murdered above the number of foure hundred small children . . . now translated out of Dutch (London, 1601).

The most cruel and bloody murder committed by an Inkeeper's wife . . . With Severall witch-crafts, and most damnable practises of one Johane Harrison and her Daughter upon seuerall persons, men and women at Royston, who were all executed at Hartford the 4 of August last past 1606 (London, 1606).

See D. C. Collins, *A Handlist of News Pamphlets* (London, 1943).

editions. Many of them are no longer extant; but the minority which survive are enough to convey some notion of the panic terror they must have spread in hall and cottage and inn over a large part of England. Every sickness of man or beast, every sudden death, every storm, every failure of crops was now unhesitatingly attributed to the satanic power exerted by some old women of the afflicted neighbourhood. Terror and a fierce desire for vengeance dominated men's minds, and continued to do so for two generations. As late as 1682 Roger North [1] describing the popular excitement at a witch trial in Exeter wrote, ' A less zeal in a city or kingdom hath been the overture of defection and revolution, and if these women had been acquitted, it was thought the country people would have committed some disorder '.

§ 4 (a) While an extensive issue of popular pamphlets deepened the convictions of the masses of the people, the presses of England and of the Continent produced a series of substantial volumes, the work of scholars of the highest repute, to influence the more literate classes in their pseudo-scientific witch-beliefs. Amongst them the first in order of time was the work of a Calvinist minister of considerable consequence, Henry Holland (d. 1604), a graduate of Magdalene College, Cambridge (M.A. 1593/4), Vicar of Orwell, Cambridgeshire, and later of St. Bride's, London. Amongst his works, which show him to have been well-read in continental Calvinist writers, was *Aphorisms of the Christian Religion : or a verie Compendious Abridgement of M. I. Calvin's Institutions, set forth in short sentences by M. I. Piscator : And now Englished according to the Author's third and last edition* (London, 1596). The long title of his propagandist volume on witchcraft indicates the urgency which he attributed to the subject: *A Treatise against Witchcraft : or a Dialogue, wherein the greatest doubts concerning that sin, are briefly answered : a Sathanicall operation in the Witchcraft of all times is truly prooved : very needful to be knowen of all men, but chiefly of Masters and Fathers of families, that they may learn the best meanes to purge their houses of all unclean spirits, and wisely to avoide the dreadfull impieties and greate daungers which come by such abominations, &c.* The book, like so many others on the same subject, was ' Printed by John Legatt, Printer to the Universitie of Cambridge ' (1590). It was dedicated to Elizabeth's favourite, the Earl of Essex.

In the course of the Dialogue (ch. ii), *Mysodaemon*, whose

---

[1] Roger North, *Autobiography*, ed. Jessopp, pp. 131 sqq.

function is to act the part of Devil's Advocate, suggests that witchcraft ' is knocked on the head, and nayled to the crosse with Christ, who hath broken the power of the deuilles '. To this Theophilus makes the thorough-going Calvinistic reply that only the elect are saved by the cross:

> For babes in Christianitie understand that Christ on his crosse, hath so farreforth broken the power of sinne, as that it shall never have strength to the condemnation of his elect. But hee never ment so to take away sinne, as that it should have no beeing in the world, much lesse to knock in the head (as thine Author saith) the sinnes of Sathan & reprobates, for they are predestinate al to burne in that lake which is prepared for the deuill and his angels.

After Theophilus has narrated from Luther a story of a pact with the Devil, Mysodaemon asks where the pact is made.

> At their common meetings [replies Theophilus] which they cal their sabboth . . . these obligations are authentically sealed. . . . In these horrible meetings, Sathan himselfe appeares sometime in one form, some time in another . . . sometimes his ministers behould him in the likeness of a man, but most commonly of a foule stinking goate. There they have sundry suits unto him : and he ministereth and teacheth them . . . and in the end he addeth (when his congregation is to be dismissed) with a terrible thundering voice, this speech, or something to this effect. *Ulciscimini vos aut mortem oppetetis. Revenge yourselves, or else die the death.*

(*b*) The outstanding work of the period was that of Nicolas Remi (1554–1600), who became Procureur-Général under Duke Henry II of Lorraine. Remi was notable in his day as one of the leading scholars, historians, and jurists. His book, *Daemonolatreia, ex judiciis capitalibus nongentorum plus minus hominum qui sortilegii crimen intra annos quindecim in Lotharingia capite luerunt* (1st ed. Lyons, 1595), owes its immense influence to the prestige of the writer and, even more, to the vividness of its style, and to the fact that all statements are authenticated with dates and with the names of the victims whose confessions he received during the fifteen years in which he acted as judge. It became the quarry from which subsequent writers hewed their material to such an extent that it largely superseded the *Malleus Maleficarum*; as is shown by the number of times it was reprinted during the subsequent century.[1]

The book begins with an impressive description of the threats

---

[1] It was reprinted at Frankfort 1596 and 1597, at Cologne 1596, and at Hamburg 1693 and 1698. German translations were published at Frankfort (1598) and Hamburg (1693).

and promises by which Satan gains power over witches, of the three powders he gives them—one to kill, one to make sick, and one to cure—and of the money they receive, which later turns to leaves and stones, &c. Remi describes the Devil's mark, which, he declares, is insensible and incapable of bleeding. He gives evidence to show (Bk. I, cap. 9) that demons can instantly assume any form, and describes in a wealth of detail the procedure of the Sabbat, where everyone has to pay tribute to the Devil on pain of severe punishment. Wives when going thither (cap. 11) throw their husbands into a profound sleep, or provide an image to represent them during their absence. The confessions of witches show the largeness of the numbers that sometimes attend a Sabbat (Bk. I, 15).

> In Lorraine, I remember, during the sixteen years in which I have acted as a judge in capital charges that not fewer than eight hundred, being clearly guilty of this offence, were condemned to death by the two of us. In addition to these there were almost as many who escaped sentence either by flight or by their stedfast endurance of torture. For so deceptive and slippery is the procedure in accusations of this kind that the accused frequently escape and frustrate the purpose of the court—a matter which we will discuss more fully in its proper place. But all those arrested for this kind of witchcraft declare with one voice that enormous numbers assemble at their gatherings. . . . Catherine Ruffa said that she saw not fewer than five hundred on the night when she first joined the Sabbat. Barbelina Rayel said the men were far outnumbered by the women, as their sex was much more inclined to the Demon &c.

More than two hundred of those whom Remi condemned to the flames voluntarily confessed that they were in the habit of going to a pond or a brook and beating the water with a rod given them by the Demon. Whereupon mists would arise and form dense clouds, upon which they would sail and direct storms of hail, rain, and lightning to burst on the spots they had selected.

> Some deny [he concludes] (Bk III, 12) that witches ought to be punished. Such persons are confuted by the evidence and the opinions of the greatest men of all ages. They are sinning against the light. ' In the words of Isaiah they are calling evil good and darkness light.'

(c) Two years after the appearance of Remi's weighty and scholarly volume came James I's *Daemonologie, in forme of a Dialogue, Divided into three Bookes*. It is a shrewd, able, and well-written book and, apart from its many merits, its royal authorship would insure its being widely read. After being published in

Edinburgh in 1597 it was republished in London in 1603. It was shortly afterwards translated into Dutch, and thence into a Latin version, which was issued at Hanover in 1604 and 1607. As it was based on a careful study of all the leading continental works, it did much to reinforce the continental beliefs in this country. The fact that James refused to accept every belief—that in werewolves, for example—gave an impression of severely critical judgement and, consequently, of exceptional trustworthiness.

In the trial of witches James considered two types of evidence of especial value—viz., the anæsthesia of the witches' marks and floating—a view which greatly increased the use of these two tests in England during the subsequent century.

> There are [he writes] (p. 80) two other good helpes that may be used for their trial: the one is the finding of their marke, and the trying of the insensiblenes thereof. The other is their fleeting (floating) on the water: for as in a secret murther, if the deade carcase be at any time thereafter handled by the murtherer, it wil gush out of bloud, as if the bloud were crying to heaven for revenge of the murtherer, God having appoynted that secret super-naturall signe, for the tryall of that secrete unnaturall crime, so it appears that God hath appoynted (for a super-naturall signe of the monstrous impietie of Witches) that the water shall refuse to receive them in her bosom, that have shaken off them the sacred water of Baptisme, and wilfullie refused the benefite thereof: No not so much as their eyes are able to shed teares (thetten to torture them as ye please) while first they repent (God not permitting them to dissemble their obstinacie in so horrible a crime) albeit the women kinde especially, be able otherwaies to shed teares at every light occasion when they wil, yea, although it were dissemblingly like the *Crocodiles*.

James urges strongly (Bk. III, 4) that all dabbling in witchcraft ought to receive the same penalty as witchcraft itself.

> PHILOMATHES. What forme of punishment thinke ye merites these *Magicians* and Witches? For I see that ye account them to be all alike gultie?
> EPISTEMON. They ought to be put to death according to the law of God, the civill and imperial law, and municipal law of all Christian nations.
> PHILOMATHES. But what kind of death I pray you?
> EPISTEMON. It is commonly used by fire, but that is an indifferent thing to be used in every cuntrie, according to the Laws or custome thereof.
> PHILOMATHES. But ought no sexe, age nor ranck to be exempted?
> EPISTEMON. None at al (being so used by the lawful magistrate) for it is the highest point of Idolatrie, wherein no exception is admitted by the law of God.

PHILOMATHES.   Then bairnes may not be spared?

EPISTEMON.   Yea, not a haire the less of my conclusion.   For they are not that capable of reason as to practice such thinges.   And for any being in company and not reveiling thereof, their lesse and ignorant age will no doubt excuse them.

PHILOMATHES.   I see ye condemne them all that are of the counsell of such craftes.

EPISTEMON.   No doubt as I said, in speaking of *Magic*, the con-sulters, trusters in, over-seers, intertainers or stirrers up of these craftes-folkes, are equallie guiltie with themselves that are practisers . . .

(*d*) Two years after the publication of James I's *Daemonologie* appeared one of the largest and most scholarly works that has ever been devoted to the inculcation of witch-beliefs, *Disquisi-tionum Magicarum Libri Sex* (1st ed., Louvain, 3 vols., 1599). The author, Martin Antonio Delrio (1551–1608), a Netherlander of Castilian origin, was regarded as the greatest prodigy of learning of the age.   He is said [1] to have spoken with equal facility Flemish, German, Spanish, Italian, and French, and to have had an unequalled knowledge of Greek, Hebrew, and Aramaic (' Chal-dee ').   At the age of nineteen he wrote in three volumes com-mentaries on the Tragedies of Seneca, in which he cited upwards of 1,300 authorities.   So great was his reputation that at the age of twenty-four he was made a member of the Supreme Council of Brabant.   He served as professor in many universities and held many important Government offices.   Though he joined the Jesuit Order (1580), he was a close friend of Justus Lipsius, the famous professor at Leyden—a fact which tended to make his work on witchcraft all the more current in Protestant circles. The large number of editions which this huge work went through shows how widely it was read [2] and the large number of copies to be found in old English libraries testifies to its influence this side of the Channel.

Delrio denounces in the most energetic terms those who show themselves half-hearted in the destruction of witches.

To omit to destroy the wicked when you can [he wrote] [3] what is that but to cherish them?   To fail to oppose error is to approve it: to fail to defend truth is to oppose it.   Those who do so are strength-ening the tyranny of the devil in the Church of Christ.   By their

[1] *Biographie Nationale de Belgique*, vol. 5 (Brussels, 1875).
[2] The best-known editions are: Lyons, 1604?, 1612; Mainz, 1603, 1612, 1617, 1624; Cologne, 1633, 1637, 1657, 1679; Venice, 1640, 1746.
[3] Delrio, *Disquisitionum Magicarum Libri Sex*, Bk. V, sec. xvi, p. 101.   Mainz ed. of 1603.

deeds is the security of the commonweal betrayed. They are accumulating lucre at the cost of the destruction of the community. Their pleasure it is to sleep soundly (*in utramque aurem dormire*) while the cunning Dragon occupies the whole body; and the poison of apostacy, idolatry and of unspeakable lusts, incredible cruelty and of daily and execrable crimes against those of tender age and against the sustenance of men, to the injury of their fatherland and that of the whole human race and the structure of society—this is gradually spreading throughout the whole Body of Christ. Who would not agree that such are guilty of the greatest possible disservice to the state and to the Church? Who would not hate and destroy them? For, if we can see anything, this is obvious: that impunity makes the witches grow in wickedness and enables them readily to enlist, all the time, more and more accomplices—and nothing do they desire more than to accomplish the constant requirement of the Devil by infecting the part that yet remains sound with the same cancer. By sparing the evil-doer the safety of the innocent is endangered. If this old saying is true of any accusation it is surely most true of all in this instance. God himself openly declared to the Babylonians by Isaiah that he would never show favour to any land in which witches were spared, but that on the contrary he would extract from it the severest penalties. 'Those two things' he saith 'shall come to thee (Babylon) in a moment in one day, the loss of children and widowhood. They shall come upon thee in their perfection for the multitude of thy sorceries and for the great abundance of thine enchantments. Thy wisdom and thy knowledge, it hath perverted thee. Therefore shall evil come upon thee; thou shalt not know from whence it riseth: and desolation shall come upon thee suddenly. Cap. 47, Ver. 9, 10 and 11.' &c.

The whole of the book does not run in this rhetorical vein. It is mostly a careful investigation of arguments against witchcraft in an apparently impartial scientific spirit. Thus, like James I, he rejects lycantrophy, and he conducts an historical investigation of the *Canon Episcopi*, which he rejects as the product of some provincial council devoid of authority. He also argues that the women described in it are not the same as modern witches, and fiercely condemns those who attempt to use it in their defence. Such a mixture of rhetoric and reasoning coming from so famous a scholar could hardly fail to have a deep and lasting influence. It is not surprising, therefore, to find allusions to Delrio's book in many subsequent English writers.

(*e*) The potent influence of the Puritan pulpit in disseminating the fear of witchcraft is strikingly exemplified in a work of William Perkins (1558–1602). His book was published after his death by Thomas Pickering, minister of Finchingfield in Essex, and printed by Cantrel Legge, Printer to the University of Cambridge, in

1608, and reprinted two years later. The main title of the work was *A Discourse on the Damned Art of Witchcraft, so far forth as it is revealed in the Scriptures*, to which is added the statement that it was *Framed and Delivered by M. William Perkins in his ordinarie course of Preaching*. Perkins, after a somewhat dissolute youth, had gone through the experience of ' conversion '—as a result, apparently, of hearing himself described as ' drunken Perkins ' and held up as a horrid example to a child. He became a Fellow of Christ's College, Cambridge, and came to be recognized in his own generation and in several following ones as the greatest Calvinist preacher, theologian, and controversialist that England had produced.

> The remarkable popularity of Perkins's writings is attested by the number of languages into which many of them were translated. Those that appeared in English were almost immediately rendered into Latin, while several were reproduced in Dutch, Spanish, Welsh and ' Irish '.[1]

Perkins wrote before the passing of the Jacobean Statute had made all witchcraft a capital offence. He therefore argues strongly that the bad and the good alike should be put to death (ch. vi):

> And now I proceed to the second point considered in this Text, the punishment of a Witch, and that is Death. . . . The cause of this sharpe punishment, is the making of a league with the devill, either secret or open, whereby they covenant to use his helpe for the working of wonders. For by vertue of this alone it cometh to passe, that Witches can doe strange things, in Divining, Inchanting and Jugling. Now let it be observed, of what horrible impietie they stand guiltie before God, who ioine in confederacie with Satan. Hereby they renounce the Lord that made them, they make no more account of his fauour and protection, they doe quite cut themselves of from the covenant made with him in Baptism, from the Communion of Saints, from the true worship and service of God. And on the contrary they give themselves unto Satan, as their god, whome they continually feare and serve. Thus they are become the most detestable enemies of God, & his people, that can be. For this cause Samuel told Saul that rebellion was as the sinne of Witchcraft: that is a most heinous and detestable sinne in the sight of God.

---

[1] *Dict. Nat. Biog., sub nomine.*
Of his collected works incomplete editions appeared at Cambridge in 1597, 1600, 1603, and 1605; a more complete edition was printed in 3 vols. in 1608, 1609, and 1612. It was also printed in London in 1606, 1612, and 1616; at Geneva in a Latin Folio in 1611 and in 2 vols. in 1611, 1618, and 1624. A Dutch translation was printed at Amsterdam in 1659. His *Discourse on Witchcraft* was published in Latin at Hanover in 1610.

The traytour, that doeth no hurt to his neighbour, but is willing and ready to do him all services that can be desired, is notwithstanding by the law of Nations, no better than a dead man, because he betraues his Souveraigne, and consequently cannot be a friend unto the Common-wealth. In like manner, though the Witch were in many respects profitable, and did no hurt, but procured much good; yet because he hath renounced God his king and governor, and hath bound himself by other lawes to the service of the enemie of God, and his Church, death is his portion iustly assigned him by God; he may not live.

He indignantly rejects the view that witches are merely 'aged persons of weake braines, and troubled with abundance of melancholie' (ch. vii). He gives many reasons, for example:—

Men of learning have observed, that all Witches through Europe, are of like carriage and behaviour in their examinations, and convictions: they use the same answears, refuges, defences, protestations. In a word, look what be the practises and courses of Witches in England, in any of these particulars, the same be the practises of the Witches of Spaine, Fraunce, Italie, Germanie &c.

So grave is the crime that torture, he urges, is admissible in the examination of those accused of witchcraft (p. 204):—

Touching the manner of Examination, there be two kinds of proceeding; either by a single Question, or by some torture. A single question is, when the Magistrate himself onely maketh enquirie, what was done or not done, by bare and naked interrogations. A torture is, when besides the enquirie in words, he useth also the racke, or some other violent means to urge confession. This course hath beene taken in some countries, and may no doubt lawfully and with good conscience be used, howbeit not in every case, but onely upon strong and great presumptions going before, and when the partie is obstinate.

In his conclusion Perkins insists forcibly upon his main theme, that good witches must be destroyed.

For this must alwaies be remembered, as a conclusion, that by witches we understand not those onely which kill and torment: but all Diviners, Charmers, Iuglers, all Wizzards, commonly called wise men and wise women; yea, whosoever doe anything (knowing what they doe) which cannot be effected by nature or art; and in the same number we reckon all good Witches, which doe no hurt but good, which doe not spoile and destroy, but save and deliver. All these come under the sentence of *Moses*, because they deny God, and are confederates with Satan. By the lawes of England, the thiefe is executed for stealing, and we thinke it iust and profitable: but it were a thousand times better for the land, if all Witches, but specially the blessing Witch might suffer death. For the thiefe by his stealing and the hurtfull Inchanter by his charming, bring hindrance and hurt to the bodies and goods of men; but these are the right hand of the deuill by which he taketh and destroieth the soules of men.

(*f*) Another preacher less famous than Perkins, but akin to him in his attitude towards witchcraft, was James Mason, a Master of Arts of Trinity College, Cambridge (1586), and probably vicar of Teversall, Notts, from 1609 until his death in 1638. His volume, *The Anatomie of Sorcerie, Wherein the wicked Impiety of Charmers, Inchanters, and such is discovered and confuted*, was published in London by John Legatte, Printer to the University of Cambridge, in 1612.

It was my chance [says Mason in his introduction] to fall into communication with a notable supporter of these wicked vanities which are spoken of in this book: who not content to practise the same himself went about to persuade others thereunto: and to that end had framed reasons and arguments to uphold his assertion.

His main thesis is (p. 22) that all that ' the magitians, witches, sorcerers, inchanters and such like' do is really done by the Devil and not by their own actions.

Howbeit nothing is brought to passe by these meanes; but the diuell himself, under the colour thereof, to wit of certain sette formes of words, or characters, of what forme or fashion soever they be, whether circular, angular, crossewise, or in figure of a man, beast, or any other thing which is used in magicke.

In speaking of the exorcists mentioned in Acts xix. 13, he argues that the distinction between witches and conjurers is of little significance:—

it is evident by the circumstances of this place, that these men were nothing but meere wicked magitians, and namely, of that sort which we cal coniurers: who although there be no difference in respect of the substance of their wicked serving of Satan in this behalf: Notwithstanding the fashion, and manner of their service seemeth somewhat to differ. For those which we cal witches, or sorcerers, seems to be in a more vile, and slavish condition, being alwaies at the diuell's commaundment: but these which we terme coniurers will make as though they commaunded the diuell, howbeit they profit nothing thereby, saving that they serve his turne herein, and sometime their own: so farre forth as their practise may stand with the furtherance of Satans purpose in the same, which is the enlargement of his owne Kingdome.

(*g*) Another preacher, better known than Mason, was Alexander Roberts, a Fellow of Caius College, Cambridge (1581–94), Headmaster of Lynn School (1590–93), Rector of

West Lynn (1593–1620), preacher of St. Margaret's, Lynn, and the author of several theological treatises. In 1616 he printed in London a work with the following lengthy title: *A Treatise of Witchcraft. Wherein sundry propositions are laid downe, plainly discovering the wickednesse of that damnable Art, with divers other speciall points annexed, not impertinent to the same, such as ought diligently of every Christian to be considered. With a true Narration of the Witchcrafts which Mary Smith, wife of Henry Smith, Glover, did practise : Of her contract vocally made between the Devill and her, in solemne termes, &c.* The book is mainly a re-statement of conventional Calvinistic theology and applied to witchcraft. In his ' Epistle Dedicatorie ' to the Corporation and people of King's Lynn he states that his work is directed against two types of people.

> The first of these mentioned are slie and masked Atheists . . . The second be Sorcerers, Wizards, Witches, and the rest of that rank and kindred: no small multitude swarming now in the world, yet supposed of many, rather worthy of pitty than punishment as deluded by fantasies, and mis-led, not effecting those harmes wherewith they be charged, or themselves acknowledge. But considering they be ioyned and linked together with Satan in a league (the common and professed enemy of mankinde) and by his helpe performe many subtile and mischievous actions, and hurtful designes, it is strange that from so great a smoake arising, they should neither decrie nor feare some fire. And therefore, in respect of these I have at your appointment and request (for whom I am willing to bestow my best labours and ever shall be) penned this small Treatise, occasioned by the detection of a late witch among you . . .

Roberts makes a special point of emphasizing the enormous powers of witches (pp. 18–19) :—

> they are permissively able through the helpe of the Diuell their maister, to hunt Men and Beasts, and trouble the elements, by vertue of that contract & agreement which they have made with him. For they endamage both in body and mind : In body, for *Danaeus* reporteth of his owne knowledge, as an eye witnesse thereof, that he hath seene the breasts of Nurces (onely touched by their hands) those sacred fountaines of human nourishment so dried up that they could yield no milk; some suddenly tormented with extreame and intolerable paine of Cholicke, others oppressed with Palsie, Leprosie, Gout, Apoplexia &c. . . .
>
> In minde, stirring up men to lust, to hatred, to love, and the like passions, and that by hindering the inward and outward sences . . .
>
> Now concerning beastes they doe oftentimes kill them out right, and that in sundry manner, or pine and waste them little by little, till they be consumed
>
> For the elements it is an agreeing consent of all, that they can

E

corrupt and infect them, procure tempests, to stirre up thunder and lightening, move violent winds, destroy the fruits of the earth . . . It were but fruitlesse labour, and ill spent, to bestow long time in confirming this so manifest a truth, and not much better than to set up a candle to give the Sunne light when it shineth brightest in mid-heaven. . . .

The shapes in which the Devil can appear are, in Roberts's opinion, almost—if not completely—unlimited (p. 31) :—

The Diuell can assume to himselfe a body and frame a voyce to speake with, and further instruct and give satisfaction to those who have submitted themselves unto him and are bound to his service. For he lost not by his transgression and fall, his naturall endowments, but they are continued in him whole and perfect, as in the good Angels, who abide in that obedience and holiness in which they were created . . . This the Diuell hath appeared to some in the forme of a Man, cloathed in purple, & wearing a crowne upon his heed : to others in the likeness of a Childe : sometime he sheweth himselfe in the forme of foure-footed beastes, foules, creeping things, roaring as a Lyon, skipping like a Goat, barking after the manner of a dogge, and the like. But it is observed by some, that he cannot take the shape of a Sheepe, or Dove. . . .

(h) Few preachers could claim to have encountered magic and witchcraft in so many parts of England as did Thomas Cooper. Like James Mason, at Cambridge, he made his first acquaintance with magic during his undergraduate days at the other university. After graduating at Christ Church, Oxford (M.A. 1593, B.D. 1600), he received the College living of Great Budworth in Cheshire (1601), where he was deeply impressed with the horror of dealings with the Devil. He records encounters with witchcraft at Northwich in Cheshire, in Lancashire, and at Coventry, where he became vicar of Holy Trinity (1604). In 1620 he was living in Whitecross Street, London, befriended by Lord Chief Justice Montague, to whom he expresses the deepest obligation. He was already the author of several volumes—one of them on the Gunpowder Plot—when he published in 1617 *The Mystery of Witchcraft, Discovering the Truth, Nature, Occasions, Growth and Power thereof. Together with the Detection and Punishment of the same. As Also, the severall Stratagems of Sathan, ensnaring the poore Soule by this desperate practize of annoying the bodie : with severall Uses thereof to the Church of Christ. Very necessary for the redeeming of these Atheisticall and secure times.*

Amongst his reasons for his writing this book he alleges his own experiences (pp. 8–15) :—

Hath not the Lord enabled me to discover the practice of Anti-Christ in the *hellish Plot of Gunpowder-treason?* Hath he not preserved me gratiously from such divelish *Practises of these Anti-Christian Instruments*, not onely in keeping mee from seeking their helpe, when my children were suspected to bee afflicted by them, that so my soule might be endangered thereby: But especially in preserving me from so many cursed snares which by these mischevious instruments have been privily laid for me, to the endangering of my life, and the hindrance of the Gospell? . . .

He admits his undergraduate admiration for skill in the magic arts:

Was there not a time when I admired some in the University famozed in this skill?

Did not the Lord so dispose of mee, that my *Chamberfellow* was exceedingly bewitched with these faire shewes, and having gotten divers books to that end, was earnest in the pursuit of that glorie which might redound thereby?

Did we not communicate our Studies together? And did not the Lord so arme his unworthy servant, that not onely the snare was gratiously espied; but, by the great mercie of my God, the Lord used me as a means to divert my *Chamber-fellow* from these dangerous Studies? . . .

Was I not purposed upon a *speciall occasion of the death of the Ladie Hales* procured by Witchcraft, to commend such observations to Posteritie, but that *good knight* her husband, for reviving and continuing of his griefe by that memoriall over-ruled that opportunity: But is not the Lord mercifull to offer another seasonable and worthy occasion to *Pay my Vowes?*

Doth not every Assise almost throughout the Land, resound of the arraignement and conviction of notorious witches; either where gross ignorance and Popery most aboundeth, or where the truth of God is withheld, and prophaned, by unrighteousnesse and hypocrisie?

Can we forget the late assise at *Lancaster*, where no lesse than fifteen were endited, and twelve condemned of that horrible crime, a Countrie abounding on that part thereof, with grosse ignorance and Popery?

Hath not *Coventrie* beene usually haunted by these hellish Sorcerers, where it was confessed by one of them, that no lesse than three-score were of that confederacie? And is not this a place famous for the glorie of the *Holy Mountaine?*

And was not I there enjoyned by a necessitie to the discoverie of this Brood?

Cooper adopts the rather unusual view that the formal witch's covenant takes place in a church (p. 88):—

She must be *covenanted solemnly in the house of God*, there to make open testimony of her subjection unto him (the Devil), by renouncing all *former covenants* with the Lord. *And heer,* Usually these things are performed in their order,

First, *Satan* blasphemously *occupying* the *Place* whence the *holy Oracles* are delivered, doth thence:

First, require of his *Proselite* an *acknowledgement of her covenant,* causing her usually in her owne person to repeate the forme thereof: As *I N do here aknowledge, that upon such conditions I have given myselfe unto Satan to bee disposed of him at his pleasure :* And

Secondly, when this *acknowledgement* is made, in testimoniall of all this subjection, Satan offers his *back-parts* to be kissed of his vassal.

Thirdly, this being done, he then *delivers* unto his *Proselite,* and so to the rest (for many are covenanted at this meeting) *the Rules of his Art,* instructing them in the manner of *hurting* and *helping,* & acquainting them with such *medecines* and *poysons* as are usuall hereunto.

Fourthly, *Taking also account of the proceedings* of his other Schollers, and so approving and condemning accordingly.

Fifthly, for their further confirmation, he yet enjoynes them *another ceremonie :* Namely, *to compasse about the Fount divers times,* there solemnely to *Renounce the Trinitie,* especially their *salvation by Iesus Christ,* and in token thereof to *disclaime their Baptism.*

Sixthly, in further *token* of their subjection unto Satan in yeelding themselves wholly unto his devotion, behold yet *another ceremonie* heere usually is performed : namely, *to let themselves bloud* in some apparent place of the body, yeelding the same to be *sucked by Satan,* as a sacrifice unto him, and testifying thereby the full *subjection* of their *lives* and *souls* to his devotion.

Lastly to gratify them somewhat for their dutifull service it pleaseth their new Maister oftentimes to offer himself familiarly unto them, to *dally and lye with them,* in token of their more neere *coniunction,* and as it were *marriage* unto him.

Like Roberts, Cooper dwells upon the almost limitless powers over men and beasts and over the weather and the crops (p. 157); and like Perkins, he argues that obstinate witches should be examined under torture. A good deal of his material was derived, as he himself acknowledges (p. 363), from earlier works. Nonetheless the book was brought out again five years later—this time under the title *Sathan transformed into an Angell of Light . . . emplified especially in the Doctrine of Witchcraft.*

(i) The works quoted above are merely a small selection of the most important that appeared during the period 1588–1618. Many others are almost equally worthy of mention and quotation. Of such are Thomas Potts' account [1] of the trial of the Lancashire witches of 1612; Dalton's *Country Justice* (1618), which demands consideration elsewhere; Edward Jorden's *Brief Discourse of the*

---

[1] Potts, *Discoverie of Witches* (London, 1613). Reprinted by the Chetham Society (Manchester, 1845) and edited by G. B. Harrison (1929).

Disease called the Suffocation of the Mother (1603). In addition are the works of George Giffard [1] and John Cotta,[2] who, while admitting the terrible reality of witchcraft, sought to curb some of the most extravagantly absurd excesses of the witch-hunter. (A later publication of Cotta will be considered in Chapter VI.) The foreign works of Paul Grillandus,[3] Pierre de Lancre, and Henri Boguet [4] were with many others imported into England and eagerly read. When the smallness of the output of books at this time is considered, it is difficult to avoid the conclusion that the great overmastering emotion of the literate classes was terror of witches, rising in intensity by force of action and reaction— the terror increasing the demand for books and the resulting books increasing the terror.

[1] Giffard, *A Dialogue concerning Witches and Witchcraftes* (London, 1593 and 1603); reprinted by the Shakespeare Association (Oxford, 1931). In 1587 Giffard had published *A Discourse of the subtle Practices of Devils.*

[2] Cotta published in 1612 *A Short Discoverie of Unobserved Dangers,* and followed this up in 1616 with a larger book, *The Triall of Witch-craft, Shewing the True and Right Methode of Discovery.*

[3] *Tractatus Duo de Sortilegiis et Lamiis* (Frankfort, 1592).

[4] de Lancre and Boguet were judges who published works based on their experiences in sending huge numbers of witches to the stake. See the Bibliography.

CHAPTER IV

JAMES I's RENUNCIATION OF HIS BELIEF IN WITCHCRAFT

§ 1. THE SEEDS of the great witch-terror had been sown by the Crown and the Council, by Parliament and by the ruling classes. The reluctant soil had been sedulously fertilized for several generations. By the middle of James I's reign an abundant harvest had appeared. Now, however, the leading cultivator began to have serious doubts about the value of his crop. James I, much as he disliked the Genevan model of church government, was a Calvinist in his theology. He had used his scholarly pen to denounce in unmeasured terms Vorstius and his anti-Calvinist movement in the United Provinces. He had sent English theologians to uphold the purity of Genevan doctrine at the Synod of Dort (1618). Ungainly, slovenly, pedantic, and naïvely self-conceited as he undoubtedly was, the British Solomon yet concealed under an unpromising exterior really great qualities, such as genuine scholarship, broad tolerance, acuteness of mind, and receptiveness to new ideas. His aims in home no less than foreign policy, though ill-advised and tactlessly pursued, were often strikingly in advance of their age. That such a man should make a radical change of his views even during the fixed stability of middle age is not out of keeping with his character. The steps by which the change in his view of witchcraft came about are not altogether obscure.

(*a*) The first was probably taken at Leicester in 1616. In that year, at the Leicestershire Summer Sessions before Humphrey Winch, Justice of the Common Bench, and Ranulf Crew, Serjeant, nine women were condemned to death for witchcraft merely on the evidence of a boy of twelve or thirteen years of age. They were all of them, presumably, hanged a few days later. Shortly afterwards when James visited the town he sent for the boy, and having put him through a searching cross-examination, came to the conclusion that he had never been bewitched at all and that, consequently, a terrible miscarriage of justice had

58

occurred. As a result Justice Winch and Serjeant Crewe suffered seriously thereafter from royal displeasure.[1]

(*b*) The change in James's views was largely completed by the more famous case of ' the Boy of Bilson '. This unhappy youth confessed at the Staffordshire Assizes (26th July 1621) that all his evidence against witches had been the merest fabrication and that he had been trained by a Roman Catholic priest in the art of simulating the symptoms of being bewitched. Fuller's references to the effect of this case upon the royal mind are unusually illuminating.[2]

The frequency of such forged possessions [he wrote] wrought such an alteration upon the judgement of King James that he, receding from what he had written in his *Daemonologie*, grew at first diffident of, and then flatly to deny, the workings of witches and devils, as but falsehoods and delusions. . . . Indeed all this king's reign was scattered over with cheaters of this kind. Some papists, some sectaries, some neither; as who dissembleth such possessions, either out of malice, (to be revenged on those whom they accused of witchcraft,) or covetousness, (to enrich themselves,) seeing such, who, out of charity or curiosity, repaired unto them, were bountiful in their relief . . .

King James . . . was no less dexterous than desirous to make discovery of these deceits. Various were his ways in detecting them; awing some into confession by his presence, persuading others by promise of pardon and fair usage. He ordered it so that a proper courtier made love to one of these bewitched maids, and quickly Cupid's arrows drove out the pretended darts of the Devil. Another there was, the tides of whose possessions did so ebb and flow, that punctually they observed one hour till the king came to visit her. The maid loth to be so unmannerly as to make his Majesty attend upon her time, antedated her fits by many hours, and instantly ran through her whole zodiac of tricks which she used to play. A third, strangely affected when the first verse of St John's Gospel was read unto her in our translation, was tame and quiet when the same was pronounced in Greek; her English devil, belike, understanding no other language . . .

(*c*) Cases of simulated possession were not the only reason for James's renunciation of his belief in witchcraft. There had always been at least a few enlightened men even in the worst of times who refused to accept the continental witch-beliefs, and whose books may well have been familiar to the well-read King. Thus, for example, Hans Sachs, the cobbler poet of Nuremberg,

---

[1] Ewen, *Witchcraft and Demonianism*, pp. 228–9 (London, 1933).
G. L. Kittredge, *English Witchcraft and James I,* pp. 57–8 (New York, 1912).
[2] Fuller, *Church History of Britain,* bk. x, Cent. XVII, 54.

had boldly disclaimed in verse all belief in demoniac agencies.[1]
Cornelius Agrippa, whom Calvin described as one of the chief
contemners of the Gospel, wrote his *De Occulta Philosophia*[2]
in an effort to stem the tide of witch mania, and exerted himself
in the courts to save old women accused of commerce with the
Devil.   Agrippa's pupil, Wierus (John Weyer, 1516–88), attacked
some of the current beliefs that led to the hasty execution of
witches; but his book, *De Praestigiis daemonum et incantationibus ac
veneficiis*, is filled with so many of the grossest superstitions[3] that
its influence, which was considerable, was not always for good.
Probably no continental writer of the sixteenth century did more
to combat belief in witchcraft than the cool and sceptical Montaigne (1533–92), who dismisses the whole subject for good with a
few smiling remarks.

> The witches about my country [he wrote][4] are in hazard of
> their life, upon the opinions of every new authour, that may come to
> give their dreams a body. . . .   Our life is over-real and essential
> to warrant these supernaturall and fantasticall accidents. . . .
> Mine ears are full of a thousand such tales. . . .   How much more
> naturall and more likely doe I find it that two men should lie, then
> one in twelve houres, passe with the windes, from East to West?
> How much more naturall, that our understanding may by the
> volubility of our loose-capring minde be transported from his place?
> then that one of us should by a strange spirit, in flesh and bone, be
> carried upon a broome through the tunnel of a chimney?   Let us,
> who are perpetually tossed to and fro with domesticall and our
> owne illusions, not seek for forraine and unknowen illusions. . . .
> When al is done, it is an overvaluing of ones conjectures, by them to
> cause a man to be burnt alive.

John Florio, the translator of Montaigne, was in a position to
influence the opinions of his King.   He was a well-known figure
in Court circles, and was made Reader in Italian to the Queen,
Anne of Denmark, immediately after James's accession—at a

---

[1] *Werke*, herausgegeben von A. von Keller, Tübingen, 1870, 5. Band.
S 287 ss.
> ' Des teuffels eh und reuttery
> Ist nur gespenst und fantasey . . .'

[2] Printed at Paris, 1531, and at Cologne, 1533.   Calvin's allusion occurs in
his *De Scandalis*.
[3] See especially Lib. I, cc. 8–16 (Basle, 1568).   In his Index of Devils
Weyer stated that there existed seventy-two chief and 7,405,926 subordinate
devils.
[4] Montaigne, *Essais*, liv. III, 11 (published originally in two vols. in 1580,
then in three in 1588).   Florio's translation was published 1603, new ed. 1618.
In the *Everyman Series*, vol. iii, pp. 284 sqq. (London, 1910).

salary of £100 a year.   The learned King's favour was shown by his appointment the following year as Gentleman-Extra-ordinary and Groom of the Privy Chamber.   In these cir-cumstances it would not be surprising if Montaigne's opinion on the burning question of witchcraft were widely discussed in Court circles.

In England itself men had not been wanting who put up resistance to the conquest of their country by continental witch-beliefs.   Thus, for example, it is recorded [1] that in 1578 a certain Dr. Browne was the subject of proceedings on the ground that he 'spread misliking of the laws, by saying there are no witches'. But the greatest onslaught against the current mania was the *Discoverie of Witchcraft*, published in 1584 by the Kentish squire, Reginald Scot, who has already been quoted.   A far greater man who threw in his influence against the prevailing superstition was Francis Bacon, James's Lord Chancellor.   S. R. Gardiner in his monumental history of the early Stuart period [2] makes the mis-leading statement that ' Bacon . . . took the existence of witches for granted '.   This is based on a careless reading of a passage in Bacon's *Sylva Sylvarum* which runs thus :—[3]

> The ointment that witches use is reported to be made of the fat of children digged out of their graves; of the juices of smallage, wolf-bane, and cinquefoil, mingled with the meal of fine wheat; but I suppose that the soporiferous medicines are likest to do it.

The last sentence shows that he assumes witches' delusions to be merely subjective and produced by drugs.   This interpretation is confirmed by another passage in the same work,[4] where he warns judges to be on their guard against believing the confessions of witches or lightly accepting evidence against them :—

> For witches themselves [he writes] are imaginative and believe ofttimes they do what they do not; and people are credulous in that point, and ready to impute accidents and natural operations to

---

[1] *State Papers, Domestic, Addenda* 1566–79, p. 551.

[2] S. R. Gardiner, *History of England* 1603–42, vol. vii, p. 323 (London, 1884); G. L. Kittredge, *Notes on Witchcraft*, p. 6 (Worcester, Mass., 1907), says Bacon ' has left his belief in sorcery recorded in a dozen places '.   *Witchcraft in Old and New England*, p. 580 (Cambridge, Mass., 1929), gives a number of references to Bacon's works.

[3] *Sylva Sylvarum*, Cent. X, 975, in *Works of Bacon*, ed. Spedding, vol. ii, p. 664 (London, 1857–8).

[4] *Op. cit.*, vol. ii, pp. 642–3, quoted in Notestein, *History of Witchcraft in England*, pp. 246–7 (Washington, 1911).   For other references to witchcraft in Bacon's works see vol. i, 193, 498, 608–9; ii, 634, 641–2, 657–8, 664; iii, 490; vi, 392–3, 395–6; vii, 738; *Life and Letters*, vii, 30–1.

witchcraft. It is worthy the observing, that . . . the greatest wonders which they tell of, carrying in the air, transporting themselves into other bodies etc. are still reported to be wrought, not by incantations, or ceremonies, but by ointments, and anointing themselves all over. This may justly move man to think that these fables are the effect of imagination.

The Lord Chancellor could hardly have spoken out more definitely without putting himself into the hands of his numerous enemies by denying the very existence of those witches which the recent Act of Parliament had been passed to destroy. It is clear that, if ever he had believed in witchcraft at all, that belief had long shrunk to vanishing-point. Bacon, be it remembered, was one of the greatest thinkers of the human race, as well as the paladin of high Royalist views and the target for the sharpest shafts of the Puritan parliamentarians. In these circumstances it is likely that his influence upon James I in the matter of witchcraft, as in so much else, was very considerable.

(d) Another influence that came into James's life—largely owing to his foreign policy—was that of Spain, a country in its attitude towards witchcraft far ahead of the rest of Europe. Early in the sixteenth century the Spanish Inquisition had won exclusive jurisdiction over witches, and its beneficent activities— in this respect, at least—soon banished witch-terror almost completely from the whole country.[1] As early as 1526 the Inquisitors only narrowly avoided a denial of the very existence of witchcraft. Henceforth, though admitting its possibility in abstract theory, they acted on the supposition that in practice it did not occur. They used their immense influence to inculcate a similar attitude amongst the mass of the Spanish people, thus saving them from the century and a half of terror and cruelty that was the lot of the rest of Europe.[2] James I, like most intelligent contemporaries, was greatly interested in Spain, which was now at the height of her cultural and intellectual ascendancy. Moreover, his plans for a marriage alliance brought him greatly under the influence of the

[1] M. Menéndez Pelayo, *Historia de los Heterodoxos Españoles*, vol. ii, p. 669 (Madrid, 1880).

[2] H. C. Lea, *History of the Inquisition in Spain*, vol. iv, pp. 206 sqq. (New York, 1907).
    In the later seventeenth century Spain, in the depths of her decline, contained many who believed in witchcraft at a time when such beliefs were being seriously challenged in the rest of Western Europe. But Kittredge, *Witchcraft in Old and New England*, p. 370 (Cambridge, Mass., 1929), writes, ' In Spain the last witch was burned in 1781 '. This is an error which has been many times repeated. See Lea, op. cit., vol. iv, pp. 241 (ft. n. 5) and 89.

Count of Gondomar, the Spanish Ambassador, who soon became one of the most intimate of his friends. His delight in the company of witty and learned Spaniards, such as the Duke of Osuna, is well known. It is therefore perhaps not unlikely—though there is not direct evidence—that Spanish influence had its share in changing the attitude of James and of many of his Court towards the alleged machinations of Satanic agencies.

§ 2. If James alone had renounced the doctrines of continental witch-belief, the renunciation could have had but small historical importance. Its main importance lies in its coming at a time when a small but enlarging circle of enlightened men—including the heir to the throne himself—had reached the conclusion that the witch-terror had no sound basis either in reason or in authority. Their scepticism was largely due to two great movements of the age, the one religious and the other scientific.

(a) The religious movement was partly a reaction against the excesses of the last generation. In the opening years of the seventeenth century the life-and-death struggle between Calvinism and the Counter-Reformation had reached its climax. Almost every thinking man in Western and Central Europe had ranged himself with ardent conviction on one side or the other. The opposing forces, like Communism and Fascism in recent times, resembled one another in many important features. Both were fanatically dogmatic; both were theocratic in their political outlook and, therefore, opposed to strong national monarchies; both were sombre and ascetic in their attitude even to the most innocent pleasures of life in this world; and both shared the conviction of the terrible reality of the Devil's power, which made them especially prone to witch-mania.

Signs of a liberal reaction began to show themselves in many parts of Europe even before the end of the sixteenth century. The strongest movement appeared in the Dutch Republic under the leadership of the famous scholar, Jacobus Arminius, Professor of Philosophy at Leyden (1602). The Arminian revolt against the Established Dutch (Calvinist) Church took the form of an insistence upon the all-embracing love of God as opposed to the doctrine of absolute predestination, which was the central pillar of the Calvinistic dogmatic system.[1] It also minimized the importance of dogma by its insistence upon the philosophical

---

[1] W. K. Jordan, *The Development of Religious Toleration in England* (1603–40), pp. 321–40 (London, 1936).

right of every man to worship as his conscience dictated.[1] Owing
to the close connexion between England and Holland in the time
of James I, Arminianism powerfully reinforced a somewhat
similar movement in the Anglican Church, which opposed a sweet
reasonableness to narrow dogmatism.

Richard Hooker (1553–1600), in his great classic, *Of the Laws
of Ecclesiastical Politie*, had brought out the principles implicit
in the Anglican Reformation in opposition to the claims of Geneva
and of Rome. Though apparently indifferent to the Apostolical
Succession of the ministry, he stressed strongly the continuity of
the Anglican Church as a portion of the Church Catholic.

'To reform ourselves is not to sever ourselves from the
Church we were of before,' he maintained; 'in the Church
we were and we are so still.' His broad tolerance as opposed
to the narrow dogmatism of Geneva and Rome appears in his
sympathy for much that he considered good in Calvinism
combined with his allusion to the rites and ceremonies of the
Medieval Church as 'those whereby for so many ages together
we have been guided in the service of God'.

Hooker's interpretation of the Anglican position was elaborated
and strengthened by a number of scholars, such as Lancelot
Andrewes [2] (1555–1626) at Cambridge and John Buckeridge
(1562?–1631) and his pupil William Laud (1573–1645) at Oxford.
By the time of James I's renunciation of witch-beliefs, Arminian
views, as they were often called, had won over the University of
Oxford and had gained a considerable following even in the
University of Cambridge.

Such views, though not incompatible with a theoretical belief
in the abstract possibility of witchcraft, would be strongly opposed
in practice to all witch prosecutions. Many an Arminian might
have said with Addison [3] in a later age, ' I believe in general that
there is, and has been, such a thing as witchcraft; but at the same
time can give no credit to any particular instances of it '. Many
more dismissed all question of witchcraft with complete unbelief
and derision. The reasons for this attitude are logically de-

---

[1] Georg Lenz, *Demokratie und Diktatur in der Englischen Revolution 1640–60*
(Munich, 1933. Beiheft 28, der Historischen Zeitschrift), pp. 53 sqq.
    S. A. A. Seaton, *The Theory of Toleration*, p. 51.
    M. Freund, *Der Idee der Toleranz in England der grossen Revolution* (Halle, 1927).
[2] For Bishop Andrewes's beliefs in marvels see M. Casanbon, *Relation of what
Passed for many years between Dr Dee and Some Spirits* (London, 1659), Preface, pp.
19, 20.
[3] J. Addison (1672–1719), *Sir Roger de Coverley*, on witchcraft—the Coverley
witch.

ducible from many of their convictions. Thus, for example, they rejected the Calvinist dogma of the total depravity of fallen man and insisted on the reality of baptismal regeneration. At the same time they rejected Predestination and Election, inclining instead to the view of certain of the early Greek Fathers that the love of God is so great that few or none will ultimately perish.[1] Such a faith militated strongly against the belief that any practising Christians could be subjected to the Devil's power by witchcraft.

At the same time they were exempted from the temptation, to which some Roman Catholic priests are said to have succumbed, of exploiting the custom of exorcism for purposes of propaganda. For the 72nd Canon of 1604 forbad any of the clergy without special permission ' to attempt, upon any pretence whatsoever, either of possession or obsession, by fasting and prayer, to cast out any Devil or Devils, under pain of imputation of imposture or cosenage, and deposition from the ministry '.

Again, they opposed the Puritan insistence upon the verbal inspiration of Scripture by the assertion that the Bible must be read in the light of the traditions of the Church and the writings of the Fathers. They strove to interpret Scripture in the light of philology and historical background, for which purpose Laud spent great sums on the purchase of Oriental manuscripts and on the founding of a professorship of Arabic at Oxford. To such men the appeal to texts of Scripture as conclusive proofs of the existence of witchcraft would lose much of its force. Thus, to give one example out of many, they often pointed out that the Hebrew word ' witch,' *mĕkashshêphâh*, in Exodus xxii. 18 was rendered in the Septuagint version by φαρμακός, ' a druggist or apothecary '.

Finally, it should be noticed that the Arminians tempered the appeal to authority of Rome and Geneva by an appeal to reason. Many of them were deeply imbued with the new scientific spirit which was destined ultimately to give witch-beliefs their *coup de grâce*. Thus, for example, Andrewes was so celebrated for his interest in physical science that the great Bacon submitted some of his scientific works to his judgement before their publication.

(*b*) In weaning a small circle from the grosser superstitions

---

[1] Origen and St. Clement of Alexandria went so far as to consider the possibility of the Devil's ultimate repentance and forgiveness. See K. R. Hagenbach, *Compendium of the History of Doctrines*, vol. i, pp. 147 sqq. (London, 1858) ; St. Clement, *Stromateis*, i, 17, p. 367.

connected with witchcraft, the new scientific spirit undoubtedly played a part in spite of the fact that great names, like that of Robert Boyle, can be cited on the side of superstition.[1] Francis Bacon's contribution to scientific method is open to much adverse criticism in matters of detail.   Its importance, however, lies in the assertion that the road to truth lies in the careful observation of nature, in experiment, in the careful tabulation of results, and above all, in the rejection of traditional authority and prejudice—the *Idola Tribus*, the *Idola Specus*, the *Idola Fori*, and the *Idola Theatri*.   'Man, who is the servant and interpreter of nature,' he wrote, ' can act and understand no further than he has observed, either in operation or contemplation, of the method and order of nature.'   The impressive style of Bacon's writings was hardly less effective than their contents in spreading the new scientific spirit amongst educated men.   Moreover, the practical defects of his inductive methods were soon to be remedied by the French mathematician and philosopher René Descartes (1596–1650), who aroused a lively interest in scientific research all over Europe, as is shown by the prolific growth of societies for the advancement of science.   'I learned', wrote Descartes in his *Discourse on Method* (1637), 'not to believe too firmly anything of which I had been persuaded merely by example and custom, and thus gradually I shook off many errors which can obscure our natural light and make us less capable of understanding reason.'   Genuine knowledge comes by way of experiments—' the further a man is advanced in knowledge so much the more are they necessary '. To trust to the authority of great teachers such as Aristotle is futile.   Those who do so ' are like the ivy, which never mounts higher than the trees which support it, and which even descends again after having reached their summit '.

Indications of the rising interest in scientific research were especially abundant in Oxford.   The foundation of professorships in Astronomy and Geometry (1619), of a lecturership in Natural Philosophy about the same time, of a lecturership in Anatomy (1624) with careful directions for the dissection of human bodies, together with the formation of a botanical garden (1621), suggest the extent to which the university had been conquered [2] by the new scientific spirit even before the death of

---

[1] G. L. Kittredge, *Notes on Witchcraft*, p. 15 (Worcester, Mass., 1907). For Boyle see Chapter X below.

[2] R. T. Gunther, *Early Science in Oxford*, 2 vols. (Oxford, 1923).

James I. The Puritan, with his complete conviction of the necessity of his dogmatic beliefs for salvation, looked with apprehension on the change of outlook. Half a century later the Puritan Poet wrote:—[1]

> That not to know at large of things remote
> From use, obscure and suttle, but to know
> That which before us lies in daily life,
> Is the prime Wisdom, what is more, is fume,
> Or emptiness, or fond impertinence,
> And renders us in things that most concerne
> Unpractis'd, unprepar'd, and still to seek.

Witch-beliefs rested so largely on tradition, prejudice, and deductive method applied to authorities that the inductive method of the scientist was bound to shake them to their foundations. One striking example of a famous scientist faced by the question of witchcraft has come down to us. It offers so sharp a contrast to the old attitude and illustrates so clearly the new spirit that it deserves notice here.

(i) Dr. Harvey (1578–1657), Charles I's physician, the discoverer of the circulation of the blood, was one of those who suspected that the phenomena of witchcraft were purely imaginary. He consequently desired to test his hypothesis by experiment; and seized the opportunity to visit a reputed witch at Newmarket.[2] On the pretence that he, too, was a practitioner in the forbidden art, he managed to persuade her to introduce her imp. This she did by uttering a peculiar cry. Whereupon a toad crawled out from beneath a chest and drank some milk which the old woman offered it. The resourceful doctor then got rid of his hostess by suggesting that she should go out and get some beer with which to celebrate their happy meeting. As soon as she was gone he induced the toad to reappear by imitating the old woman's peculiar cry. He then seized it with the tongs and opened its belly with his dissecting-knife. After a most careful examination he satisfied himself that it was merely a common toad which the old woman had tamed. On her return she was

---

[1] Milton, *Paradise Lost*, bk. viii, 11, 191–7.

Cf. *The Memoirs of Colonel Hutchinson*, written by his widow, Lucy. At Peterhouse, Cambridge, ' He was enticed to bow to their great idol, learning, and had a higher veneration for it a long time than can strictly be allowed ' (p. 41 in the *Everyman Library* ed.). Hutchinson was one of the regicides and a strict Puritan.

[2] *The Gentleman's Magazine*, May 1832, pp. 407–8. Unfortunately the date of this incident is not given.

furious at the slaughter of her familiar. But Harvey managed to get away, and reported the incident to Charles I. By this experiment [1] was confirmed his hypothesis that those accused of witchcraft were often merely old women suffering from delusions; and that their confessions, upon which witch-hunters laid such heavy stress, were devoid of evidential value.

(ii) This view of witches' confessions rapidly gained ground amongst those of scientific outlook. A conversation between the great Royalist leader, the Duke of Newcastle, and Thomas Hobbes at the end of the First Civil War is significant illustration of this and of the change that had come over a small circle of enlightened men brought up in the new scientific outlook.

> Some other time they falling into a Discourse concerning witches [wrote the Duchess of Newcastle [2]] Mr Hobbes said, That though he could not rationally believe that there were Witches, yet he could not be fully satisfied to believe that there were none, by reason that they themselves would confess it, if strictly examined.
>
> To which my Lord answered, That though for his part he cared not whether there were witches or no; yet his opinion was, That the Confession of Witches, and their sufferings for it proceeded from an erronious belief, viz., That they had made a contract with the Devil to serve him for such Rewards as were in his power to give them; and that it was their Religion to worship and adore him; in which Religion they had such a firm and constant belief, that if anything came to pass according to their desire, they believed the Devil had heard their prayers, and granted their requests, for which they gave him thanks; but if things fell out contrary to their prayers and desires, then they were troubled at it, fearing they had offended him, or not served him as they ought, and asked him for forgiveness for their offences. Also (said my Lord) they imagine their dreams are real exterior actions; for example, if they dream that they flye in the Air, or out of the Chimney top, or that they are turned into several shapes, they believe no otherwise, but that it is really so: And this wicked Opinion makes them industrious to perform such Ceremonies to the Devil that they may worship him as their God, and chuse to live and dye for him.

§ 3. It has sometimes been argued that many Royalists continued to believe in the reality of witchcraft.[3] Such a view is not

---

[1] Compare Sir Kenelm Digby's *Séance* described below at the end of this chapter.

[2] *Life of the Duke of Newcastle* (1667), ed. C. H. Firth, p. 107.

[3] For example, G. L. Kittredge, *Notes on Witchcraft*, pp. 8 sqq. (Worcester, Mass., 1907), and *Witchcraft in Old and New England*. In the latter volume the writer seeks to put the best face on the New England witch-hunts of 1690 by collecting alleged examples of believers in witchcraft who were not Puritans. Many of those adduced have a *floruit* after 1660 and, consequently, do not affect the argument here. They will receive notice in Ch. X below.

antecedently improbable, especially as many persons in the middle of the seventeenth century held a middle position in which they suspended judgement on the question, sometimes inclining to affirm, and at others to deny the possibility of the black art.[1] Nonetheless the examples of Royalist believers in witchcraft which are commonly adduced are not entirely convincing— viz., James Howell, Jeremy Taylor, Joseph Hall, and Robert Burton.

(a) The important fact to remember about Howell (1594?– 1666) is that he was 'a pure cadet not born to land, lease or office'. His main preoccupation during the greater part of his life was the problem of earning a comfortable living. Under Charles I he sought the favour of Royalists such as Strafford. Under the Long Parliament he made several bids for the favour of that body, as, for example, in his *Preheminence and Pedigree of Parliaments* (1644), in which he described the Long Parliament as 'that high Synedrion wherein the wisdom of the whole Senate is epitomized'. Later he sought the favour of Cromwell and commended him for having destroyed Parliament. His imprisonment in the Fleet may have been due to the suspicion that he was a Royalist spy, though even this is not completely certain. Anthony à Wood stated that he was imprisoned as an insolvent debtor. While in the Fleet (1643–51) he wrote his *Familiar Letters*[2] 'to relieve his necessities'. He is thus one of the earliest Englishmen to make a livelihood out of literature. He did so at the demand of Humphrey Moseley, the great publisher of the period, who in all probability dictated the tone of his writings. It is usually rash to assume that a publisher's hack is expressing his own personal views. When, therefore, Howell discourses on

[1] Richard Corbet (1582–1635), Bishop of Oxford, preaching (1631) at the consecration of Lincoln College Chapel, appears to have compared the resemblance between false preaching and true preaching with the resemblance between the miracles of God and the wonders worked by witches (*Collectanea, Fourth Series*, Oxford Historical Society, 1905, pp. 147–8). 'This place above all hath most need of consecration, the Pulpit. If this be not sanctified to the preacher, and the preacher to this, all the whole chappel is the wors for it. . . . All this beauty, all this worship, shall go for abomination, if the sorcerers will have it so (for such preaching is but witchcraft). It is like preaching, I confes, as the sorcerers were like Moses. . . . They did tricks before Pharoah. . . . So here they call up spirits, and in this circle they conjur, but the right spirit comes not up, or very seldom here of late. . . .' His words, as rather confusedly summarized, might almost be taken to imply some belief in the existence of witchcraft in his own day. In certain verses of his, however, he writes in a playful spirit of fairies, witches, &c.

[2] James Howell, *The Familiar Letters*, ed. Jacobs (London, 1890–92).

F

witchcraft for the benefit of the witch-ridden Londoners [1] he could scarcely be expected to deny its existence. Nonetheless he writes in a detached and somewhat academic way, describing the universality of the belief in witches and the increase of witch executions since the beginning of the Civil War. He may well be suspected of writing with his tongue in his cheek, especially when he attributes the renewed activity of the Devil to the Puritans' destruction of crosses. 'The Devil may walk freely up and down the streets of *London* now, for there is not a cross to fright him anywhere.' Thus Howell's royalism and his belief in witches may both well be questioned.

(*b*) In considering Jeremy Taylor (1613–77) it is important to remember that he excelled even his contemporary prose-writers in his exotic richness of phraseology, florid rhetoric, and wild luxuriance of comparison and allusion. It is therefore unsafe to seize upon some sentence or phrase and use it as a pin for fastening some particular belief upon him. Thus, for example, the oft-quoted passage from one of his sermons,[2] 'Witchcraft, or final impenitence and obstinacy in any sin, are infallibly desperate . . .' is probably merely a rhetorical reminiscence of I Samuel xv. 23 in the Authorized Version: 'For rebellion is as the sin of witch-craft, and stubbornness is as iniquity and idolatry'. Similarly the passage adduced from his *Rule and Exercise of Holy Living*,[3] 'Of all carnal sins it is that alone which the Devil takes delight to imitate and counterfeit—communicating with witches and impure persons in the corporal act, but in this only,' is quite possibly only a highly rhetorical way of saying that there is some-thing peculiarly devilish about the sin of fornication. Taylor frequently ranged over vast areas of classical paganism and folk-lore in order to enforce his lessons. There is little in Taylor's life to suggest that he had any more belief in witchcraft than he had in Jupiter. Such a conclusion is confirmed by his denunciation of the forms used for exorcising devils in the Roman Catholic Church,[4]

---

[1] Op. cit., pp. 506, 515, 547, 551.

[2] *The Works of Jeremy Taylor*, ed. R. Heber, vol. vi, p. 61. For another of his allusions to witchcraft in his sermons see vol. v, p. 363. 'For, as envy is in the evil eye, so is cursing in the reproachful tongue; it is a kind of venom and witchcraft, an instrument by which God oftentimes punishes anger and uncharitableness. . . .' Here the context shows clearly that he is speaking figuratively.

[3] Ch. ii, sect. iii, Malleson's ed., p. 47 (London, 1894).

[4] *The Works of Jeremy Taylor*, ed. R. Heber, vol. x, pp. 233–8 (London, 1822).

and by his insistence that the freedom of man's will survived the Fall.[1]

(c) Joseph Hall (1574–1656) was the outstanding exception among the bishops of his age. For he was always much more a Puritan than an Arminian in his theology. When Archbishop Laud on his trial was taxed with giving preferment ' only to such men as were for ceremonies, popery, and Arminianism ', he replied in his *History of his Troubles* that he was responsible for the preferment of Bishop Hall to Exeter.[2] The reply was a good one; for Hall had been brought up a strict Calvinist. In the words of his biographer, he may be ' said to have almost imbibed Calvinism with his mother's milk ',[3] and ' when he went up to Cambridge, Calvinism was just reaching its climax '.[4] Though in later life he receded from the more extreme positions with regard to church government and rites and ceremonies, he was still commonly regarded as a Puritan. His sermon at the Synod of Dort (1618), where Calvinists were in the majority, was well received. In his *Christian Moderation* (1639) he expressed approval of the burning of Servetus: ' kind Master Calvin did well approve himself to God's Church in bringing Servetus to the stake at Geneva '. As Bishop of Exeter he was viewed with the deepest suspicion by Laud owing to his conciliatory attitude towards Puritans and his disinclination from enforcing the reading of the declaration for Sports on Sunday (1633).[5] Though he defended episcopacy in the Long Parliament with much courage (1641), he was clearly regarded as a semi-Puritan by the Committee of the Eastern Counties, who tried to assign him a pension of £400 a year (1643) after his expulsion from the See of Norwich. That a man with such a record should evince in his early writings a strong belief in witchcraft[6] does not severely prove the rule that Calvinists were

---

[1] Op. cit., vol. ix, pp. 85–9. Taylor's treatment of a man who claimed to be visited by a ghost suggests almost the detached scientific attitude of a member of the Society for Psychical Research. For this see Glanville, *Sadducismuss Triumphatus*, ed. More, pp. 243–53 (London, 1682).
On the danger of assuming that Taylor's random statements represent his considered opinions see Henry Hallam's *Literature of Europe*, ch. xix, ss. 53 sqq. ' In no other writer is it more necessary', wrote Hallam, ' to observe the *animus* with which he writes. . . . He probably revised hardly at all what he had written before it went to the press. This makes it easy to quote passages, especially short ones, from Taylor, which do not exhibit his real way of thinking . . .'
[2] G. Lewis, *Life of Joseph Hall*, p. 276 (London, 1886).
[3] Op. cit., p. 5.   [4] Op. cit., p. 72.
[5] *Dict. of Nat. Biog., sub nomine.*
[6] Hall's *Works*, vol. vi, pp. 136–7; vol. vii, pp. 245–6.

witch-hunters and Arminians, protectors of those accused of witchcraft. On the contrary, it would have been surprising had Hall been sceptical.

(*d*) Robert Burton (1577–1640), to judge from many pages of *The Anatomy of Melancholy*, was no Puritan. He was probably a Royalist, though he died before his Royalism could be put to the test of civil war. He belonged to a generation that had grown to full manhood in the reign of Elizabeth, when belief in witch-craft was almost universal amongst educated men. But he was above all things a bibliophile—not to say a bibliomaniac—and his belief about witchcraft, as about a multitude of more exotic superstitions, was curiously detached and academic. His usual argument seems to be that the majority of writers concur in such and such a belief, therefore it should be accepted. Thus, for ex-ample, in writing of Chiromancy and Metoposcopy he concludes :—

> But I am over-tedious in these toys, which howsoever, in some men's too severe censures, they may be held absurd and rediculous, I am bolder to assert, as not borrowed from circumforanean rogues and gipsies, but out of the writings of worthy philosophers and physicians. . . .[1]

On such an argument from authority, belief in the reality of witchcraft was obviously well-founded :—

> Many deny witches at all, or if there be any they can do no harm; of this opinion is Wierus, *lib* 3, *cap* 53, *de praestig. daem.* Austin Lerchemer, a Dutch writer, Biarmannus, Ewichius, Euwaldus, our country man Scot; with him in Horace,
>
> > *Somnia, terrores, magicos, miracula, sagas,*
> > *Nocturnos lemures, portentaque Thessala risu*
> > *Excipiunt.*
>
> They laugh at all such stories; but on the contrary are most lawyers, divines, physicians, philosophers, Austin, Hermingius, Danaeus, Chytraeus, Zanchius, Aretaeus etc., Delrio, Sprenger, Niderius, *lib.* 5 *Formicar.*, Cujacius, Bartolus, *consil.* 6. tom 1, Bodine, *Daemoniant. lib* 2. *cap.* 8, Godelman, Damhoderius, &c., Paracelsus, Erastus, Scribanius, Camerarius, &c.[2]

There is nothing here or elsewhere to suggest that Burton's interest in the subject was anything more than an academic one, or that he was in earnest about anything except finding pegs on which to hang the abundance of his inconsequent erudition. It is recorded that Burton used to go 'down to the Bridge-foot in

---

[1] *Anatomy*, pt. 1, sec. 2, mem. 1, subs. 4.
[2] Op. cit., pt. 1, sec. 2, mem. 1, subs. 3.

Oxford ' to hear ' the Barge-men scold and storm and swear at one another, at which he would set his hands to his sides, and laugh most profusely '.[1]   Such a man's words should not be interpreted narrowly as an expression of his deepest convictions. Thus, for example, he sometimes quotes with approval the words of Beza and other Calvinist divines.   Yet, in the light of other passages in his book, it would be absurd to argue that he had Calvinistic leanings.   Similarly his discussions on witchcraft and demonianism should be read in the light of his many scornful remarks on the subject of superstition, and not rashly taken to imply approval of witch-hunting.   The result of such reading is to leave some uncertainty as to Burton's genuine convictions on the subject of witchcraft.   But even on the highly improbable assumption that Burton really was a deeply convinced believer in black arts, such an eccentric and altogether exceptional man would not be a disconcerting exception to the general rule.

Two other alleged Royalists who believed in witchcraft, Meric Casaubon and Sir Matthew Hale, are reserved for mention in another connexion.[2]

§ 4. Whether there were or were not exceptions to it, the rule seemed to be generally accepted even before the death of James I that the Royalist Church rejected belief in witchcraft, which had become the peculiar domain of Puritans and a few of the Roman Catholics.   So much is implied by Edward Fairfax [3] when, in seeking to obtain credence for his account of the bewitching of his daughters, he protests in his preface that he was ' neither a fantastic Puritan nor a superstitious Papist, but so settled in conscience that I have the sure ground of God's word to warrant all I believe, and the commendable ordinances of our English Church to approve all I practise '.

Outside Puritan circles some were, in fact, so indifferent to the alleged terrors of witchcraft that they were not averse from attending spiritualistic *séances* either out of curiosity or from the urge for scientific investigation.   Lilly the astrologer (and witch-believer) describes [4] an instance in which Sir Kenelm

[1] Bishop Kennet's *Register and Chronicle* (1728).
[2] Chapter IX.
[3] *A Discourse of Witchcraft.   As it was enacted in the Family of Mr Edward Fairfax of Fuystone in the County of York in the Year 1621.*   This volume will be considered in the next chapter.
[4] *William Lilly's History of his Life and Times from the year 1602 to 1681. Written by himself in the sixty-sixth year of his age, to his worthy friend Elias Ashmole Esq.* (London, 1826), pp. 26–8, in the edition of 1715, pp. 20–3.

Digby, son of one of the Gunpowder Conspirators of 1605, was involved.

> It happened [he wrote] on one Sunday, 1632, as myself and a justice of the peace's clerk were, before service, discoursing of many things he chanced to say, that such a person was a great scholar, nay, so learned that he could make an almanack, which to me was strange: one speech begot another, till at last, he said, he could bring me acquainted with one Evans in Gunpowder-alley, who had formerly lived in Staffordshire, that was an excellent wise man that studied the Black Art. . . . Now something of the man: he was by birth a Welshman, a master of Arts, and in sacred orders: he had formerly had a cure of souls in Staffordshire, but now was come to try his fortunes in London, being in a manner enforced to fly for some offences very scandalous, committed by him in those parts where he had lately lived; for he gave judgements on things lost, the only shame of astrology. . . . Sometime before I became acquainted with him, he then living in the Minories, was desired by lord Bothwell [1] and Sir Kenelm Digby to show them a spirit. He promised to do so: the time came; and they were all in the body of the circle, when, upon a sudden, after some time of invocation, Evans was taken out of the room, and carried into a field near Battersea Causeway, close to the Thames. Next morning a countryman going by to his labour, and espying a man in black cloathes, came unto him and awakened him, and asked how he came to be there ? Evans by this understood his condition, inquired where he was, how far from London, and in what parish he was; which when he understood, he told the labourer he had been late in Battersea the night before, and by chance was left there by his friends. Sir Kenelm Digby and the lord Bothwell went home without any harm, and came next day to hear what was become of him; just as they, in the afternoon came to the house, a messenger came from Evans to his wife, to come to him at Battersea. I inquired upon what account the spirit had carried him away: who said, he had not, at the time of invocation, made any suffumigation, at which the spirits were vexed.

The latter part of the narrative about Evans waking up in Battersea may be disregarded on account of the astrologer's bibulous habits. ' He was much addicted to debauchery,' wrote Lilly, ' and when in drink he would be very abusive and quarrelsome, so that he would seldom be without a black-eye or one bruise or another.' The interest of the narrative lies in Sir Kenelm Digby's attitude towards witchcraft, since he was a

---

[1] Francis Stewart Hepburn, fifth Earl of Bothwell, was deprived of his title and fled from Scotland to the Continent in 1595, dying near Naples in 1624. His eldest son Francis obtained a rehabilitation under the Great Seal (1614) which was ratified by Parliament (1633), but his title was never restored. He is, possibly, the person here described (incorrectly) as ' Lord Bothwell '. Wood, *Athenae Oxonienses*, ed. Bliss, vol. i, p. 579, writes of ' one who called himself Lord Bothwell '.

typical example of many who combined staunch Royalism [1] with zeal for scientific research. His Royalism is shown by his close friendship with Archbishop Laud; by his duel to the death with a Frenchman who made an offensive statement about Charles I; by his sufferings at the hands of the Long Parliament, and by the office which he held of Chancellor to Henrietta Maria. His zeal for scientific research is shown by his chemical experiments, some of which were witnessed (1651) by Evelyn; by his lectures at Gresham College (1661) on the vegetation of plants; by his intimate friendship with Descartes; by his position on the Council of the Royal Society, and by his scientific treatises. He is said to have been the first to notice the importance of oxygen—'vital air', as he called it—in the life of plants.

One would naturally assume that a man with such a record would be sceptical about the existence of witchcraft, but that, like Dr. Harvey already mentioned, he would be interested in investigating the matter in a scientific spirit; hence his visit to Evans's *séance*. This assumption is verified by a passage (p. 35) in his *Observations on Religio Medici* (London, 1644). Commenting on Sir Thomas Browne's contention that to deny the existence of witchcraft is to deny the existence of spirits and of God, he wrote :—

> I acknowledge ingeniously our *Physicians* experience hath the advantage of my *Philosophy* in knowing there are witches. Yet I am sure, I have no temptation to doubt of the Deity; nor have any unsatisfaction in believing there are Spirits. I do not see such a necessary conjunction between them, as that supposition of the one, must needs inferre the other. Neither do I deny there are witches. I oneley reserve my assent till I meet with stronger motives to carry it. And I confesse I doubt as much of the efficacy of those magicall rules he speaketh of, as also the finding out of mysteries by the courteous *Revelations of Spirits*.

Here Digby voices the typical Royalist attitude of Charles I's time—an attitude that has already been exemplified in Dr. Harvey, the Duke of Newcastle, Hobbes, and others—not a dogmatic denial of the possibility of witchcraft, but a scientific sceptical attitude, to which witch-hunting would be utterly abhorrent.

---

[1] Digby was brought up a Roman Catholic. He became an Anglican in 1630; but five years later reverted to Roman Catholicism. During the Protectorate he engaged in certain obscure negotiations with Cromwell—presumably with the purpose of mitigating the persecution of his co-religionists.

CHAPTER V

THE ATTEMPTS OF JAMES I AND CHARLES I TO EXTINGUISH WITCH-MANIA, 1618–42

§ 1. MUCH OF the power of the Tudor monarchy remained in the hands of the early Stuarts. When, therefore, they had made up their minds that witchcraft was a delusion, they were able to save from execution most of the victims of superstition. They could not, indeed, secure a repeal of the terrible Statute of 1604—the intense hostility of Parliament would have made any such attempt futile. But they had in their hands the appointment to all the great offices of authority and influence in Church and State, the great though vague power of the Council in its many forms, and the censorship of the Press. These they used with considerable effect in an attempt to turn back the tide of witch-terror. As vacancies occurred on the Bench of Bishops or the Bench of Judges these were filled with men opposed to the prevailing superstition, so that it became almost impossible to secure the conviction of a witch in spite of the fanaticism of her enemies.

(a) (i) The influence of the new bishops was so important a factor in preventing convictions that it is necessary to give a few examples of its exercise. One of the oldest of the Arminian clergy was Samuel Harsnett (1561–1631), who, as early as 1584, had been censured by Whitgift for a sermon directed against the Calvinist dogma of predestination. In 1629 he was translated from the See of Norwich to become Archbishop of York. His record in the matter of witchcraft had made him famous throughout the country. He had played a conspicuous part in detecting the frauds of one John Darrell, a Puritan minister, who had created a great sensation (1597–8) by pretending to exorcise those possessed by devils. Darrell's frauds had done much to spread the terror of witches in the Northern Midlands when he was unmasked by Harsnett's widely read treatise, *A Discovery of the Fraudulent practises of Iohn Darrell, Bachelor of Arts . . . detecting in some sort the deceitful trade in these latter days of casting out Devils.* (London 1599.) This was extremely effective in spite of the strenuous defence of Darrell put up by the Puritans of Cambridge. (S. Clarke, *Lives of Two and Twenty English Divines*, pp. 41 sqq. London, 1660.) Shortly afterwards Harsnett discovered that some Roman Catholic priests were adopting Darrell's methods in the hope of regaining popular support by exploiting the prevailing superstition. He thereupon denounced the pretended exorcisms of a supposed Jesuit priest in a pamphlet that has been made famous by Shakespeare's use of it,[1] *A Declaration of Egregious Popish Impostures, . . . under pretence of casting out devils. Practiced by Edmunds, alias Weston, a Iesuit, and divers Romish Priests, his wicked associates.* This was published in 1603, with copies of the confessions and of the examination of the persons concerned. So great was the demand that it was republished two years later. The new Archbishop of York was, therefore, one of the first of the Anglican clergy publicly to oppose the great Witch Scare. Charles I rewarded him with the highest preferment available.

A few years later Harsnett, with two other prelates, took his part in the detection of another case of simulated possession. Anne Gunter, of South Moreton near Wallingford in Berkshire,[2] a girl of about fourteen years of age, accused three women of bewitching her. Though she performed many miraculous feats in her native village and in Oxford, she found the people of these parts far less credulous than their contemporaries in the Eastern Counties would have been; and a jury at the Abingdon Assizes (1st March 1604/5) acquitted two of the accused. As Anne and her father persisted in their accusations, the girl was handed over to the care of Henry Cotton, Bishop of Salisbury, whose experience as the father of nineteen children apparently gave him some insight into the ways of small girls. As one of Anne's favourite manifestations of diabolical possession was the vomiting or sneezing up of pins, the good Bishop had certain pins secretly marked and put in a place where she could easily find them. When she proceeded a little later to vomit and sneeze up these marked pins, her credibility was seriously shaken.

Nonetheless her father, hoping for a more credulous attitude from the author of the *Demonologie*, took her to Oxford to see King James (27th August 1605). As a result she was placed in charge of Harsnett and a medical man, who induced her to confess

[1] It is the source of the names of the Spirits mentioned by Edgar in *King Lear*, Act III, sc. iv.

[2] For a full account of this interesting case see Ewen, *Witchcraft in the Star Chamber* (printed for the author, 1938).

that all her symptoms of possession had been feigned at the instance of her father and others.

(ii) Another prelate who contributed to the detection of Anne's frauds was Richard Neile (1562–1640), then Dean of Westminster. For he is recorded (1st March 1605/6) as having received £300 to be distributed to 'divers persons employed in the discovery of a pretended witchcraft in the case of Anne Gunter'.[1] Neale's part in this detection is important for two reasons. First, because Charles I promoted him to succeed Harsnett as Archbishop of York (1631) and made much use of his services in the High Commission Court and in the Star Chamber. Secondly, he is even more important as the patron and friend of Archbishop Laud, who became his chaplain in 1608, and owed to him much of his advancement and much also of his intellectual make-up. When Neile became Bishop of Durham in 1617, Laud, then Dean of Gloucester, took up permanent residence with him at Durham House in the Strand.

(iii) A later example of a prelate who set himself to stem the tide of witch-mania is Thomas Morton (1564–1659), who became successively Bishop of Chester (1616), of Lichfield and Coventry (1618), and of Durham (1632). His stand against witch-mania is of the first historical importance, for it resulted in the detection of the fraud of the famous 'Boy of Bilston'— a thirteen-year-old boy who had been taught, apparently by a Roman Catholic priest, to simulate diabolical possession. The boy created a considerable sensation in his neighbourhood by casting 'out of his mouth rags, thred, straw, crooked pins' and by falling into fits and spasms. He attributed his seizures to the witchcraft of a certain Jane Clarke, thus putting the unhappy old woman in imminent danger of the gallows. Morton thereupon interposed. He took the boy to his house, and with the help of his secretary put him through a series of well-planned tests, and had him secretly watched. One of his tests proved particularly devastating. The boy regularly underwent a furious seizure on hearing read the first verse of the first chapter of St. John's Gospel.

> 'Boy,' said the Bishop, 'it is either thou or the Devil that abhorrest these Words of the Gospel: and if it be the Devil (he being so ancient a Scholar, as of almost six thousand Years' standing) knows, and understands all Languages; so that he cannot but know when I recite the same sentence out of the Greek Text: But if it be

[1] Ewen, *Witchcraft in the Star Chamber*, p. 14 (printed for the author, 1938).

thyself then thou art an execrable Wretch, who plays the Devil's part. . . . Wherefore look to thyself, for now thou art to be put to Trial, and mark diligently, whether it be that same Scripture that shall be read. . . .[1] The Bishop then read out another verse in the Greek, and the boy thinking it was the first verse, had at once a furious seizure. Later, when the Bishop read out the first verse in Greek, the Boy, believing that this verse had already been read, remained unmoved.

After many such tests the boy was induced to confess his trickery in court before ' the face of the County and Country there assembled ' and to beg forgiveness of the old woman he had falsely accused (1621). This piece of detection had its repercussions far beyond Staffordshire. For, as has been noticed elsewhere, it served to complete James I's renunciation of his former witch-beliefs.

(iv) No less important was the resistance to superstition put up by John Bridgeman (1577–1652), who was appointed Bishop of Chester in 1619, and whose diocese included witch-ridden Lancashire. Though he exerted himself at times to repress the Puritans of that shire, he was a man of a notoriously indolent and dilatory disposition, and failed to do as much as might have been done to assuage the witch-terror of his diocese. Nonetheless his action in the second great outburst of witch-mania in Lancashire (1634) helped to save many lives. At the Lent Sessions and General Jail Delivery held at Lancaster no fewer than seventeen persons were found guilty of witchcraft. The judge, however, appears to have been dissatisfied with the findings of the jury and, probably for that reason, the execution was respited and the proceedings reported to the King in Council. Consequently Bridgeman was ordered to examine some of the prisoners.[2] The result of his examination was seriously to shake the case against them. He came to the conclusion that some of the accusations were made with a view to blackmail, and a few from personal hostility; and that others were due to the crudest superstition. Thus, for example, one of the accused, a girl of twenty years of age named Mary Spencer, had been found guilty merely because she was in the habit of rolling her pail down a hill to the well and running in front of it, calling it in fun to follow her. The ' witches' marks ' asserted to have been found on some of

[1] *The Boy of Bilson : or, A True Discovery of the Late Notorious Impostures of Certaine Romish Priests, &c.*, p. 59 (London, 1622).
[2] *Calendar of State Papers*, 1634–35, pp. 26, 77–9, 98, 129–30, 141, 152–3.

the accused were said by Bridgeman to be merely natural growths. In view of the law it would have been worse than useless to assert the innocence of the accused on the ground that there was no such thing as witchcraft. The only way of saving them was to show that the evidence against them was not sufficient. Bridgeman therefore sent them on to London, where a number of medical men headed by the King's physician, Dr. Harvey, made short work of the alleged witches' marks, and where the chief witness, a small boy, admitted to a Middlesex Justice of the Peace that all his evidence in court had been completely untrue. Thereupon all the accused escaped the gallows—to the horror and dismay of the population of London, who fully believed in their guilt. The part played by bishops in the rescue of these women from the hangman may well have contributed to the zeal of the London mob for the abolition of episcopacy 'root and branch' seven years later.

(v) Another example of an Arminian prelate exerting himself to allay the witch-mania is William Piers (1580–1670), who had, largely by Laud's influence, been made Bishop of Peterborough (1630) and been translated two years later to Bath and Wells. In Staffordshire in 1637 he interposed on behalf of an old woman named Joyce Hunniman,[1] who was accused of witchcraft. He not only saved her, but exerted himself to discredit certain apparitors who went about spreading the terror of sorcery.[2]

(b) (i) Hardly less important than the Arminian prelates in the attempt to extinguish witch-mania were the new Royalist judges. Formerly the judicial Bench had been filled with witch-hunters of the type of Sir Edward Coke (1552–1634), the great Parliamentarian.[3] Since James I's renunciation of his witch-beliefs the influence of the new judges came to be felt with increasing power in the courts. The earliest example of the change

[1] *Historical Manuscripts Commission 2nd Report*, Appendix, p. 48 b; Ewen, *Witchcraft and Demonianism*, pp. 435–6 (London, 1933).

[2] Another prelate who used his influence against witch-mania was Godfrey Goodman (1583–1656), Bishop of Gloucester (1625). In his *Court of James I* (printed by J. S. Brewer, 1839) he praised James on the ground that he 'was ever apt to search into secrets, to try conclusions (i.e., experiments), as I did know some who saw him run to see one in a fit whom they said was bewitched'.

[3] For Coke's views on witchcraft see his *Institutes*, p. III, ch. 6. Several books on witchcraft were dedicated to him—e.g., William Perkins's *Discourse on the Damned Art of Witchcraft* and John Cotta's *Triall of Witchcraft*. He assisted the Lords' Committee in framing the Act of 1604 against witchcraft.

comes in the famous case (1621) in which **Edward Fairfax**, an uncle of Thomas Fairfax, the Parliamentary generalissimo, believed that he himself and two of his daughters had been bewitched. On his evidence six women were arrested and sent for trial at the Spring Assizes at York. Details of their trial have not survived. It appears, however, that most at least of the accused were acquitted, and that Fairfax with the help of his powerful family managed somehow to get them put on trial a second time.[1] They were again acquitted, owing largely to the scepticism of the judge. Fairfax's own description [2] of the event is eloquent of the new attitude that was so rapidly winning supremacy in Royalist circles. His family, he stated, was troubled by six witches, five of whom were known to him.

> The first is called Margaret Waite, a widow that some years ago came to dwell in these parts, with a husband, who brought with them an evil report for witchcraft and theft. The man died by the hand of the executioner for stealing, and his relict has increased the report she brought with her for Witchery. Her familiar spirit is a deformed thing with many feet, black of colour, rough with hair, the bigness of a cat, the name of it unknown.
> The next is her daughter. . . . Her Spirit is a white cat, spotted with black and named Inges.
> The third is Jennit Dibble, a very old widow, reputed a witch for many years; and a constant report affirmeth that her mother, two aunts, two sisters, her husband, and some of her children have all been long esteemed Witches, so that it seemeth hereditary to her family. Her Spirit is in the shape of a great black cat, called Gibbe, which hath attended her now above 40 years.
> These are made up to a mess [3] by Margaret Thorpe, daughter to Jennit Dibble. . . . Her familiar is in the shape of a bird, yellow of colour, about the bigness of a crow; the name of it is Tewhit.
> The fifth is Elizabeth Fletcher . . . a woman notoriously famed for a Witch, who had so powerful a hand over the wealthiest neighbours about her, that none of them refused to do anything she required; yea, unbesought, they provided her of fire, and meat from their own tables, and did what else they thought would please her, *ne illis noceat*.
> Within the forest of Knaresborough [Fairfax argued [4]] dwell many more suspected for Witches, so that the inhabitants complain much by secret murmurings of great losses sustained in their goods, especially in their kine which should give them milk . . .

[1] W. Notestein, *A History of Witchcraft in England*, p. 144 (Washington, 1911).
[2] *A Discourse of Witchcraft : As it was enacted in the Family of Mr Edward Fairfax of Fuystone in the County of York in the Year 1621*, pp. 226 sqq.
[3] ' A group of four persons.' O.E.D.; cf. Shakespeare 3 *Henry VI*, Act 1, sc. iv, ' where are your mess of sons '.
[4] Op. cit., p. 11.

On the other hand, Fairfax was much troubled by sceptics

> who think that there be no Witches at all. Of this opinion I hear
> and fear there be many, some of them men of worth. . . .   Other
> sceptics were less worthy. Neither be thou moved with their bare
> assertions or silly arguments for they proceed from men ill-affected
> to the cause, and perhaps not clear from the crime. . . . [1]

When he brought up the women for trial, the judges, he found, exerted themselves to secure an acquittal.

> These are the particulars of the afflictions of my poor children . . .
> they are also given in evidence at two sundry assizes, and two several
> juries . . . well satisfied that these women were the offenders . . .
> indicted them and put them to their trials. . . . But it pleased mercy
> to interpret the law in their favour . . . the proceedings which made
> the way easy for their escape, I fear, were not fair : either the hardness
> of hearts to believe, which made some of the best sort incredulous, or
> the openness of hand to give, which waylaid justice, untying the fetters
> from their heels, unloosing the halters from their necks, which so
> wise juries thought they had so well deserved. . . .

The grand jury, so he asserts, ' received also a good caveat, by a message from the judge to be very careful in the matter of Witches. . . .' [2] Finally ' the Judge, upon what occasion moved I know not, after some good plausible hearing of the evidence for a time, at last told the jury that the evidence reached not to the point of the statute, and withdrew the offenders from their trial by the jury of life and death, and dismissed them at liberty, at which manner of proceeding many wiser men than I am greatly wonder '.[3]

(ii) The name of the judge, who evidently exerted himself a great deal to baulk Fairfax of his prey, is unknown. Also unknown is the name of the judge, already mentioned, who, having failed to secure the acquittal of the Lancashire witches of 1634, saved them by referring the case to Charles I.

(iii) Four years later, at the Essex Jail Delivery of the summer of 1639, a certain Robert Garnett was brought before Sir Richard Weston, Baron of the Exchequer, who was later impeached by the Long Parliament, and Edmund Reeve, Judge of the Common Pleas. Garnett was accused of ' putting his trust in witches and conversing with them to the great dishonour of God '. Such a charge might easily have been construed as a capital one under the Statute of James I. The judges, however, ignored the witchcraft and treated the accused merely as a vagabond, sentencing

---

[1] Op. cit., p. 39.   [2] Op. cit., p. 234.   [3] Op. cit., p. 237–8.

him to be put to work for one week in a house of correction. The judge responsible was probably Weston, he being senior to Reeve, who afterwards adhered to the Parliamentary side in the Civil War.

(iv) The change in the attitude of Charles I's judicial Bench towards witchcraft was facilitated by the death or removal of many of the witch-hunting judges early in the reign.[1] Robert Houghton died in 1624, while James I was still on the throne. Henry Hobart, who had been one of the judges in the famous Lancashire case of 1612 and in the Margaret Flower case of 1618/19, died in 1625. Humphrey Winch died in the same year, and John Doderidge three years later (1628). Henry Montague, afterwards Earl of Manchester, one of the Commons' Committee that helped to frame the Act against witchcraft of 1604, and father of the Parliamentarian general, ceased to function as a judge as early as 1620, when he became a member of the King's Council. Ranulf Crewe, who with Humphrey Winch had sent nine witches to the gallows at Leicester in 1616, was dismissed by Charles I (9th November 1626). The reason for his dismissal is unknown. The one commonly given is that he had refused to sign a document affirming the legality of forced loans. But, as all his colleagues made the same refusal and were not dismissed, this makes Parliamentarian propaganda, but not sense.[2] Sir John Walter, to whom Bernard's great defence of witch-beliefs, the *Guide to Grand Jurymen*, was dedicated, was inhibited by Charles I from sitting in court (22nd October 1630), in spite of the fact that he is commonly accused of being unduly obsequious to the Crown in dealing with questions of the right to raise revenue by extra-parliamentary means. The bench of judges which resulted from these dismissals ' were never charged

---

[1] Ewen, *Witch Hunting and Witch Trials*, pp. 50 sqq. (London, 1929), gives a list of judges who are known to have sentenced witches.

[2] In the Long Parliament in 1641 Denzil Hollis moved to petition the King to compensate Crewe. On Charles I's dismissals of judges see Tanner, *English Constitutional Conflicts of the Seventeenth Century*, pp. 40, 60 (Cambridge, 1928), and S. R. Gardiner, *History of England 1603–42*, vol. vii, pp. 112–13 (London, 1891). On 14th September 1634, Sir Robert Heath, Chief Justice of the Common Pleas, was suddenly dismissed. 'No reason was assigned for the unexpected blow, and the special grant of professional precedence which was accorded to him after his dismissal excludes the supposition that he had committed any actual offence ' (Gardiner, op. cit., vol. vii, p. 361). Heath was a strong upholder of prerogative and a devoted admirer of the King. Evidently judges were dismissed for reasons other than lack of subservience to the Crown.

with incapacity or negligence',[1] and all were sceptics on the matter of witchcraft.

§ 2 (a) In addition to bishops and judges, many of the Justices of the Peace and other local gentry of Royalist convictions contributed their quota towards saving old women from the gallows. One such example has only recently come to light.[2] In Kent, on the eve of the Civil War, Henry Oxinden writes to his kinsman, Robert Bargrave of Bifrons, to enlist his support in protecting a certain Goodwife Gilnot, who was accused by a neighbour, one Brake, of using the black art to make him ill and to cause the loss of many of his sheep. Brake also asserted ' that she hath a wart or Teat uppon her body wherewith she giveth her familiar suck '. Oxinden appeals to reason against the absurdity of such charges, and concludes with the notable words descriptive of the majority of his countrymen

> such is the blindness of men in these latter days that . . . the poore woman's cry, though it reach to heaven, is scarce heard heere uppon earth . . . for the world is now come to such a passe that . . . if any woman, bee she never so honest, be accused for a witch they cry ad ignem; and no marvel if common people be mistaken in this matter, when almost all divines, physitions and lyers (lawyers) . . . have given to much credit to these fables . . . (23rd September 1641).

Henry Oxinden, though a relative of Charles I's Lord Treasurer, Cottington, was a moderate at the beginning of the Great Rebellion, and inclined to favour the Parliamentary cause. Soon, however, he moved in a Royalist direction, became a satirist of Puritan sects, and died an Anglican parson. His correspondent, Robert Bargrave, showed no such hesitancy, and devoted himself heart and soul to the Royalist cause from the outset, leaving to posterity his epitaph in Patrixbourne Church:—

> *Bello civili ex partibus regiis*
> *Stetit et cecidit familia.*

(b) Oxinden and Bargrave did not stand alone amongst the gentry of Kent in supporting the Government's efforts to suppress the prevailing witch-mania. Sir Robert Filmer of East Sutton is known to history chiefly as the most formidable of defenders of the doctrine of the Divine Hereditary Right of Kings. His finely reasoned case for Royalism in the *Patriarcha*

---

[1] S. R. Gardiner, op. cit., vol. vii, p. 361.
[2] Dorothy Gardiner, *The Oxinden Letters, 1607-42*, pp. 220 sqq. (London, 1933).

earned him the execration and ridicule of more than two centuries of Whig posterity. His urgent desire to protect the victims of superstition produced his *Advertisement to the Jury-men of England Touching Witches, Together with a difference between an English and Hebrew Witch* in 1653, during a period of witch-killing in Kent which accompanied the inauguration of the Commonwealth. With exquisite satire he places William Perkins,[1] the Puritan preacher, and Delrio,[2] the Jesuit, side by side as teaching substantially identical doctrines about witchcraft. Perkins's advocacy of torture he rejects as contrary to the laws and customs of the country.

> Touching Examination Mr *Perkins* names two kinds of proceedings, either by *simple Question* or *by Torture, Torture, when besides the enquiry by words, the Magistrate useth the Rack, or some other violent means to urge Confession ;* this he saith, *may be lawfully used howbeit not in every case, but only upon strong and great presumptions, and when the party is obstinate.* Here it may be noted that it is not lawful for any person, but the Judge only to allow Torture, superstitious neighbours may not of their own heads use either Threats, Terrors or Tortures. . . .[3]

As the witch-hunters based so much of their belief upon certain passages of Scripture, Filmer takes great pains to give them a lesson in exegesis, showing that they were guilty of most serious misinterpretations. Thus, for example, the belief that God would allow witchcraft is, he maintains, contrary to the teaching of the Bible.[4]

> Setting aside the case of *Job* (wherein God gave a speciall and extraordinary Commission) I doe not finde in Scripture that the Devill, or Witch, or any other had power ordinarily permitted them, either to kill or hurt any Man, or to medle with the Goods of any : for though for the triall of the hearts of men God doth permit the Devill ordinarily to tempt them; yet hath he no Commission to destroy the Lives or Goods of Men, it is little less than blasphemy to say any such thing of the admirable Providence of God, whereby he preserves all his Creatures.

Coming to more specific texts—especially Deuteronomy xviii. 10, 11—Filmer demolishes them by a careful consideration of the Hebrew original.[5]

---

[1] William Perkins, *A Discourse of the Damned Art of Witchcraft* (Cambridge, 1608). The book passed through many editions.

[2] M. A. Delrio, *Disquisitionum Magicorum Libri Sex* (Louvain, 1599). Delrio entered the Society of Jesus in 1580 and died 1608.

[3] *Advertisement, &c.,* p. 10.

[4] Op. cit., p. 15.

[5] Op. cit., pp. 17 sqq.

G

The Hebrew word for a Witch properly signifies a Jugler, and is derived from a word which signifies *changing* or *turning*, and *Moses* teaches Exod. 7. that Witches wrought by Enchantments, that is, *by secret Juglings, Close Conveyance, or of Glistering like a flame of Fire, or a Sword wherewith Men's Eyes were dazled.*

A consulter with a Familiar Spirit means merely a consulter with a ventriloquist:—

If we draw neerer to the words of the Text, it will be found that these words Consulte with a Familiar Spirit are no other than *a Consulter with Ob.* Where the question will be what *Ob* signifieth. Expositors agree that originally *Ob* signifieth a Bottle, and they say is applied here to one possessed of an evill Spirit, and speaketh with a hollow voyce as out of a Bottle; but for this I finde no proofe, they bring out of Scripture that saith, or expoundeth that *Ob* signifieth one possessed with a Familiar Spirit in the Belly; the onely proofe is that the Greek Interpreters of the Bible translate it *Engastromuthi,* which is, speaking in the Belly, and the word anciently, and long before the time of the Septuagint Translators was properly used for one that had his cunning or slight to shut his mouth, and seeme to speake with his Belly, which that it can be done without the helpe of a Familiar Spirit, experience of this age sheweth in an Irish-man. . . .

The incident of the Witch of Endor (I Samuel xxviii), upon which contemporaries laid so much stress, Filmer explains as a piece of trickery:—

It may well be that . . . her intention was to deceive *Saul* and by her secret voyce to have made him believe that *Samuel* in another roome had answered him; for it appeares that Saul was not in the same place where she made a shew of raising *Samuel,* for when she cried out in a loud voyce, *Saul* comforted her, and bid her not to be afraid, and asked her *what she saw ? and what forme he is of ?* which questions need not have beene if *Saul* had beene in the Chamber with the Witch.

Finally Filmer strikes a shrewd blow at the foundation of witch-persecution by questioning the accepted meaning of the commandment (Exodus xxii. 18), ' Thou shalt not suffer a witch to live '.

The *Hebrew* Doctors that were skild in the Lawes of *Moses,* observe that wheresoever one was to die by their Law, the Law always did run in an *affirmative precept;* as, the Man shall be stoned, shall be put to death, or the like *;* but in this Text, and nowhere else in Scripture the sentence is onely a *Prohibition negative, Thou shalt not suffer a Witch to live,* and not Thou shalt put her to death, or stone her or the like. Hence some have beene of opinion that not to suffer a Witch to live, was meant not to relieve or maintain her by running after her, and rewarding her.

The Septuagint have translated a Witch, an Apothecary, a Druggister, one that compounds poysons, and so the Latin word for a Witch is *venefica*, a maker of poysons . . .

There is consequently no case for supposing that there is any covenant with the Devil.

Filmer was a man of very considerable influence in his neighbourhood. He had been knighted by Charles I, at the beginning of his reign, and had married a daughter of the Bishop of Ely (Martin Heton). Though the *Advertisement* may not have been written till after the Civil War, there is no reason to doubt that his views about witchcraft dated back to the period under discussion (1618–42), when he probably played his part in putting obstacles in the way of the witch-hunter. If this is so, it may help to explain the special vengeance directed against him by the Parliamentarian troops, who plundered his house ten times and in 1644 imprisoned him in Leeds Castle, Kent.

In other shires besides Kent there were not a few loyal Justices of the Peace [1] scattered here and there who used their power and influence to support the Government's great offensive against witch-killing, and thus brought upon themselves and their King the hatred of the countryside.

§ 3. Of the efforts of the Government at the centre, the King's Council, to stem the tide of witch-mania only a few fragmentary records are extant. They are insufficient to be formed into anything like a complete picture. They merely suggest a faint outline, like some badly faded fresco, of the activities that were continually proceeding. The case of the Lancashire Witches of 1634 has been mentioned more than once. Here, it should be remembered, it was the Royal Council who ordered the intervention of Bishop Bridgeman and who had four of the witches and their accusers brought up to London for examination. It was the Council who ordered Alexander Baker and Sergeant William Clowes, his Majesty's Surgeons, 'to make choice of

---

[1] In Royalist Yorkshire the magistrates had long been opposed to witch-hunting. Edward Fairfax, in the preface to his *Discourse of Witchcraft* (1621), wrote: 'When I first questioned by way of justice some of these women, they wanted not both counsellors and supporters of the best, able, and most understanding about them. These men, at feasts and meetings, spread reports, and moved doubts inferring a supposal of counterfeiting, and practice in the children, and that it was not serious but a combination proceeding of malice.

' These things they suggested to our next justices, where it found a welcome, ether for the person's sake who presented it, or for that those magistrates were incredulous of things of this kind, or perhaps for both those reasons.'

midwives to inspect and search the bodies of the women lately brought up by the Sheriff of Co. Lancaster indicted for witch-craft, wherein the midwives are to receive instructions from Dr. Harvey, the King's physician, and themselves '[1] So in-terested in the case were the Council and the King himself that after the medical examination they found time to interview the witches.[2] They also took elaborate measures to get the true story out of the boy, Edmund Robinson, whose amazing assertions about the old woman who took the form of a dog and then changed a boy into a horse had given the initial impulse to the witch-hunt. Their efforts resulted in his admission to the King's Coachman at Richmond that he had ' framed the tale out of his own invention '.[3] It was Sir Francis Windebank, the Secretary, who sent him to a J.P. for examination, and thus obtained a full confession that did much to discredit belief in witchcraft amongst those whose minds were still open to reason.

The following year (Feb. 1634/5) ' certain women late of Wigan ' were lodged in Lancaster Jail to await trial for witchcraft. Again the Council ordered Bishop Bridgeman to intervene. Bridgeman replied that he was ill and that Lancaster was a long way from Chester. ' Nevertheless,' he concluded ' . . . I sent my servant to the judges at Lancaster with a copy of your letter, that they might know His Majesty's pleasure and proceed accordingly.' [4] In May he rode to Lancaster and announced that the evidence against those who had survived the rigours of imprisonment was insufficient.[5] They had all been condemned to death at the last Assizes. They were now presumably reprieved.

Three years later (1638) Janet Home and Edward South were accused of witchcraft, in Lincolnshire apparently. Accordingly the Council set to work to unravel a tangled skein of simulated possession, bribery, threats, accusations, and counter-accusations; and finally showed that the whole affair was entirely free from supernatural ingredients. The whole complicated story survives

[1] *Calendar of State Papers, Domestic, Charles I*, 1634–5, p. 98 (London, 1865).
[2] J. Webster, *Displaying of Supposed Witchcraft*, p. 277 (London, 1677). Webster had himself seen Edmund Robinson when the boy was taken to various churches during service time so that he might detect witches among the congregations.
[3] *Calendar of State Papers, Domestic, Charles I*, 1634–5, p. 141 (London, 1864).
[4] *Historical MSS. Commission*, 1888, MSS. of Earl of Cowper, vol. ii, p. 77.
[5] Op. cit., p. 80.

in a page and three-quarters at the Record Office, which deserve quotation as an instance of painstaking enquiry.

Examination of Margaret Cley, taken before Peregrine Bertie,[1] Sir Anthony Irby,[2] and others. Her uncle, Thomas Stennett, carried her before the Earl of Lincoln, and by the way told her that she had undone her aunt Field, and might never look her in the face any more, and said he would give her some new clothes if she would deny what she had confessed to Lord Willoughby, and deny that her aunt Field had taught her to do any counterfeit tricks, which she was willing to do. The Earl of Lincoln examined her whether Lord Willoughby or any of his servants had beaten her, or used any violence towards her to make that confession. She told the Earl that her confession was true. The Earl told her she was a naughty girl, and had wronged her aunt, and so sent her out of the room with her uncle Stennett, who persuaded her and she promised to say as he would have her. One of the Earl's men brought her again to the Earl, and then she denied that her aunt had taught her to counterfeit herself possessed, but that she was really possessed, and that Janet Home and Edward South had bewitched her.

Examination of Anne Coleson, taken before the same persons. Thomas Stennett, brother of Elizabeth Field, her dame, came and fetched examinant before the Earl of Lincoln, and by the way Stennett desired her to deny what she had said before Lord Willoughby, and Elizabeth Field should give her 2 s. to accuse her dame, and Jane Thompson had given her 12 d. to accuse her said dame. The Earl examined deponent, and said she was a naughty girl, and worthy to be sent to a House of Correction, for she had caused Margaret Cley to confess that which was not true. After persuasion by Stennett, she said she had done her dame wrong, and denied what she had confessed before Lord Willoughby. The Earl wished her to put her hand to her examination, which she refused to do, though threatened by the Earl to be sent to the House of Correction for not doing it.[3]

§ 4. The attitude of the Star Chamber towards witchcraft was so widely known that accused persons sometimes appealed to it for protection.[4] Thus, for example, a certain Mary Prowting in Berkshire was accused of being a witch. She appealed to the Star Chamber (November 1635); and notes in the hand of

[1] Peregrine Bertie (1685–40) was the second son of Lord Willoughby de Eresby (1555–1601) and brother of the Earl of Lindsey, the Lord High Admiral, who died of wounds received at Edgehill whilst fighting on the Royalist side.

[2] Sir Anthony Irby was later one of the members of the Long Parliament who took the Covenant. Rushworth, *Historical Collections*, Pt. III, vol. ii, p. 481 (London, 1692).

[3] *Calendar of State Papers, Domestic, Charles I*, 1637–8, ed. John Bruce, p. 586 (London, 1869).

[4] For further examples see C. L'Estrange Ewen, *Witchcraft in the Star Chamber* (1938).

Secretary Windebank survive to show that the accusation was based on ' pretended convulsions and fasting, which were ultimately confessed to be mere deception '.[1] It is unfortunate that no record of the Star Chamber's further action in this case appears to be extant.

Witchcraft was well within the province of the Ecclesiastical Commission, where the offence was classed as heresy.[2] Several small fragments of its records are sufficient to arouse the suspicion that its activities in curbing the witch-hunters were considerable. As, however, the Registers which contained details of the cases that came before it are lost, the suspicion cannot be confirmed.

§ 5. It has been noticed that witch-mania used the printing-press as a potent means of propaganda. This was soon prevented by the censorship of Charles I's Government. The Press was subject to certain ordinances of the Star Chamber issued in the reign of Elizabeth, chiefly that of 1586,[3] which prohibited the printing of books without the licence of one of the Archbishops or of the Bishop of London, and allowed presses only in London, Oxford, and Cambridge. So long as the Calvinist Abbott continued to exercise his rights as Archbishop a copious stream of books and pamphlets on witchcraft continued to pour from the presses to spread terror and destruction over the country. In 1627, however, Abbott was virtually retired, and the following year William Laud, who had long been powerful at Court, became Bishop of London. From this time till the outbreak of the Civil War the stream was arrested. Only a few new editions of older works, a few new books in which allusions to witchcraft formed only a small portion of the total contents, and a few plays in which witches figured were allowed to pass.

The flood of terrifying witch pamphlets was stayed completely. The most exhaustive list of such pamphlets [4] shows that fifty-one are extant for the period between the accession of James I and the Restoration (1603-60). Of these fourteen were printed

---

[1] *Calendar of State Papers, Domestic, Charles I,* 1635, p. 477 (London, 1865).
[2] R. G. Usher, *The Rise and Fall of the High Commission,* p. 257 (Oxford, 1913).
[3] G. W. Prothero, *Statutes and Documents of Elizabeth and James I,* pp. 169 sqq. (Oxford, 1913). The Censorship of the Press was further strengthened by a Star Chamber Ordinance of Charles I (1637). On the censorship as a whole see W. M. Clyde, *The Struggle for the Freedom of the Press from Caxton to Cromwell* (Oxford Univ. Press, 1934).
[4] Montague Summers, *The History of Witchcraft and Demonology,* pp. 329-38 (London, 1926).

between 1603 and 1622, and thirty-seven between the outbreak of the Civil War and the Restoration (1642–60). Not one was printed in England during the last three years of James I and the whole of Charles I's reign up to the outbreak of the Great Rebellion (1622–42). During the whole of this twenty-year period the only witch pamphlet to appear—one dealing with the death of Dr. Lamb, which will be noticed later—was printed in Holland and smuggled into England. These figures are not, of course, complete, many witch-pamphlets having disappeared leaving no trace. Yet they are a remarkable tribute to the determination of Charles I's ministers to banish witch-mania from the kingdom. For witch-mania deprived of literature might well have died out for lack of nourishment.

Much of the credit for this deprivation is due to Laud, who, becoming Chancellor of Oxford University in 1629 and Archbishop of Canterbury in 1633, largely controlled the University presses as well as the printers of London. Like most of the school of thought to which he belonged, he had no belief in witchcraft—at least in the current connotation of the term. It is true that his Visitation Articles for the Diocese of St. David's [1] contain the query (No. 24), 'Whether have you . . . any which have used any enchantments, sorceries, incantations, or witchcrafts, which are not made felonies by the statutes of this realm; or any which have committed perjury,' and that his Visitation Articles of 1635 for the Diocese of London [2] have a similar query (No. 24). But these were probably only copied from the Visitation Articles of his predecessors [3] and allowed to stand for the purpose of securing information about the extent of the prevailing superstition. It should be noticed that his Articles for the Peculiars of Canterbury (1637),[4] which were, apparently, Laud's own work, contain no allusion to witchcraft. His attitude is made fairly clear by an entry in his Diary [5] for 23rd January 1624. ' Sunday

---

[1] *Works of Laud*, vol. v, pt. ii, p. 392 (Oxford, 1853).

[2] Op. cit. *Articles to be Inquired of in the Metropolitical Visitation*, vol. v, pt. II, p. 417.

[3] Though Harsnett had been Archbishop of York till 1631, the ' York Articles of Inquiry ' continued up to 1640 to contain the question, ' Whether there be any man or woman in your parish that useth witchcraft, sorcery, charmes, or unlawfull prayer, or invocations in Latine or English, or otherwise, upon any Christian body or beast, or any that resorteth to the same for counsell or helpe '.

[4] *Works of Laud*, vol. v, pt. ii, pp. 439 sqq. (Oxford, 1853).

[5] Op. cit., vol. iii, p. 157.

night the discourse which L.D. (the Duke of Buckingham) had
with me about witches and astrologers '. Buckingham's wife was
Lady Catherine Manners, one of the children said to have been
bewitched in 1617 by Margaret and Philip Flower, who were
duly hanged at Lincoln (11th March 1618/9). It is, therefore,
to be supposed that Laud exerted himself to disabuse his friend's
mind of any relics of witch-beliefs that had remained after the
celebrated trial in which his wife was so deeply concerned.
The Duke had, apparently, consulted him about using superstitious means for restoring his brother, Lord Purbeck, to
health.[1]

Laud was one of those persons who are subject to vivid and
impressive dreams. He frequently entered them in his Diary;
and this fact, together with his interest in astrology, has often
been used as a ground for charging him with superstition. Such
a charge is refuted by the Diary itself, in which the narrative of a
dream is concluded with some such remark as ' *Somniis tamen
haud multum fido* '[2] or ' I am not moved by dreams; yet I thought
fit to remember this '.[3] Moreover, there are abundant evidences
in his writings to show that Laud shared with those of his school
the sceptical scientific attitude. Thus, for example, he records
in his Diary (11th August 1634):—

> One Rob. Seal, of St Alban's, came to me to Croydon; told me
> somewhat wildly about a vision he had at Shrovetide last, about not
> preaching the word sincerely to the people. And a hand appeared
> unto him, and death; and a voice bid him go tell it the Metro-
> politan of Lambeth, and made him swear he would do so; and I
> believe the poor man was overgrown with fancy. So I troubled not
> myself further with him, or it.[4]

Like a typical modern man, Laud shows himself sceptical in his
attitude to alleged supernatural occurrences without committing
himself dogmatically to a total denial that events can happen
sometimes contrary to what is known of nature. ' Shut out all
superstition in God's name, the farther the better ', he said in his

---

[1] *Calendar of State Papers, Domestic, Charles I*, 1625-6, ed. John Bruce
(London, 1858), June 1626, p. 363. Laud's Diary, p. 13 (ed. of 1695),
says, ' *Septembr* 9. *Thursday*, My Lord of *Buckingham* consulted with me
about a Man, that offered him a strange way of Cure for himself and his
Brother '.
[2] Op. cit., vol. iii, p. 227.
[3] Op. cit., vol. iii, p. 230. 24th January 1639/40, ed. 1695, p. 57.
[4] *Laud's Works*, vol. iii, pp. 221-2 (Oxford, 1853).

sermon at the opening of Parliament (19th June 1625), 'but let in no profaneness therewhile'.[1] Witch-mania was based on the precise cast-iron dogmatism of Geneva and Trent. It could find no resting-place in the broader tolerance of Laud. 'The Church of England', he declared in his Controversy with Fisher the Jesuit, 'never declared that every one of her Articles is fundamental', and 'I will never take it upon me to express that tenet or opinion, the denial of the foundation only excepted, which may shut any Christian, even the meanest, out of heaven'.[2] It is not surprising, therefore, that during the period in which Laud was in virtual control of the Press all over the country witch-literature ceased. The effect of its cessation upon public opinion, though doubtless very important, is one of the imponderables of history. It probably did much to abate the fury of the witch-mania, and at the same time served to infuriate the majority, whose belief in witches remained unshaken.

§ 6. The examples of the Government's attempt to restrain the persecution of witches during the period under review (1618–42) are obviously fragmentary and, in not a few cases, obscure. The results of their attempt stand out much more clearly. On the Home Circuit, which contained by far the most witch-ridden part of England, not one witch was executed during the whole period of twenty-four years.[3] This fact becomes impressive when it is recognized that during the twenty years before 1618 no fewer than twenty-two witches were hanged on the Home Circuit and that the same number were hanged on the same circuit during the five years after 1642. To find another period of twenty-four years' immunity for witches on the Home Circuit it would be necessary to go back before the accession of Elizabeth or forward to the middle years of Charles II's reign. Throughout England south of the Trent, which contained more than 80 per cent of the total population, witches enjoyed a similar immunity from the accession of Charles I to the outbreak of the Civil War. The only possible exceptions are one in Somersetshire

---

[1] W. H. Hutton, *History of the English Church 1625–1714*, p. 7 (London, 1903).

[2] Ibid., pp. 42–3.

[3] Ewen, *Witch Hunting and Witch Trials*, pp. 99 and 214 sqq. (London, 1929). One Katherine Kinge of Shaulford is said to have been hanged for witchcraft in 1626. But there has evidently been some confusion, for 'the prisoners' names do not correspond with those on the gaol delivery roll'. The whole MS. may belong to another period. See Ewen, op. cit., p. 213 ft. n.

and one mentioned in a letter written in 1688; but the accounts are so late, vague, and unverifiable that they can probably be rejected.[1]

North of the Trent was a region largely outside the control of the Government in London. It was separated from the South by a broad belt of fen, mountain, forest, and quicksands, almost impassable during the winter months. It was a land of perpetual anarchy, where the King's writ did not run smoothly till nearly the end of the eighteenth century. In this region alone, in the few Puritan patches it contained, did witches suffer the supreme penalty during the period between the accession of Charles I and the Great Rebellion. The most serious case was in Lancashire in 1633—shortly after Strafford's departure to Ireland had weakened the Council of the North—when four witches were condemned and hanged at Lancaster.[2] This may have been due to the notorious indolence of Bishop Bridgeman of Chester, in whose diocese Lancashire was situated. It may have been this, too, that stimulated the Government to such prompt action the following year when a witch-killing on a much larger scale was threatened. At Pocklington in Yorkshire, too, it is said that in 1631/2 a certain ' Old wife Green ' was ' burnt in the Market for a witch '.[3] This burning, if it ever occurred, may have been the deed of some mob rather than the due execution of the sentence of any court. Sibil Marcer of Acton was found guilty of witchcraft at the Chester Sessions (18th April 1631) and

---

[1] The letter is given in the *Gentleman's Magazine*, 1832, pt. i, p. 408. It runs: ' such was John Barlowes wife, convicted and executed for witchcraft about 55 years since ' (at Salisbury). The execution in Somerset rests on another vague statement: Meric Casaubon, *Of Credulity and Incredulity* (1670), pp. 170–1. A third-hand narrative in a *Collection of Modern Relations* (1693), pp. 48–9, speaks of a witch execution in Oxford ' in the time of King Charles the First . . . but the year not remembered '. This is unconfirmed anywhere in the voluminous records of Oxford and is, on other grounds, in the highest degree unlikely. Equally vague and unlikely is the tradition of ' the Widow Drew hanged for a witch ' some time in the reign of Charles I at Sandwich (W. Boys, *Collections for an History of Sandwich*, p. 714 (Canterbury, 1792)). J. Aubrey (1626–97), *Remains of Gentilism and Judaism*, p. 61 (Folk Lore Soc. Publ., 1881), has a vague reference to an accusation and possible hanging for witchcraft in Westminster in 1641. This, again, is unconfirmed and unlikely.

[2] Ewen, *Witchcraft and Demonianism*, pp. 408–10 (London, 1933). Strafford left for Ireland in January 1633, retaining his office of Lord President of the Council of the North.

[3] *The Yorkshire Archæological Journal*, vol. xiv, p. 115. Witches were burned in England only for causing the death of their husbands or masters—i.e., for ' petty treason '. In Scotland and many continental countries they were burnt for witchcraft practised against anyone.

hanged.[1] Cheshire still retained something of the independence of a sovereign state separate from England.

There may, of course, have been witch executions under Charles I which have left no surviving record. But as far as extant records go, it seems to have become virtually impossible to compass the death of a suspected witch by legal means so long, and so far, as he was in effective control of his kingdom.

---

[1] Ewen, op. cit., p. 416. The judges of the County Palatine of Chester (Sir John Bridgeman and Sir Marmaduke Lloyd) were appointed at the beginning of the reign and less amenable to the influence of the Central Government than the ordinary judges of assize.

CHAPTER VI

INDIGNATION AROUSED BY THE PROTECTION OF WITCHES, 1618–42

§ 1. HISTORY SEEMS to show that a government which acts in advance of the public opinion of its day arouses far more indignation than one which errs by excessive conservatism. This opinion is confirmed by the storm of indignation aroused by the enlightened attitude of James I and his successor towards superstition. The choice between King and Parliament was not for most Englishmen a very difficult one. Much was to be said on both sides. Did the immunity of the hated witch finally turn the scale against the Royalist cause? In order to attempt to answer this question, public opinion on the policy of protecting the reputed agents of the Devil needs some investigation.

Until the retirement of Archbishop Abbott in 1627 opinion on the policy of protecting witches could be, and was, expressed through the Press. Books and pamphlets defending the current superstition appeared in considerable numbers. In face of the small but influential body of sceptics that were monopolizing power in the State, defenders of witch-beliefs were prepared to throw a little of their cargo overboard in order to save the rest. They abandoned a few minor items of their faith in order to concentrate greater defensive strength upon the larger ones.

(a) A typical example of the *reculer pour mieux sauter* tactician is John Cotta, a Northampton physician, who had taken his medical doctorate at Cambridge, and whose professional zeal led him to stress the importance of the medical man in detecting witchcraft. As early as 1612 he had published *A Short Discovery of Unobserved Dangers*, in which he devoted a chapter to the relation between witchcraft and sickness. He followed this up four years later with his better-known volume, *The Triall of Witchcraft and the True and Right Methode of Discovery* (London, 1616). In view of the Government's movement to discourage witch-hunting he produced his book in an amended and enlarged form under the title *The Infallible True and Assured Witch* (1625). Here he concedes to the sceptic the admission that the traditional method of trial by water is unsound, and that 'witches' marks' are no conclusive proof of guilt. Then, having made these small concessions, he argues strongly that witches are able to travel through the air. 'To perform some manner of asportation, and local translation of the bodies of Witches and sorcerers, it seemeth in reason a thing to which the Devill is not unable.'[1] He goes on to support the argument with all the authority of his long experience as a medical practitioner.

> Some sick men also have revealed and declared words gestures and actions done in farre distant places, even in the time and moment of their acting, doing and uttering, as I have known myself in some, and as is testified to have beene heard, knowne, and seene by divers witnesses worthy of credit in our country, in divers bewitched Sicke people. (See *A Treatise on the Witches* of Warbozyes.)

He gives in the introduction a hint, as broad as circumstances allowed, of the purpose of his book:

> The Author perceiving that his former Tractate or first edition thereof, either not diligently read, or not truly by many men understood, he hath now by a second edition thereof offered more ease and light unto such as are willing to search after truth, both by the addition of many things before omitted, as also by this plaine direction unto all the most special points in the whole Treatise.

(*b*) Two years later Richard Bernard (1568–1641) took a stronger line in his *Guide to Grand Jurymen with respect to Witches* (London, 1627). Bernard was a Puritan of the most nonconformist type, a protégé of Frances, Countess of Warwick, the stepmother of the Earl of Warwick who commanded the fleet for Parliament in the Civil War, and who condemned to death so many witches at Chelmsford in 1645. As vicar of Batcome in Somerset, he had taken part in a witch trial at Taunton Assizes[2] the year before his book appeared.

He adopted Cotta's tactic of ceding a few points to the sceptic, admitting that strange diseases may come from natural causes[3] and that persons have been known to counterfeit possession by evil spirits.[4] At the same time, unlike Cotta, he refuses to yield

---

[1] J. Cotta, *The Infallible True and Assured Witch*, p. 41 (London, 1625).

[2] For details see Ewen, *Witchcraft and Demonianism*, p. 452 (London, 1933). Edward Bull and Joan Grudie were indicted at Taunton Assizes (13th August 1626) for bewitching Edward Dynham. Their fate is unknown. See T. Wright, *Narratives of Sorcery and Magic*, vol. ii, p. 143 (London, 1851). The case will be considered in a later chapter.

[3] R. Bernard, *A Guide to Grand Jurymen with respect to Witches*, bk. i, ch. ii (London, 1627).

[4] Op. cit., i, iii.

an inch on the subject of ' witches' marks '.[1]   He insists that
Grand Jurymen should make an especial point of searching for
these as the first evidence of a league with the Devil.   A suspect
may be proved guilty

> by a *Witches marke*, which is upon the baser sort of witches, and this
> by sucking, or otherwise by the Devils touching, experience proveth
> the truth of this, and innumerable instances are brought for examples.
> *Tertullian* found this true, and saith, *It is the Devils custom to mark his :
> God hath his mark for his*, Exek 9. Rev. 7 and 14.   *The Beast will have
> his marke*.   Rev 13. (who is the Devils Lieutenant) So the Devil
> himself will have his marke: see the relations of witches and the
> witness of many learned men, writing of Witches and Witchcraft.
> Therefore where this mark is, there is a league and a familiar spirit.
>   Search diligently therefore for it in every place, and lest one be
> deceived by a naturall mark, note this from that.   This is *insensible*
> and being pricked will *not bleede*.   When the mark therefore is found,
> try it, but so as the Witch perceive it not, seeming as not to have
> found it, and then let one pricke in some other places, and another in
> the meane space there: its sometimes like a little *teate*, sometimes but
> a *blewish spot*, sometimes *red spots* like a fleabiting, sometimes the
> *flesh is sunke* in and hollow, as a famous witch confessed, who also
> said that Witches cover them, and some have confessed, that they
> have bin taken away; but, saith that Witch, they grow againe, and
> come to their old forme.   And therefore, though this mark be not
> found at first, yet it may at length: once searching, therefore must
> not serve: for some out of fear, some other for favour, make a
> negligent search.   It is fit therefore searchers should be sworn to
> search, and search very diligently, in such a case of life and death,
> and for the detection of so great a height of impiety.

Bernard seeks to refute the sceptic not only by the appeal to
Scripture, but by the wider appeal to all experience of all nations,
ancient and modern, Christian and heathen; to the confessions
of witches themselves and to so many recent convictions.[2]   The
question as to whether there really are witches or not seems to him,
in the light of such abundant evidence, to be completely absurd.
' It is idle to spend time further in so manifest a truth. . . .'

But sceptics often asked the question why women so much
more often than men became witches.   Bernard is ready with a
series of reasons, drawn partly from earlier writers :—

>   1. Satan is setting on these rather than on men, since his unhappy
> onset and prevailing with *Eve*.
>   2. Their more credulous nature, apt to be misled and deceived.
>   3. For they are commonly impatient, and more superstitious,
> and being displeased, more malicious, and so more apt to bitter

[1] Op. cit., pp. 218 sqq.   [2] Op. cit., pp. 89 sqq.

cursing, and farre more revengeful, according to their power, then men, and so herein more fit instruments of the Divell.

4. They are more tongue ripe, and less able to hide what they know from others, and therefore in this respect, are more ready to be teachers of Witchcraft to others, and to leave it to children, servants, or to some others, then men,

5. And lastly, because where they thinke they can command, they are more proud in their rule, and more busie in setting such on worke whom the may command, then men. And therefore the Divell laboureth most to make them Witches: because they upon every light displeasure, will set him on work, which is that which he desireth . . . for he will ask and press to be commanded: and if he be called upon, and not set on worke, it may cost the party his or her life: so displeased is hee, if he be not set on worke, which women will be ready enough to doe.

After this almost Miltonic view of the moral incapacity of women he is ready to maintain that the Devil regularly appears to witches in visible form

in the shape of a Man or Woman, or a Boy, of a browne and white Dogge, of a Foale, of a spotted Bitch, of a Hare, Moale, Cat, Kitling, Rat, dunne Chicken or Owle, of a Toade or Crab; of these have I read in the narratives of Witches, to which more may be added; for no doubt he can, if God permit, take any forme upon him, for his advantage to deceive; though some write, that he cannot take the forme of a Dove or a Lambe.[1]

He asserts the compact between the witch and the Devil as a ' certain truth '. If anyone asks ' how it may be possible, that any reasonable soul, endued with any knowledge of God, and of the nature of the Devill, should be thus enthralled ', he answers by an appeal to Calvinistic teaching about the Fall of Man :—

1. That man hath lost the image of God, in which he was created, and is wholly polluted with sinne and corruption

2. That hereby he is become of very neere kin unto the Divell, even his own babe.

3. That being his child, he will doe his father's lusts, and that, no doubt in one thing as well as in another. . . .[2]

Though Bernard had conceded to his adversaries that some diseases may be due to natural causes, he draws up a long list of symptoms which should point to witchcraft. Thus, for example, ' when learned Physicians can find no distemper in the body ' or ' when a very healthy body on a suddaine shall feel violent torture . . .' or ' when two or moe in one family, or dwelling

---

[1] Op. cit., p. 107.   [2] Op. cit., p. 136.

asunder, one or more in one town, and some in another, are taken in the like strange fits . . .', witchcraft is clearly indicated.

§ 2 (a) Bernard's volume is the last full-fledged attempt to resist the Government's offensive against superstition. For shortly after its publication the virtual retirement of Archbishop Abbott resulted in a censorship of the Press that, as has been noticed before, was by no means friendly to such propaganda. Henceforth the discontent of the frustrated witch-hunters found vent only in fresh editions of older books and in the passages newly inserted into them. One of the most interesting, as well as the most important, of these is the work of Thomas Beard (d. 1632), who is known to history chiefly as the schoolmaster to whom Oliver Cromwell, the Lord Protector, owed his education. Beard was also the lecturer of the town of Huntingdon. He published a volume made up from his sermons, under the grim title *The Theatre of God's Judgements*, as early as 1597, and brought out a new edition in 1612. In these editions of the sombre, but eminently readable, volume there are such solemn warnings against witchcraft as might be expected in a Puritan homiletical work of the period. When in 1631 it was reprinted for the second time the portions added to this third edition are far more insistent upon the dangers of witchcraft and magical practices. It is impossible to read them without feeling that public opinion was deeply moved, in Beard's circle at least, by the practical immunity of witches from punishment under Charles I. History and the writings of the great fathers of Protestantism are ransacked for the most terrifying stories they contained.[1]

> John Faustus [wrote Beard] a filthie beast, and a sinke of many divels, led about with him an evill spirit in the likenesse of a dog; being at Wittenberg, when as by the Edict of the Prince hee should have been taken, he escaped by his magicall delusions, and after at Noremberg being by an extraordinarie sweat that came upon him as he was at dinner, certified that he was beset, payed his host suddenly his shot;[2] and went away: and being scarce escaped out of the walls of the city, the Sergeants and other officers came to apprehend him. But God's vengeance following him, as he came into a village of the dukedome of Wittenberg, he sat there in his Inne very sad: the host required of him what was the cause of his sadnesse: he answered that he would not have him terrified, if he heard a great noise and shaking of the house that night: which happened according to his

---

[1] Thomas Beard, *The Theatre of God's Iudgements ; Now thirdly printed and increased with many more examples*, ch. vi, pp. 553 sqq. (London, 1631).

[2] I.e., *reckonong* (Old English *scéotan*, to pay).

presage: for in the morning hee was found dead, with his necke wrung behind him; the Divell whom he served having carried his soule into hell. . . .

Anno 1553, two witches were taken which went about by tempest, haile and frost, to destroy all the corne in the countrey; these women stole away a little infant of one of their neighbours, and cutting it in pieces, put it in a Cauldron to be boiled: but by God's providence the mother of the child came in the meanwhile, and found the members of the child thus cut in pieces and boyled. Whereupon the two Witches were taken, and being examined, answered, That if the boyling had been finished, such a tempest of raine and haile would have followed, that all the fruits of the earth in that countrey, would have been destroyed; but God prevented them by his just iudgement, causing them to be put to death.

Anno 1558, in a village neere to Ihaena in Germany, a certaine Magitian being instructed by the divell in the composition of divers herbs, restored many unto their healths. Hee had dayly commerce with that evill spirit, and used his counsell in the curing of diseases: but it happened that there fell a quarrell betwixt him and a neighbour of his a carpenter, who so exasperated him with his taunting words, that in a few days after he caused the Carpenter, by his magicall art, to fall into a grievous disease. The poore Carpenter sent for this Magitian, and entreated him to helpe him in his need. The Magitian feigning an appeased minde, but desiring to revenge the injuries done to him, gave unto him a potion confected of such venomous hearbs and roots, that being taken, the poore man presently died. Whereupon the Carpenters wife accused the Magitian of murther: the cause is brought to the Senate of Ihaena; who examining the matter, caused him by torments to confesse the murther, and many other wickednesses for which he was fastened to a stake and burnt to death.

In a further chapter [1] of new material for his edition of 1631, Beard collects further examples of the 'molestation of evill Spirits '.

Philip Melanchthon reporteth That he heard of two men credible and faith-worthy, that a certain Bottonian young woman two years after her death, returned againe to humane shape, and went up and downe in the house, sat at meat with them, but eat little. This young seeming woman, being at a time amongst other virgines, a certain Magitian came in, skilfull in diaboliticall Artes; who said to the beholders, This woman is but a dead carkasse carried about by the Divell; and presently he took from under her right arme hole, the charme; which he had no sooner done, but she fell down a filthie carkasse.

Martin Luther reporteth the like of a woman at Erford in Germanie, who being animated by the Divell, accompanied a young student that was in love with her, and went up and downe divers

---

[1] Op. cit., pp. 572 sqq.

H

years: but at last, the Divell being cast out by the prayers of the Church, she returned to a dead and filthie carkasse.

The same *Luther* in his Colloquies telleth us how Satan oftentimes stealeth away young children of women lying in Child-bed, and supposeth[1] others of his owne begetting in their stead, in the shapes of *Incubus* and *Succubus*; one such child *Luther* reporteth of his own knowledge at Halberstad; which being carried by the parents to the Temple of the Virgine *Marie* to bee cured, the Divell asked the childe (being in a basket on the river) Whether it was going ? the young infant answered, That hee was going to the Virgine *Marie*: whereupon the father threw the basket and the child into the river. The like he reporteth of another at Pessovia, which representing in all lineaments a human shape, it was nothing else than a mere elusion of the Divell: this child, saith he, delighteth in nothing but in stuffing itself with food, and egesting the same in a filthie manner, but was discovered and disrobed, and cast out by the prayers of the Church.

Beard goes on in this tone multiplying instances of the Devil's intervention in a variety of terrifying shapes in the affairs of men. At last he concludes with a world of half-suppressed indignation at the modern men who were making light of witchcraft:—

But enough, enough, of this unsavourie subject: onely let us learne hereby to beware of this ambitious enemie of mankinde, who as Saint Peter sayth, Goeth about sometime like a Lyon to devour us: other times like a subtill Serpent to molest us, but all with a desire of our destruction.

I may be thought too prolix in this Argument of Gods Iudgements; but considering the fiercenesse of Gods wrath against notorious sinners, and the hardnesse of mens hearts to be drawne to repentance, nothing I think can be judged too much. . . .[2]

(i) One of the chief interests of the book, and one which should justify such full quotation, is that Beard was among the best-known of those lecturers, who had been set up by the Puritans in so many towns—men who devoted their whole time to preaching alone and took no part in parochial duties.[3]   It was these men that Charles I's Government had striven so hard to restrict.   An indenture of 23rd March 1625/26 shows that Beard held a lecturer-

[1] Suppose, *substitute by artifice or fraud* (Oxford Eng. Dict.).
[2] Op. cit., p. 582.
[3] Thomas Ady, *A Candle in the Dark* (London, 1655), pp. 167–8. ' Some Ministers for want of due examining of the Scriptures, have taught in the Pulpits unwarily and inconsiderately, the Doctrine of Witches Power. . . .' S. R. Gardiner, *History of England 1603–1642*, vol. vii, pp. 130–1 (London, 1891). Puritan ministers often maintained their prestige amongst the masses by trading upon their fear of witchcraft and diabolical possession. For example of this see Samuel Clarke, *Lives of Two and Twenty English Divines*, pp. 41–4 91–3, 216–17 (London, 1662).

ship at Huntingdon. 'All the said parishes and town of Huntingdon', states the Indenture, 'were for a long time . . . utterly
destitute of a learned preacher to teach and instruct them in the
word of God; but . . . the said Thomas Beard . . . painfully
preached the word of God.' [1] The lecturership was in all Saints'
Church, Huntingdon, the church of the annual witch lecture;
and it is probable that when Laud was Archdeacon of Huntingdon
in 1615 he sought to abolish it. For Beard expressed the desire
in his *Preface* ' to shew my thankfulness to all those who stood by
me in the late business of this lecture, notwithstanding the opposition of some malignant spirits '. It is probably not far wrong to
assume that *The Theatre of God's Iudgements* contains the typical
repertory of a lecturer of the time. Indeed, William Perkins's
Discourse on the Damned Art of Witchcraft is stated on the title-page
to have been ' framed and delivered by M. William Perkins, in his
ordinary course of Preaching '.[2] Such volumes help to explain the
attitude of the Government towards Puritan lectures. It was not
till after Beard's death in 1633 that Laud was able to secure the
suppression of his lecturership.

(ii) Beard is of interest for another reason. He was the lifelong friend—perhaps the most intimate of all the friends—of the
Cromwell family at Huntingdon. He was one of the four witnesses of Robert Cromwell's will in 1617.[3] His interest in Robert's
son, Oliver, the Lord Protector to be, extended far beyond his
schooldays. For he helped his former pupil in the local politics
of Huntingdon in 1627,[4] and it was in his defence that Oliver first
opened his mouth in Parliament (11th February 1628/9).

Cromwell's anxious concern for his old master and his teaching
ring insistently through his variously—and probably inaccurately
—reported speech.[5] Speaking of the preferment of one who
was known to be a defender of the Divine Right of Kings and
' popery ', he continued:—

> If these be the steps to preferment what may we not expect?
> Dr Beard told me some time ago that one Dr Alablaster, in a ser-
> mon at St Paul's Cross, had preached flat popery. Dr Beard was to

---

[1] Add. MS. British Museum, 15665, p. 126.
[2] *Victoria County History of Huntingdonshire*, p. 366 (London, 1926).
[3] W. C. Abbott, *Writings and Speeches of Oliver Cromwell* (Harvard Univ.
Press, 1937), vol. i, p. 30.
[4] Abbott, op. cit., vol. i, p. 67.
[5] Abbott, op. cit., vol. i, p. 62. W. Notestein and F. H. Relf, *Commons
Debates for 1629*, pp. 59, 139, 192–3, 249 (Minneapolis, 1921).

rehearse (? refute) Alablaster's sermon at the Spittle, but Dr Neale, Bishop of Winchester, sent for him and charged him as his diocesan [1] to preach nothing contrary to Dr Alablaster's sermon. He went to Dr Fenton, Bishop of Ely [2] who charged him as a minister to oppose it, which Beard did; but he was then sent for by Dr Neale, and was exceedingly rated for what he had done.

So successful was Cromwell's advocacy that Beard was requested to appear before the House of Commons that very day.

(b) Another example of an emphatic assertion of the reality of witchcraft, that eluded the censorship through its insertion into a new edition of an older work, is to be found in the fourth [3] edition of Michael Dalton's *Countrey Justice* (1630). In the first and second editions (1618 and 1619) Dalton had contented himself with a brief and somewhat perfunctory statement of the provisions of the Jacobean Statute of 1604. '*Now to proceed with Felonies by Statute* . . .' he had written:—

1. Conjuration or Invocation of any evill spirit, for any intent &c or to be counselling or aiding thereto, is felony, without any benefit of Clergie. See Exod. 22, 18.

2. To consult, covenant with, entertaine, imploy, feede, or reward any evill Spirit is felonie in such offenders, their aydors, and counsellers.

3. To take up any dead body, or any part thereof to be imploied or used in any manner of witchcraft, is felony in such offenders, their aydors and counsellers.

4. Also to use and practise Witchcraft, Inchantment, Charme, or Sorcery, whereby any person shall be killed pined or lamed in any part of their body, or to be couselling thereto, is felony.

5. Also the second time to practise Witchcraft &c. thereby to declare where any treasure may be found:

6. Or where any goods lost, or stolen, may be found.

7. Or where any cattle or goods shall be destroied or impaired.

8. Or to the intent to provoke any person to love.

---

[1] This incident occurred some time not later than 1617. See S. R. Gardiner, *History of England 1603–42*, vol. vii, p. 55 (London, 1891). Richard Neale (1562–1640) was elected Bishop of Winchester in 1627. He succeeded Harsnett as Archbishop of York in 1631. From 1614 to 1617 he was Bishop of Lincoln, in which see Huntingdon was situated, and so was Beard's diocesan. It will be remembered that Neale helped to detect the simulated bewitchment of Anne Gunter of South Moreton (1605), and thus removed the shadow of the gallows from three village women accused of witchcraft. He was one of the earliest opponents of Continental witch-mania.

[2] Nicholas Fenton (1556–1640) was one of the last of the old Puritan bishops. He had helped to translate the Epistles for the Authorized Version.

[3] *Dictionary of National Biography, sub.* Dalton, says, 'A third edition appeared in 1630'. The title-page of the volume, however, describes it as 'Now the fourth time published and revised, corrected and inlarged, &c.'

9. Or to the intent to hurt any person in their body, though it be not effected: All these are felony, *scz* the second offence; and without benefit of Clergy.

Now against these Witches the Justices of the peace may not alwaies expect direct evidence, seeing all their workes are the workes of darknesse, and no witnesses present with them to accuse them: And therefore for their better discovery, I thought good here to insert out of the booke of the discovery of the witches that were arraigned at Lancaster, *ann. Dom.* 1612. before *Sir James Altham*, and *Sir Edward Bromeley* Judges of Assise there;

1. These Witches have ordinarily a familiar, or spirit, which appeareth to them.

2. The said familiar hath some bigg or place upon their body, where he sucketh them.

3. They have often pictures of Clay or Waxe (like a man, &c.) found in their house.

4. If the dead body bleed upon the Witches touching it.

5. The testimony of the person hurt, upon his death.

6. The examination and confession of the children, or servants of the Witch.

7. Their owne voluntarie confession, which exceeds all other evidence.

That is all Dalton had to say in his earlier editions. In the 1630 edition the space and emphasis bestowed on witchcraft are the most distinctive feature. The volume as a whole is only about 10 per cent. longer than the edition of 1619 (i.e., 410 pages against 372), yet the space devoted to witchcraft is increased by about 250 per cent. First the passage quoted above is reprinted with various additions intended to emphasize the importance of the subject. Thus, for example, in clause 1 of the earlier part he adds two more Scriptural references—Deuteronomy xviii. 11 and Leviticus xx. 27—as a stronger antidote against scepticism. In clause 4 he adds regretfully, ' By the ancient common law such offenders were to be burnt. *Fitzherbert* 269 *b*.' At the beginning of the second half of his exposition he puts in parenthesis that witches are ' the most cruell, revengeful, and bloudie of all the rest '. To clause 1 of the second half he adds that witches' familiars appear to them ' sometimes in one shape, sometimes in another; as in the shape of a Man, Woman, Boy, Dogge, Cat, Foale, Fowle, Hare, Rat, Toad &c. And to these their Spirits they give names, and they meet together to christen them (as they speke) *Bernard.* 107. 113.'

Then follows the long addition which Dalton derived partly, as he says, from Bernard's *Guide to Grand Jurymen.*

2. Their said familiar hath some big or little teat upon their body, where he sucketh them. And besides their suckings, the Devill leaveth other marks upon their body, sometimes like a blew spot, or a red spot, like a Flea-biting: sometimes the flesh suncke in and hollow (all which for a time may be coverd, yea taken away, but will come again to their old forme) And these the Devill makes to be insensible, and being pricked will not bleed, and be often on their most secretest parts, and therefore require careful and diligent search. *Ber.* 112. 219.

These first two are the maine points to discover and convict these Witches; for they prove fully that those Witches have a familiar, and make a league with the Devil. *Ber.* 60.

So likewise if the suspected be proved, to have been heard to call upon their spirit, or talke to them, or have offered them to others.

So if they have been seene with their spirit, or seene to feed something secretly; these are proofs they have a familiar, &c.

3. They often have pictures or clay or waxe (like a man &c. made of such as they would bewitch) found in their house, or which they roast, or bury in the earth, that as their picture consumes, so may the parties bewitched consume.

4. Other presumptions against Witches; as, if they be given to usuall cursing and bitter imprecations, and withall use threatenings, to bee revenged, and their imprecations, or some other mischiefe presently followeth. *Ber.* 61. 205.

5. Their implicite Confession; as when any shall accuse them for hurting them or their cattell, they shall answer, You should have let me alone then; or I have not hurt you as yet: these and the like speeches are in a manner of a Confession of their power for hurting. *Ber.* 206.

6. Their diligent enquiry after the sicke party, or comming to visit him or her, unsent for; but especially being forbidden the house.

7. Their apparition to the sicke party in his fits

8. The sicke party in his fits naming the parties suspected; & where they be or have beene, or what they doe, if truely.

9. The common report of their neighbours, especially if the party suspected be of kinne, or servant to, or familiar with a convicted Witch.

10. The testimony of other Witches, confessing their owne witch-crafts and witnessing against the suspected, that they have spirits or markes; that they have beene at their meetings; that they have told them what harme they have done &c. Ber. 212. 223.

11. If the dead body bleed upon the Witches touching it.

12. The testimony of the person hurt upon his death.

13. The examination and confession of the children (able and fit to answer) or servants of the Witch, especially concerning the first six observations, *sc* of the party suspected; her threatenings and cursings of the sicke party; her enquiry after the sicke party; her boasting or rejoicing at the sicke parties trouble. Also whether they have seen her call upon, speak to, or feed any spirit, or such like, or have heard her foretell of this mishap, or speak of her power to hurt or of her transportation to this or that place, &c.

14. Their owne voluntary confession (which exceeds all other evidence) *sc* of the hurt they have done, or of the giving of their soules to the Devill, or of the Spirites which they have, how many, how they call them, and how they came by them.

15. Besides, upon the apprehension of any suspected, to search also their houses diligently, for pictures of Clay or Waxe &c. haire cut, bones, powders, bookes of witchcrafts, Charmes, and for pots and places where their Spirits may be kept, the smell of which place will stinke detestably.

Now to show you further signes, to know whether the sicke party be bewitched.

1. When a healthfull body shall bee suddenly taken, &c, without probable reason, or naturall cause appearing, &c. *Ber* 169.

2. When two or moe, are taken in the like strange fits, in many things.

3. When the afflicted party in his fits doth tell truely many things, what the Witch, or other persons absent are doing or saying, or the like.

4. When the parties shall doe many things strangely, or speake many things to purpose, and yet out of their fits know not any thing thereof.

5. When there is a strength supernaturall, as that a strong man or two, shall not be able to keepe down a child, or weake person, upon a bedde.

6. When the party doth vomit up crooked pinnes, needles, nayles, coales, lead, straw, haire, or the like.

7. When the party shall see visibly some Apparition, and shortly after some mischief shall befal him. *Ber.* 173.

Note, for the better riddance of these Witches, there must good care bee had, as well in their examinations taken by the Iustices, as also in the drawing of their Indictments, That the same be by both of them set downe directly in their material points &c.

> That the Witch (or party suspected) hath used Invocation of some Spirit.
> That they have consulted or convenanted with their Spirit.
> That they imployed their Spirit.
> That they have killed, or lamed &c. some person &c.
> And not to indict them generally for being Witches &c.

The difference between Coniuration, Witchcraft and Inchantment &c., is this: *sc* Coniurers and Witches have personal conference with the Devill, or evill Spirit, to effect their purpose. See I Sam. 28, 7. &c. The Coniurors beleeve by certain terrible words, that they can raise the Devill, and make him to tremble. . . .

And so Dalton proceeds at some length to distinguish between witches, conjurors, enchanters, and sorcerers.

He was a sufficiently staunch Parliamentarian to be appointed during the Civil War (1648) Commissioner of Sequestrations for the County of Cambridge. His book had a large sale, and passed through many editions for more than a century. It was regarded as the standard manual for the procedure of the lower courts both in England and in the American Colonies, where it was used with deadly effect against the New England witches in 1692.[1] It is difficult to read the elaborated passage just quoted in the light of the circumstances in which it was written without perceiving that it is something more than a mere instruction in the duties of a Justice of the Peace. Under only the thinnest of disguises it is a reasoned defence of the claims of the witch-hunter and an implicit condemnation of a government that was putting every possible obstacle in the witch-hunter's path. In view of this prominent feature of the book, its widespread use may perhaps be regarded as some measure of the resentment aroused by the determination of the Government to dissipate the prevailing superstition.

(c) Cotta, Bernard, Beard and Dalton were all of them Puritans, and consequently prone to the more exaggerated forms of witch-mania. Sir Thomas Browne (1605–82) is a representative of the opposition to the Government's witch-policy from a different quarter. He was no dogmatic Calvinist. Indeed, his religious views were so enigmatical that some accused him of being a Crypto-Romanist, while the Roman Church placed his book on the Index. Internal evidence seems to show that the *Religio Medici* was written in 1634.[2] It is, therefore, highly probable that the place of writing was Shipden Hall near Halifax, not much more than twenty miles from Pendle Forest, whence seventeen witches had been condemned to death that very year—to escape the gallows only through the efforts of the King's Council. It may have been this governmental intervention that stirred Browne to his protest. As his book was not intended for publication, and was not in fact published till after the outbreak of the Civil War, he was able to express himself with a directness that could not be emulated by those who hoped to see their words in print. Browne was reputedly a Royalist, yet he lived at Norwich, in the heart of the most Roundhead part of England, placid, popular, and prosperous throughout all the troubles. The Civil Wars, the execution of the King, and the Protectorate passed him by almost

---

[1] G. L. Burr, *Narratives of the Witchcraft Cases 1648–1706*, pp. 163, 304, &c (New York, 1914).
[2] *Religio Medici*, p. 76. 'As yet I have not seen one revolution of Saturn nor hath my pulse beat thirty years' (ed. London, 1886).

unheeded. How far the neutrality of the good doctor and of many others was due to reluctance to champion a government which spared witches it is impossible to determine. One thing is certain: that Browne clung to his conservatism in the matter of witch-beliefs, as in the matter of the Ptolemaic System, till the end of his days. As late as 1664 he gave evidence at the Bury St. Edmunds witch trial, where two women were sent to the gallows at Cambridge—largely as a result of his very authoritative expression of opinion. In the *Religio Medici* he makes belief in witches a corollary of a belief in the spirit world:—

> It is a riddle to me, how this story of Oracles hath not wormed out of the World that doubtful conceit of Spirits and Witches; how so many learned heads should so far forget their Metaphysics, and destroy the ladder and scale of creatures, as to question the existence of Spirits: For my part, I have ever believed, and do now [1] know, that there are Witches: they that doubt of these, do not onely deny them, but Spirits; and are obliquely, and upon consequence a sort, not of Infidels, but Atheists. Those that to confute their incredulity desire to see apparitions, shall questionless never behold any, nor have the power to be so much as Witches; the Devil hath them already in a heresie as capital as Witchcraft; and to appear to them were but to convert them.[2]

Browne doubted indeed whether human beings could be converted into animals; yet he believes quite firmly in *incubi* and *succubi* and in the conveyance of witches through the air:

> that invisible hand that conveyed Habakkuk to the Lyon's den, or Philip to Azotus . . . hath a secret conveyance, wherewith mortality is not acquainted.[3]

The belief that devils appear in visible form he regards as perfectly well-founded.

> Those apparitions and ghosts of departed persons are not the wandring souls of men, but the unquiet walks of Devils. . . . But that those phantasms appear often, and do frequent Coemteeries, Charnel-houses and Churches, it is because those are the dormitories of the dead, where the Devil, like an insolent Champion, beholds with pride the spoils and Trophies of his Victory over Adam.[4]

§ 3. The popularity of Browne's book may be gauged from

---

[1] Possibly an allusion to the witches of Pendle Forest, who were condemned to death in 1634, the probable date when this was written.

[2] *The Works of Sir Thomas Browne*, ed. G. Keynes, vol. i, pp. 38–9 (London, 1928). Browne, however, wrote in his *Commonplace Book* at an unknown date: ' We are noways doubtful that there are witches, but have not always been satisfied in the application of their witchcrafts '.

[3] *Works*, ed. Keynes, vol. i, p. 42 (London, 1928).

[4] *Works*, vol. i, p. 47.

the fact that in 1642 two unauthorized editions were made; and that after the author himself had published it (1643) a Latin translation by John Merryweather was issued twelve months later—and all this while the Civil War was at its height. How much of its popularity was due to its outspoken condemnation of those who sought to stand between witches and the gallows? No definite answer can be returned; but the atmosphere of witch-terror in which so many of the Parliamentarians waged their war shows, when it is properly appreciated, that the question is not an idle one.

The printed word in an age of Press censorship can only be a faulty barometer of public opinion. Even more significant, therefore, than the writers quoted is the behaviour of the people in the greatest centre of population. London, as has been noticed, had long been to the fore in the execution of witches; and it soon became clear that the scepticism of the Government was not shared by the citizens of the Capital. John Aubrey (1626–97), the antiquary, remarked: ' It is a thing very common to nail horseshoes to the thresholds of doors : which is to hinder the power of witches that enter into the house. Most houses of the West end of London, have the horseshoe on the threshold.' [1] Some impression of the fury that raged beneath the surface of London opinion may be gathered from the fate of John Lambe, a notorious Worcestershire magician. His death is often explained on the ground that he was a reputed follower of the unpopular Duke of Buckingham. Yet contemporary narratives make it clear that it was his sorcery rather than his politics that caused the outburst.[2]

On Monday, 12th June 1626, London was startled by a fearful storm of wind and rain and by a mist over the river, in which many mysterious shapes were discerned by the witch-haunted citizens. While the terror was at its height Dr. Lamb appeared on the river, and everything was attributed to ' his art of conjuring '. So fierce was the feeling aroused that henceforth he dared not go out

---

[1] J. Aubrey, *Miscellanies*, p. 197 (new ed., London, 1784). ' The nailing of horse-shoes on the threshold ', says a writer in *The Gentleman's Magazine* for March 1814, ' may possibly have taken its origin from their resemblance to the Crescent of Diana, who, in her character of Hecate, was supposed to preside over enchantments.'

[2] See a rare pamphlet in the British Museum, *A Brief Description of the notorious life of John Lambe, otherwise called Dr Lambe, together with his ignominious Death*. Printed in Amsterdam, 1628. See also G. L. Kittredge, *English Witchcraft and James I*, p. 51 (New York, 1912), and Rushworth, *Historical Collections*, vol. i, p. 391 (London, 1659).

except in disguise. Two years later, during the proceedings for Buckingham's impeachment, the rumour was spread abroad that Lambe was using sorcery in defence of the Duke. Consequently, when someone recognized him in spite of his disguise as he was leaving the Fortune Theatre in Finsbury he immediately became the centre of a murderous mob. He was dragged through the streets and stoned near St. Paul's Cross, the crowd roaring the while, ' Kill the wizard, kill the poisoner '. Charles I, on hearing of the riot, rode out at once from Whitehall, but arrived too late. For the following morning Lambe died of his injuries. The Privy Council acted with vigour. It demanded the arrest and punishment of those guilty of the murder. The London authorities were, however, determined that none should suffer for doing what they regarded as an act of plain justice on a servant of the Devil. Though many constables were arrested for their negligence in failing to protect Dr. Lambe, none of the culprits was ever disturbed.[1] At last the Lord Mayor was summoned before the King in Council and threatened with the forfeiture of the City Charter should there be any more delay in bringing the murderers to justice. But threats were powerless against the firm convictions of the citizens. The Privy Council was at last compelled to content itself with the imposition of a fine of £6,000 upon the Corporation—a fine subsequently reduced in accordance with custom to 1,500 marks.

It is noteworthy that the witch-hunters' version of the death of Dr. Lambe had to be printed abroad, at Amsterdam. The censorship of the Press was now too strong to allow such appeals to superstition to proceed from the English presses. There was, however, still one hole in the system through which the indignation of Londoners might find expression. This was the theatre. For plays were commonly acted without being published; and, as they were acted from hastily produced manuscript copies, the censorship of necessity allowed considerable latitude. Thus the theatre offers itself as a useful pressure-gauge for measuring the increasing resistance of the Capital to the witch-protecting policy of the Government.

§ 4 (a) In the early days of James I's movement against the superstition, witchcraft was sometimes regarded as not too serious a subject for mirth. Thus, for example, Jonson's *The Devil is an Ass*, first acted in 1616, delights in the exposure of the pretended

[1] Overall, *Remembrancia*, p. 455.

demoniacs and witch-finders of the day.   When Fitzdottrel finds
himself in business difficulties he seeks a solution by pretending to
be bewitched:

> ·It is the easiest thing, Sir, to be done,
> As plain as fizzling: roll but with your eyes.
> And foam at the mouth. A little castle-soap will do it.

He has little difficulty in deceiving a Justice by his simple fraud.
But the funniest episode of all concerns Pug, ' a lesser devil ',
who has been allowed by Satan to try his hand at iniquity on
earth for one day.   He finds himself completely outwitted by
human knaves, outdone in wickedness, and finally sent to Newgate.   Jonson, who was strongly anti-Puritan, had shown in
The Masque of the Queenes (1609) a very thorough acquaintance
with the witch-beliefs of his age.   In *The Devil is an Ass* he satirizes
them with unbridled scorn, making pointed allusions to the
credulity of Middlesex juries and of the witch-ridden populace
of Lancashire.   The Devil twits Pug with his manifest incompet-
ence and suggests that he was only capable of dealing with such
easy dupes.

> And you'll go sour the citizens' cream 'gainst Sunday,
> That she may be accused for't, and condemn'd,
> By a Middlesex jury, to the satisfaction
> Of their offended friends, the Londoners' wives,
> Whose teeth were set on edge with't . . .
> You would make, I think,
> An agent to be sent to Lancashire. . . .

Such a play was calculated to offend the deepest convictions
of a London audience.   Small wonder that it was such a complete
failure as to cause the author to abandon writing for the stage for
nearly ten years.   Henceforth play-writers, warned by his example,
took care to assert their belief in witchcraft; and, as the determination of the Government to protect witches became increasingly apparent, the London drama became gradually a
vehicle of protest.

(*b*) The earliest signs of this protest are to be found in *The
Witch of Edmonton* by Dekker, Ford, Rowley, and others.   It was
probably first performed in 1623, after the Government's change of
policy had become apparent.   Here, it is true, the old woman,
driven by the persecution of her neighbours to sell her soul to
the Devil, arouses sympathy, as Dekker's under-dogs often do.
Nevertheless she becomes a thorough-paced witch, capable of the
lowest depths of wickedness.   The dread reality of witchcraft is

never for a moment questioned; and it is very far from being regarded as a subject for light-hearted mirth. The play's attitude was such that it could not, apparently, pass the censorship. For it was not published till the time of the Protectorate (1658).

(c) In Thomas Middleton's play, *The Witch*, written two or three years after *The Witch of Edmonton* (before 1627), the protest is more obvious. Here, in the main plot and in the subordinate intrigue, the witch Hecate and her five sister-witches are involved. The vast extent of their powers and of the injuries they inflict are impressively described. They anoint themselves with the fat of an unbaptized infant in order to be able to fly through the air. They are ever ready to help those who seek vengeance upon their neighbours. They devote their powers to the injury of man and beast. In Act I, scene ii, Hecate is shown roasting the images of a farmer and his wife who had refused to give her what she had demanded. ' Their marrows ', she boasts, ' are melting subtilly,

> And three months' sickness sucks up life in 'em.
> They denied me often flour, barm and milk,
> Goose grease and tar, when I ne'er hurt their churnings,
> Their brew-locks nor their batches, nor forespoke
> Any of their breedings. Now I'll be meet with 'em.
> Seven of their young pigs I have bewitch'd already
> Of the last litter, nine ducklings, thirteen goslings and a hog
> Fell lame last Sunday, after even-song too.
> And mark how their sheep prosper; or what soup
> Each milch-kine gives to th'pail: I'll send these snakes
> Shall milk 'em all before hand: the dew'd skirted dairy wenches,
> Shall stroke dry dugs for this, and go home cursing. . . .

Thus the dramatist lays his finger unerringly upon just those ills of frequent occurrence that were regularly ascribed to witchcraft and that kept the mass of the people in many districts of England in a constant ferment of indignation.[1]

---

[1] Compare the evidence against Margaret Moon of Thorpe, April 1645, ' She confessed witchcraft, having twelve imps, and that she had killed cows, horses, and had spoiled brewings, and batches of bread of her neighbours . . . destroyed Joan, the daughter of Henry Cornwall. . . . The jury of life and death brought in a verdict of guilty . . . and the arraigned woman was condemned and hanged.' C. L'E. Ewen, *Witchcraft and Demonianism*, pp. 275–6 (London, 1933).
The Confession of Anne Leach of Mistley (14th April 1645), ' Three years ago, Elizabeth, daughter of Robert Kirk of Manningtree, having refused to give her a coif, she dispatched a grey imp to destroy her, and after languishing a year she died '. Anne Leach was executed with seventeen Suffolk witches on 27th August 1645. Ewen, op. cit., pp. 274–5.
These are typical of hundreds of accusations that were being made at the one.

(*d*) The strongest protest from the stage was yet to come. It has been noticed that the intervention of the Privy Council on behalf of the witches condemned at Lancaster in 1634 deeply stirred the Londoners, who were completely convinced of their guilt. While the case was still under consideration Thomas Heywood [1] and Richard Broome produced their play, *The Late Lancashire Witches*. Heywood, though a Lincolnshire man by birth, was ' a Londoner every inch of him '. [2] ' His attachment to the City of London, though not, so far as we know, due to any official or hereditary tie, was very strong and enduring, and comprehended both the town and the inhabitants.' It might reasonably be expected that this play would reflect faithfully London public opinion on the Government's witch-policy, particularly as it was specially written for the occasion, and not a rehashing of older work, as has sometimes been suggested. [3] It is therefore impressive to find that *The Late Lancashire Witches* marks the climax in the indignation against the practical immunity of traffickers with demons. It tells with utmost force of conviction of ridings through the air, unholy assemblies, and other ghastly rites. It drives home its case by the poignant characterization of a sceptic who was at last convinced by completely unanswerable evidence. Generous asks Arthur why a neighbouring household is all topsy-turvy:

> *Arthur.* 'Tis thought by Witchcraft.
> *Generous.* They that think so dreame,
>   For my belief is, no such thing can be,
>   A madnesse you may call it: Dinner stays. . . .

Generous's married life has been one of exceptional happiness and affection, and yet as the play develops the evidence of his wife's wandering in the forms of various animals, changing a servant-man into a horse, and other diabolical practices, becomes so complete that at last he cheerfully hands her over to the gallows. This is the most effective part of an otherwise poorly constructed play, the supreme object of which must have been to intensify public feeling against witches and to confound sceptics by following as closely as possible the evidence given at the trial at Lancaster.

§ 5. Thomas Heywood was already famous for his knowledge

---

[1] A. M. Clarke, *Thomas Heywood*, p. 123 (Oxford, 1931).
[2] *Cambridge History of English Literature*, vol. vi, p. 83.
[3] A. M. Clarke, op. cit., pp. 125–6.

of witchcraft. That is probably the reason why he was associated with Brome in a production which was no less than the strongest possible protest against the Government's leniency. He had given evidence of his views in his Γυναικειον, published in 1624,[1] and even before the production of *The Late Lancashire Witches* he had been at work on a ponderous volume, which stated in the most ample proportions his system of demonology, *The Hierarchy of the Blessed Angels. Their Names Orders and Offices. The Fall of Lucifer with his Angels.* That such a work should pass the censorship at this time is curious. It was licensed for the Press by the author's friend and namesake, Dr. William Heywood, Laud's domestic chaplain (7th November 1634). The fact that it was dedicated to the Queen (in gratitude for her approval of the masque *Love's Mistress*) may have assisted its passage; and perhaps the well-known hostility of the author to William Prynne and his *Histriomastix* (1633) found him favour in the eyes of the authorities.[2]

However this may be, the book was the heaviest piece of artillery ever set up by those who sought to demolish the prevailing scepticism in Court circles. It treats the most extravagant claims of the witch-hunters as the soberest of facts. Its striking description of the Witches' Sabbath is a sufficient indication of the lengths to which it goes.[3]

> The manner of this homage (and others) done to the Divell, is as followeth: First the Magitian or Witch is brought before the Tribunal of Sathan, either by a familiar spirit, or else by a Mage or Hag of the same profession: he sits crowned in a Majesticke Throne, round ingirt with other Divels, who attend on him as his Lords, Barons and Princes, richly habited . . .
>
> Then steps forth a Divell of venerable aspect and saith, O most potent Lord and Master . . . this man I present before thine Imperial Throne. . . .
>
> This done, the miserable wretch is commanded to renounce his Faith and Baptism, the Eucharist, and all other holy things, and to confess *Lucifer* as his only Lord and Governor. Which is done with

---

[1] T. Heywood, Γυναικειον, *or nine books of Various History concerning Women*, lib. viii, 399, 407 (London, 1624).

[2] A. M. Clarke, *Thomas Heywood*, p. 129 (Oxford, 1931).

Prynne himself, as might be expected from one of his Puritan convictions, believed in witchcraft. In his *Histriomastix* he records that when Marlowe's *Doctor Faustus* was being performed the Devil himself ' appeared on the stage it the *Belsavage* Playhouse in Queen *Elizabeth's* days . . . the truth of which I have heard from many now alive who well remember it '.

[3] Thomas Heywood, *The Hierarchie of the Blessed Angels*, pp. 472 sqq. London. Printed by Adam Islip, 1635.)

many execrable ceremonies, not fit to be here remembered. Then is the Writing delivered, (as was before spoken of *Theophilus*) written with the bloude of the left thumbe. Then doth the Divell marke him either in the brow, neck or shoulder, but commonly in the more secret parts, with the stamp or character of the foot of a Hare, a blacke Dog, or Toad, or some such figure, by which he brands him (as the custom was of old to mark their slaves and captives whom they brought in the market for money) to become his perpetual slave and Vassal. . . .

As the Divell is alwayes adverse to his Creator, so he will be worshipped with contrarie Rites and Ceremonies. Therefore when Magitians and Witches present themselves unto him, they worship him with their faces from, and their backs towards him, and sometimes standing upon their heads, with their heels upward : but which is most beastly and abominable of all, in signe of homage hee presents unto them his taile to kisse.

In Books vii and viii of this massive work Heywood gives one of the largest of the many collections of witch-stories ancient and modern in order to emphasize the evils that came from tolerating witches. After reinforcing the argument with the usual cento of Biblical texts he concludes this part of his argument,

Thus we see by the Scriptures themselves, as by the Civill Lawes of Kingdomes, all such as shall separate themselves from God, and enter into converse and fellowship with Sathan, are cursed in the act, and ought to be exterminated from all Christian Churches and Commonwealths.

Heywood's voice was the voice of London raised in final protest against the policy of saving witches from the penalties prescribed by the Law of England and by Scripture. For he represented the Capital more completely than any other man of his time. Almost at the beginning of the century, in his *A Woman Kilde with Kindnesse*, he has marked himself out from the general run of dramatists by his exaltation of the middle-class point of view, of middle-class morality, and even, as he hints more than once, of Puritanism.[1] He therefore leaves little room for doubt that among the many causes that alienated London from Charles I, leniency towards witches was not the least. On the importance of the hostility of London Macaulay expressed himself a century ago.

In truth, it is no exaggeration to say that, but for the hostility of the City, Charles the First would never have been vanquished, and that, without the help of the City, Charles the Second could scarcely have been restored.[2]

[1] *Cambridge History of English Literature*, vol. vi, ch. iv.
[2] Macaulay, *History of England*, ch. iii.

§ 6. Since the true Puritan hated the theatre, dramatists who voiced discontent at the tolerance of witchcraft are to be regarded as representing a less Puritanical public driven into opposition by the scepticism of the royal Government. The discontent of the out-and-out Puritan is recognizable rather in the emigration to the New England States during the period before the Great Rebellion. Between 1630 and 1643 nearly 200 ships carried some 20,000 persons thither. That this great emigration was in part a protest against the toleration of witchcraft is suggested by the conduct of the emigrants after they had crossed the Atlantic. Their long-repressed fury against witches found immediate expression. Massachusetts in 1641 made witchcraft a capital offence; Connecticut followed in December 1642; and in 1655 New Haven Colony based a similar law explicitly upon Exodus xxii. 18, Leviticus xx. 27, and Deuteronomy xviii. 10–11. Among the first recorded victims were one Alse Young in Windsor, Connecticut, and Margaret (or Martha) Jones of Boston, who was hanged there in 1648. Ann Hibbins, widow of a reputable merchant of the same city, was executed 19th June 1656. One Mrs. Basset suffered the death penalty at Stratford, Connecticut, in 1651, and Mrs. Knapp at Fairfield in the same colony in 1653. Thus the witch-hunt went on gathering momentum to reach its notorious climax in the Salem Episode of 1689–93.[1] It is surely not without significance that Royalist, Anglican Virginia [2] passed through the whole period of the great witch scare with scarcely one recorded example of witch-mania, which was virtually confined to the Puritan New England States.

[1] C. W. Upham, *History of Salem Witchcraft*, 2 vols. (Boston, 1867). M. W. B. Perley, *A Short History of Salem Village Witchcraft* (Salem, Mass., 1911). G. L. Burr, ' New England's Place in Witchcraft' (*Proceedings of The American Antiquarian Society*, New Series, xxi [1911], 185–217).

[2] G. L. Burr, *Narratives of Witchcraft Cases 1648–1706*, p. 435 (New York, 1914), ' To those who know what elements made up the earliest population of Virginia it is needless to point out why we find no such abiding fear of the Devil and his minions as among the religious exiles of New England. There no Mosaic law was enacted into statute; and the well-known Cavalier sympathies of the Colony suggest why the mid-century witch-panic of England's Presbyterian counties found there no echo. Fear of witches, indeed, Virginia did not wholly escape; but her witch-terrors found their source in folk-lore more than in theology, and, though her courts could not keep altogether clear of the matter, their influence seems to have been almost wholly a restraining one.'

I

CHAPTER VII

PARLIAMENT AND WITCHCRAFT, 1625-49

§ 1. THE REACTIONS of public opinion to Government measures in the seventeenth century are never easy to assess. Nineteenth-century historians often eluded the difficulty by making the facile assumption that Parliament represented the English people. Hence they frequently spoke of the Parliamentary faction as the popular or the national party. Such an assumption is obviously unfounded. Thus, for example, many of the most important Parliamentary leaders occupied at one time or another some of the forty-four seats belonging to Cornwall,[1] yet the Civil War left no doubt that Cornwall was one of the most Royalist regions in the Kingdom—so Royalist, indeed, that its efforts in 1643 almost decided the fortunes of the war. Those whom the majority of members of Parliament really represented were the squires, the wealthier yeomen, the merchants and captains of industry mainly of the south-eastern parts of the country. That is to say, they represented those regions and those classes that were most deeply imbued with continental witch-beliefs. For the rest of England, with the exception of certain regions of Cheshire, Lancashire, and Yorkshire, was still largely uninfected with the imported superstition.

Such being the extent of Parliamentary representation, it might well be expected that members would be especially prone to witch-mania. The available evidence goes far to show that this expectation was justified in both Houses.

The proceedings for the impeachment of the Duke of Buckingham were not uninfluenced by reports that he had dabbled in the black art under the guidance of Dr. Lambe. He was said to have resorted to unholy means in an attempt to cure the mental disease of his brother, Lord Purbeck, and ' to be also indebted to them for more important help in his conflicts with parliament and his favour with the king '.[2] The terror aroused by the storm

---

[1] M. Coate, *Cornwall in the Great Civil War*, pp. 32 sqq. (Oxford, 1933). Though ' the gentry of Cornwall was fairly evenly divided between the two parties ', the mass of the people soon left no doubt about their Royalism.

[2] John Forster, *Sir John Eliot*, vol. ii, p. 315 ft. n. (London, 1864).

of 12th June 1626 was shared by members of Parliament who were busy with their proceedings against the Duke at the very moment of its outburst.

About this time ther happened, at three a clock in the afternoon [wrote Rushworth [1]] a terrible storm of Rain and Hail in and about the City of London, and with it a very great Thunder and Lightening: The graves were laid open in S *Andrews* Church-yard in Holborn, by the sudden fall of the Wall which brought away the Earth with it, whereby many Coffins, and the Corps therein were exposed to open view, and the ruder sort would ordinarily lift up the lids of the Coffins to see the posture of the dead Corps lying therein, who had been buried of the Plague but the year before.

At the same instant of time there was a terrible storm and strange spectacle upon *Thames* by the turbulency of the waters, and a Mist that arose out of the same, which appeared in a round Circle of a good bigness above the waters. The fierceness of the Storm bent it self towards York-house (the then habitation of the Duke of *Buckingham*) beating against the Stairs and Wall thereof: And at last this round Circle (thus elevated all this while above the water) dispersed itself by degrees like the smoak issuing out of a Furnace, and ascended higher and higher till it quite vanished away, to the great admiration of the beholders. This occasioned the more discourse among the Vulgar, in that Dr Lamb [2] appeared then upon *Thames*, to whose Art of Conjuring they attributed that which had happened. The Parliament was then sitting, and this spectacle was seen by many of the Members out of the windows of the House.

The raising of tempests, be it observed, was one of the commonest activities attributed to witches; and though Rushworth, who survived into a more sceptical age (d. 1690), speaks of ' the Vulgar ' being specially moved by these manifestations, there is abundant evidence to show that continental witch-beliefs were held by many of the most highly educated and highly placed persons in the realm.

That these beliefs were shared by Sir John Eliot, the most influential member of the House of Commons of his time, is shown by a speech preserved in the MSS. of Port Eliot and delivered, apparently, in 1628.[3] In condemning the favour

[1] J. Rushworth, *Historical Collections*, vol. i, p. 391 (London, 1659). The Speaker of this House of Commons of 1626 was Sir Heneage Finch (d. 1631), who, as Recorder of London, had condemned to death (1621) Elizabeth Sawyer of Edmonton. Ewen, *Witchcraft and Demonianism*, pp. 237 sqq. (London, 1933).
[2] For popular views about Buckingham's share in the sorceries of Lamb see F. W. Fairholt, *Poems and Songs relating to George Villiers, Duke of Buckingham*, pp. 30, 64, 65, 69-70, &c. (London, Percy Society, 1850).
[3] Forster, *Sir John Eliot*, vol. ii, p. 131 (London, 1864); S. R. Gardiner, *History of England 1603-42*, vol. vi, p. 234 (London, 1884).

shown by the Court to Arminians and to Roman Catholics, he went on:—

> Apply to religion what has been propounded as to moneys exacted for the loan. We possess laws providing first in general against all forms of innovation, and also careful in particular to prevent the practice of our enemies by exclusion of their instruments, by restraining of their proselytes, by restricting their ceremonies, by abolishing their sorceries.[1] Sir, while these laws continue, while they retain their power and operation, it is impossible but that we should in this point be safe. Without that change also in our policy by which law is set at nought, there could not be an innovation in religion.

Here it is important to dwell somewhat upon an important fact—viz., that Eliot's remark about sorcery in connexion with religious grievances should be read in the light of the current witch literature, which still regularly associated witchcraft with Roman Catholicism. Thus, to give a few examples out of many, James I in his *Demonologie* (Edinburgh, 1597) compares a conjurer raising the Devil to ' a *Papist* priest, dispatching a hunting *Masse* ' (p. 18). He argues (p. 54) that devils appear more readily in bodily form amongst papists than amongst those of the reformed religion.

> This we find by experience in this Ile to be true. For as we know, moe Ghostes and Spirits were seene, nor tongue can tell, in the time of blinde *Papistrie* in these Countries, where now by the contrarie, a man shall scarcely all his time here once of such things . . . in the time of *Papistrie*, our fathers erring grosslie, and through ignorance, that mist of errors overshaddowed the Devill to walke the more familiarlie amongst them: And as it were by barnelie and affraying terroures, to mock and accuse their barnelie erroures.

Bernard in *A Guide to Grandjurymen* (London, 1627), already quoted, includes among those likely to become witches (pp. 99 sqq.)

---

[1] Eliot's well-known speech of 10th May 1626, in which he compares Buckingham with Sejanus, was not unsuggestive of an accusation of witchcraft. For Sejanus was a native of Etruria—a land especially notorious for sorcerers (A. Lehmann, *Aberglaube und Zauberei*, p. 53, Stuttgart, 1898), and he was much involved in the magic practices so frequent in the reign of Tiberius (Tacitus, *Hist.*, i, 22; *Ann.*, ii, 69; vi, 29; Pliny, *Nat. Hist.*, viii, 197; Dio, *Rom. Hist.*, lviii, v, 5, &c.). That his audience appreciated his suggestion of witchcraft is shown by his subsequent disclaimer (Rushworth, *Hist. Coll.*, vol. i, p. 362), ' Nor did he apply the Veneries and Venefices of Sejanus to the Duke '. *The Oxford English Dictionary* defines *venefice* as ' the practice of employing poison or magical potions; the exercise of sorcery by such means '. It is unlikely that Eliot's reference is simply to the poisoning of Drusus. See F. Hutchinson, *Historical Essay Concerning Witchcraft* (London, 1718), pp. 15, 16 on witchcraft in Rome in the time of Tiberius.

Those that be superstitious and idolatrous, as all Papists be. That of these very many the Divell works upon to make Witches is not to be doubted: for Sorcerie is the practice of that Whore, the Romish Synagogue, Revel. 18. 23.   Secondly it is found true, that healing Witches doe use many of their Superstitious Ceremonies, Lip-prayers, Ave-Maries, Creeds and Paternosters by set numbers. Thirdly when Poperie beare sway heere, then Divels and Spirits often appeared, and at that time there were many more Witches than now. Fourthly, they allow of Coniurers and Diaboliacll Exorcismes, Witcherie trickes, inventions of Satan. . . .   Sixthly, and lastly, wee may reade in the *Admirable History of a Magician,* set out by Papists, and dedicated to the Q. Regent of France, that the Divell, called Verrine, justified most of the superstitious and idolatrous practices of that Church, as *Transubstantiation, Worshipping of the Host, Invocation of Saints and Angels,* with the rest: Is it not likely then, that there the Divel can have power over the Professors of that Religion, which he so well liketh and approveth of?   This is evident in this one thing, that so many Priests, Religious men, and religious women of their orders, have been found to be Witches, as *Bodinus* hath left to be recorded to posterities in his *Daemonomania.*

Thomas Beard wrote in a similar strain in his *Theatre of God's Judgements* (3rd ed., 1631, p. 122) :—

Moreover it is to be observed, That within these two hundred yeares hitherto, more Monkes and Priests have been found given over to these abominations and divellishnesses, than all other degrees of people whatsoever. . . .

Fifteen years later John Gaule made exactly the same accusation in his *Select Cases of Conscience touching Witches and Witchcrafts* (London, 1646).   He asserted (p. 48) :—

That there has been, are, and are likely still to be, more Witches under Popish; then in the Protestant Religion.   For not only their Popes, Priests, Fryers, Nuns, (many of them) have been notoriou Witches: but their praestigious miracles, and superstitious rites little better than kindes of Witch-craftes.

Rushworth, after describing the terrifying storm of 12th June 1626, follows up his account with the significant statement: ' The Commons agreed upon the ensuing Petition to his Majesty concerning Recusants. . . .' [1]

It would be easy to multiply quotations from the authorities

---

[1] John Rushworth, *Historical Collections,* vol. i, p. 391 (London, 1659). See also William Perkins, *A Discourse of the Damned Art of Witchcraft,* p. 150 (Cambridge, 1608).

The eighty-year-old Anne Bodenham, who was executed for witchcraft at Salisbury in 1653, is described as ' a woman much addicted to Popery and to Papistical Fancies that she commonly observed ', vide *Dr. Lamb Revived,* p. 1 (London, 1653).

on witchcraft to show the intimate connexion that was supposed
to exist between Roman Catholicism and the Black Art. Such a
connexion had been declared, it will be remembered, ever since
the beginning of Elizabeth's reign. But the important thing to
recognize in the reign of Charles I is that from the Puritan
standpoint the ditch—albeit so deep—that separated Laudian
churchmen from Roman Catholics was well-nigh invisible.
To the Puritan, Anglo-Catholicism and Roman Catholicism were
distinctions that implied little difference. 'An Arminian will
take a papist by the hand,' said Mr. Rous [1] in the Parliamentary
session of 1629, 'he a Jesuit, he the pope and King of Spain.'
A Royalist army in the Civil War was commonly called an 'army
of the Papists', however few of its personnel were actually in
communion with the See of Rome. It was therefore assumed by
Eliot and his co-religionists that the Laudian churchmen, no less
than the Papists, were in the habit of using sorcery to achieve their
purposes. Such an assumption was confirmed by the protection
notoriously given to witches by Charles I's Government. For
Jean Bodin had stated that those who deny the existence of
witchcraft are almost always witches themselves. The ecclesiastical ceremonial advocated by Laud bore, in the Puritan imagination, a close resemblance to magic practices; and the Sunday
games encouraged by the Government included such recreations
as maypole dances, which were regarded as closely connected
with witchcraft.[2]

§ 4. The Puritans' fear that witchcraft was somehow mixed
up with the religious practices of their opponents was easily
aroused owing to an astonishing ignorance of the nature and
significance of Laudian ceremonial. Such ignorance is curiously
illustrated by an item of evidence solemnly received by Parliament
in 1628/9 from Dr. Moore, who had been summoned to give
evidence of the popish practices of Neile, Bishop of Winchester.
According to the *Notes of Sir Edward Nicholas* (13th February
1628/9)

> Dr Moore att the barr testifyeth . . . that Dr Theodore Price
> some tymes principall of Hart Hall hath used oft att his house to have
> two napkins laid a crosse, which done he maketh a low obeisance to
> that crosse, and causes his man to put at one end of that a glasse of

[1] W. Notestein and F. H. Relf, *The Commons Debates for 1629*, p. 109
(Minneapolis, 1921).
[2] M. A. Murray, *The Witch-Cult in Western Europe*, pp. 130 sqq. (Oxford,
1921).

sack, att another end a glasse of clarrit, at another a cupp of beere, att another a cupp of ale, and in the midst a cupp of March beere. Dr Moore is to deliver in writing the effect of his examination and what he knoweth of the same.[1]

That this amazing entry is not due to any mental aberration on Nicholas's part is shown by Sir Richard Grosvenor's notes of the same evidence:—

Dr Theodor Price: made several crosses: at the foote of one a Cup of Sacke, Ale, other march beare, Ale, Beare and Clearitt. Dr More to deliver his testimony in writing.[2]

There were, unquestionably, many reasons, religious, political, and social, for the antagonism of the Puritan towards the so-called Arminians. Those whose religion centred in the pulpit could have little understanding of those who found in the altar the well-spring of their spiritual life. Enthusiasts for the Protestant cause in Germany could have little love for those to whose ineptitude they attributed its decline. The rising capitalist class—now, as usually, permeated with Puritanism—could hardly fail to oppose a government that devoted itself to the enforcement of the Poor Laws, the prevention of profiteering in food, and the maintenance of the level of wages.[3] Nonetheless the part played by witch-beliefs in aggravating the antagonism of Parliament can hardly have been negligible.

The parliamentary session of the early months of 1629, which ended in a tumultuous assault on the Speaker, began in a re-markably friendly atmosphere, which vanished immediately when the Arminians came to be considered. Charles I had accepted the Petition of Right in a manner that had given wide-spread and unmistakable satisfaction. He had acted with a tact that was far from habitual to him in meeting many minor grievances. Every augury was good. Then the question of the pardons granted to Montague, Cosin, Manwaring, and Sibthorpe and the preferments granted to Anglo-Catholics transformed the whole attitude of Parliament and caused grievances of a minor character to assume gigantic proportions.[4]

---

[1] W. Notestein and F. H. Relf, *Commons Debates for 1629 Critically Edited*, p. 144 (Minneapolis, 1921).

[2] Op. cit., p. 204.

[3] S. R. Gardiner, *History of England 1603-42*, vol. vii, pp. 160 sqq., 228 sqq. (London, 1891).

[4] S. R. Gardiner, *History of England 1603-42*, vol. vii, pp. 30 sqq. (London, 1891). Notestein and Relf, *The Commons Debates of 1629*, pp. 108 sqq. (Minneapolis, 1921).

The first of the three resolutions recited by Holles while the Speaker was held in the Chair shows the dominant part played by religion in the whole quarrel.

Whosoever shall bring in innovation in religion, or by favour seek to extend or introduce Popery or Arminianism, or other opinions disagreeing from the true and orthodox Church, shall be reputed a capital enemy to this kingdom and commonwealth.

That innovation in religion included attempts to interfere with the working of the Jacobean Act of Parliament against witchcraft is suggested by the words of Eliot already quoted about ' abolishing their sorceries '.

§ 5 (a) This suggestion is confirmed by the fact that so many members of the Long Parliament who played a leading part in the Civil War are known to have been deeply concerned about the alleged prevalence of witchcraft. Of these perhaps the most remarkable were the Fairfaxes, Ferdinando, Lord Fairfax (1584–1648), who represented Yorkshire, and his son Thomas, who rose to be commander-in-chief of the Parliamentary armies in 1645. Thomas was strongly influenced in his boyhood by his bastard great-uncle, Edward Fairfax, who had tried so hard to secure the execution of six women in 1621, and whose work *A Discourse of Witchcraft, As it was enacted in the Family of Mr Edward Fairfax of Fuystone in the County of York in the year 1621* has already been noticed.[1]

In view of his upbringing, it is not surprising to find that Thomas was afterwards imposed upon by the famous astrologer, William Lilly.[2] Long afterwards, in 1664, he was concerned with a wizard, who was put on trial[3] for declaring by witchcraft that some money stolen from him had been hidden in a sack and that the sack, ' by reason of the waters ', could not be discovered for five months. The whole family seem to have been deeply concerned about witchcraft over a long period. Thus, for example, the Worcestershire wizard, John Lambe, already mentioned, is said in a pamphlet[4] to have told Lady Fairfax about 1610 that within a few days her heart would ache by occasion of an accident

---

[1] M. A. Gibb, *The Lord General. A Life of Thomas Fairfax* (London, 1938), p. 5, ' Living at Fewstone, not many miles from Denton, he (i.e. Edward Fairfax) exercised from the beginning a strong influence upon the boy's character '. Edward is best known as the translator of Tasso.

[2] *Mr. William Lilly's History of his Life and Times from the Year 1602–81*, pp. 56–7 (London, 1715). Lilly was the Sidrophel of Butler's *Hudibras*.

[3] *Surtees Society*, vol. 40, p. 101.

[4] *A Brief Description of the Notorious Life of John Lambe* (Amsterdam, 1628).

by water, and that three days later her brothers were drowned. Again during the Civil War (31st December 1646), four women of Heptenstall, in the West Riding of Yorkshire, are recorded to have been examined by Charles Fairfax and another Justice of the Peace.[1] This Charles (1597–1673) was an uncle of Thomas, the commander-in-chief. Richard Ashe, who sent at least six and probably eight women to the gallows for witchcraft at the Kent Summer Sessions of 1652, was a grandson of Sir Thomas Fairfax of Denton, and two of his aunts married into the Fairfax family.[2] In view of these few facts that have survived fortuitously when so many have left no record, it is difficult to avoid the conclusion that the Fairfaxes lived in constant terror of witchcraft, and that their opposition to the King was in no small measure due to his protection of those accused of making covenants with the Devil. For they were strongly Royalist by tradition, and had suffered little in person or property from the Crown.

(b) The Parliamentary general at the outset of the Civil War, Robert Devereux, third Earl of Essex (1591–1646), had long shown himself hostile to the King. He supported the Petition of Right in 1628, and voted for the death of Strafford in 1641, contrary to Charles I's expectations. Like Fairfax, he had more than once come into contact with witchcraft and magical practices. Thus, for example, in June 1612 a certain Mrs. Mary Woods was put on trial at Norwich on various charges, which included cozening and palmistry. In the course of the proceedings she alleged that she had received a diamond ring and money from Frances, Countess of Essex, with a promise of £1,000 if she would procure poison for the purpose of killing the Earl. Here it should be remembered that poisoning and witchcraft were closely associated, as the Latin word for witch, *venefica*, implies. This association is confirmed by Mrs. Woods's further admission that she had supplied the Countess of Essex with a certain powder to wear round her neck as a charm to enable her to bear a child.[3] The following year (1613) occurred a more sensational case, when the Countess brought her action for nullity of marriage against Essex. The court pronounced in her favour on the ground that the Earl was incapacitated by witchcraft from consummating the marriage.[4] During the Civil War he was, apparently, concerned

---

[1] *Surtees Society*, vol. 40, pp. 6–9.
[2] Foss, *Judges of England*, vol. iv, p. 417 (London, 1857).
[3] *Calendar of State Papers, Domestic Series 1611–18*, p. 187 (London, 1858).
[4] Howell, *State Trials*, vol. i, pp. 307–12 (London, 1730).

in the very curious incident of the shooting of the Witch of Newbury (1643), which will be noticed later.

(c) A first cousin of the bewitched Earl of Essex was another of the great Parliamentary leaders, Robert Rich, Earl of Warwick (1587–1658). He had become estranged from the Court early in Charles I's reign. He refused to subscribe to the forced loan of 1626 or to pay ship-money, and was an energetic supporter of Puritan clergy.[1] In July 1642 he brought over the fleet to the Parliamentary side, and was soon afterwards appointed Lord High Admiral. During the Commonwealth he was one of the closest personal friends of Oliver Cromwell, one of whose daughters, Frances Cromwell, was married to his grandson, Robert Rich. All his life Warwick had been in touch with fervent believers in the horrors of witchcraft. His step-mother, Frances, showed the utmost favour to Richard Bernard, whose *Guide to Grandjurymen with respect to Witches* has already been quoted. It was she who paid most of the expenses of Bernard's education at Cambridge and did much to assist his later career. Warwick had himself been educated at Cambridge at a time (1603) when the witch-mania of that University was approaching its climax. Later he sat in the House of Commons for Maldon in witch-fearing Essex, where most of his property lay (1610–14). (It was at Maldon that a certain Ellen Smythe was executed in 1597 for bewitching three persons to death.) In view of such antecedents it is hardly surprising to find Warwick presiding at one of the most terrible witch-trials of the Civil War—at Chelmsford in the summer of 1645. The recently discovered Jail Delivery roll[2] shows that thirty-two women were indicted on this occasion for witchcraft (all but one being arraigned). Of these no fewer than nineteen were found guilty and duly hanged. Most of the others appear to have died in jail, either before or after being brought to trial. Only three were acquitted by Warwick's court. These executions created such a sensation that a thirty-six-page pamphlet was shortly afterwards 'published by authority' in London:—

> A true and exact Relation of the severall Informations, Examinations, and Confessions of the late Witches, arraigned and executed in the County of *Essex*. Who were arraigned and condemned at the

[1] He had suffered heavily in the resumption of royal forest lands in 1634. S. R. Gardiner, *History of England, 1603–42*, vol. vii, p. 365 (London, 1891).
[2] Ewen, *Witch Hunting and Witch Trials*, p. 231 (London, 1929), contains the full transcript made by the discoverer.

late Sessions, holden at Chelmesford before the Right Honourable Robert, Earle of *Warwicke*, and severall of his Majestie's Justices of the Peace, the 29th of July 1645.

Wherein the severall murthers, and devillish Witchcrafts, committed on the bodies of men, women, and children, and divers cattell, are fully discovered.

Were one to select the staunchest Parliamentarians who sat in the Lower House at the outbreak of the Civil War it would not be difficult to make a fairly long list of those who—in addition to Ferdinando Fairfax—by some chance or other, are known to have been deeply concerned about witchcraft. Here a very few examples must suffice.

(*d*) One of the most outspoken critics of Charles I's Government in general, and of Archbishop Laud in particular, was Sir Harbottle Grimston (1603-85), the member for Colchester. He described the Archbishop as

the Sty of all Pestilential filth, that hath infected the State and Government of this Commonwealth . . . the only Man that hath raised and advanced all those, that together with himself, have been the Authors and Causers of all our Ruines, Miseries, and Calamities we now groan under.[1] It is not safe that such a Viper should be near His Majesty's Person to distil his Poyson into his Sacred Ears. . . .

Grimstone's credulity in the matter of witchcraft was virtually boundless. In 1638 he committed three women to Colchester Castle on a charge of witchcraft.[2] During the latter part of March 1645 he sat with another Justice of the Peace, Sir Thomas Bowes, to receive depositions from witnesses against the unhappy women who were tried at Colchester by the Earl of Warwick three months later. The evidence he collected is given in the pamphlet, already mentioned, *A true and exact Relation of the severall Informations, Examinations, and Confessions of the late Witches, arraigned and executed in the County of Essex, &c.* The evidence that Sir Harbottle accepted might have been expected to tax even the credulity of a seventeenth-century Puritan. It is so amazing that one deposition—that of the infamous witch-finder Matthew Hopkins (pp. 2-3)—is worth quoting at some length as a fair sample of the contents of the whole pamphlet.

The Information of *Matthew Hopkins*, of *Mannintree*, Gent *taken upon oath before us* the 25th *day* of March 1645.

This Informant saith, That the Said *Elizabeth Clarke* (suspected

---

[1] Rushworth, *Historical Collections*, pt. iii, vol. ii, p. 122 (London, 1692).
[2] Ewen, *Witch Hunting and Witch Trials*, p. 218 (London, 1929).

for a Witch as aforesaid) being by the appointment of the said Justices watched certain nights, for the better discovery of her wicked Practises, this Informant came into the roome where the said Elizabeth was watched as aforesaid, the last night, being the 24th of this instant *March*, but intended not to have stayed long there. But the said Elizabeth forthwith told this Informant and one *Master* Sterne, there present, if they would stay and do the said *Elizabeth* no hurt, shee would call one of her white Impes, and play with it in her lap; but this Informant told her they would not allow of it; And that staying there a while longer, the said *Elizabeth* confessed she had carnall copulation with the Devill six or seven years; and he would appeare to her three or foure times a week at her bedside, and goe to bed with her, and lye with her halfe a night together in the shape of a proper Gentleman, with a laced band, having the whole proportion of a man, and would say to her, *Besse I must lye with you*, and she did never deny him: And within a quarter of an houre after there appeared an Impe like a Dog, which was white, with some sandy spots, and seemed to be very fat and plumpe, with very short legges, who fortwith vanished away: And the said *Elizabeth* said the name of the Impe was *Jarmara*: And immediately there appeared another Impe, which shee called *Vinegar Tom*, the shape of a Greyhound with long legges: And the said *Elizabeth* then said that the next Impe should be a black Impe, and should come for the said Master *Sterne*, which appeared, but presently vanished: And the last that apeared was in the shape of a Polecat, but the head somewhat bigger. And the said *Elizabeth* then told this Informant that she had five Impes of her owne, and two of the Impes of old Beldam *Weste* (meaning one *Anne Weste*, Widow) who is now also suspected of Witchcraft: And said sometimes the Impes of the old Beldam sucked on the said *Elizabeth*, and sometimes her Impes sucked on the old Beldam *Weste*. And the said *Elizabeth* further told this informant, that Satan would never let her rest or be quite, until shee did consent to the killing of the Hogges of one Mr *Edwards* of *Manningtree* aforesaid, and the Horse of one *Robert Tayler* of the same Towne: And this Informant further saith . . . That coming into his own Yard that night, he espied a black thing proportioned like a Cat, oneley it was thrice as big, sitting on a strawberry-bed, and fixing the eyes on this Informant; and when he went towards it, it leapt over the pale towards this Informant, as he thought, but ran quite through the Yard, with his Greyhound after it to a great Gate, which was underset with a paire of Tumbrell Strings, and did throw the said Gate wide open, and then vanished; And the said Greyhound returned againe to this Informant, shaking and trembling exceedingly.

So the pamphlet goes on with thirty-six pages of information in this strain; and Sir Harbottle betrays no knowledge of the terrible tortures of mind and body—hunger, thirst, and sleeplessness extended over many days—that elicited these fearful confessions.

(*e*) Even stronger in his opposition to Charles I than Grimston was John Wilde (1590–1669), who sat as Knight of the Shire for Worcester in the Long Parliament. He had distinguished himself by the violence of his attack on Buckingham in the Parliament of 1626, where he argued from Bracton that common fame would be a sufficient ground for accusations against the hated Minister. In 1640 he was Chairman of the Committee appointed to prepare the impeachment of thirteen bishops. Later he was one of the managers of the impeachment of Archbishop Laud. ' His speeches against the Primate were more conspicuous for political and religious rancour than for argument and good taste.' [1] (12th March 1643/4.) He accused Laud of surreptitiously introducing Roman Catholicism into England:—

> He conveys this poyson in a guilded pill, with Baits and pretences of Reconciliation; a pleasing Snare, *Laqueus Diaboli ad miserorum animas ad infernum detruendas* . . . This Man's Leprosy hath so infected all, as there remains no other Cure, but the Sword of Justice. . . . [2]

In 1646 he was appointed Chief Baron of the Exchequer, in which office he is said to have amassed a considerable fortune by accepting bribes for making unjust judgements.[3] He was nominated by Parliament a member of the High Court of Justice for the trial of the King, though he was too astute to take any part in the proceedings.

At the Lent Assizes at Salisbury in 1653 he sentenced to death an eighty-year-old woman named Anne Bodenham. The fantastic charges which caused Wilde to send her to the gallows are sufficiently indicated on the title-page of a pamphlet published in London the same year:—

> Dr Lamb's Darling: or, strange and terrible news from Salisbury, being A true exact, and perfect Relation, of the great and wonderful *Contract* and *Engagement* made between the Devil and Mistris Anne Bodenham; with the manner how she could transform herself into the shape of a *Mastive Dog a black Lyon, a white Bear, a Woolf, a Bull and a Cat ;* and by her Charmes and Spels, send either man or woman 40 miles an hour in the Ayr. . . .

At the same time another pamphlet describing the witchcrafts of the old woman in a somewhat fuller form was published, also in London, with, as the dedication states, the approval of Lord Chief Baron Wilde.

---

[1] *Dictionary of National Biography, sub nomine.*
[2] Rushworth, *Historical Collections*, pt. iii, vol. ii, pp. 829–30 (London, 1692).
[3] Wood, *Fasti*, vol. i, p. 336.

(*f*) The County of Chester was represented in the Long Parliament by Sir William Brereton (1604–61), who was, in Clarendon's opinion,[1] ' most considerable for a known averseness to the government of the Church '.

He was appointed Commander-in-Chief of the Parliamentary forces in Cheshire and the neighbouring counties to the South. In this capacity he won several notable victories, defeating Sir Thomas Aston near Nantwich (28th January 1642/3) and Lord Ashley at Stow-in-the-Wold (22nd May 1646) in the last battle of the First Civil War. Brereton's views on witchcraft are preserved by the merest chance in a passage from his diaries,[2] where he records a conversation he had with Elizabeth, titular Queen of Bohemia, the daughter of James I, on 3rd June 1634.

> " Here Mr Stones, one of her Majesty's principal gentlemen, invited me solemnly to stay and sup with him, and afterwards came to fetch me to see the queen at supper, where after the queen had put me upon a discourse of the discovery of our Lancashire witches, she answered it with a relation of a discovery of witches in Westphalia, where a whole village, all witches; and amongst them was the Bishop of Wurzburg's Chancellor and his page, all whom deservedly burnt.

The date of the passage makes it fairly clear that the ' Lancashire witches ' in question were those rescued by the Government in 1634 and not those of 1612. The tone suggests that Brereton had little doubt of their guilt. He spent the rest of the evening exchanging with the Queen of Bohemia fearful narratives of supernatural visitations.

Marlow was represented in the Long Parliament by Bulstrode Whitelock (1605–75), one of the most pertinacious of Charles I's opponents. He acted as chairman of the committee which managed the prosecution of Strafford, and was a member of the committee of 1648 for drawing up a charge against the King and considering the method of conducting his trial. He held many important offices under the Protectorate, and was an intimate friend of Oliver Cromwell, whom he urged to accept the Crown. His unquestioning belief in the most extravagant accusations against witches is one of the most remarkable features of his *Memorials*. Thus, for example, he refers to the terrible witch-slaughter at Newcastle in 1649 in the most casual way:

---

[1] Clarendon, *History*, vol. i, p. 270, ed. Macray.
[2] Sir William Brereton, *Travels in Holland, &c., 1634–35*, pp. 33–4 (Chetham Society, vol. i, 1844).

From Newcastle of the unanimous subscription of the engagement by that garrison. That many witches were apprehended thereabout of late; that the witch-trier taking a pin, and thrusting it into the skin in many parts of their bodies, they were insensible of it; which is one circumstance of proof against them.[1]

In the same casual tone he records a case at Boston the following year (1650):—

Letters, of one man and two women about Boston committed for witches; that the man confessed he had a familiar sucked him at some paps he then showed; that he had signed a writing to deny God and Jesus Christ, and the familiar drew blood from those paps, and appeared to him in the shape of a white chicken.[2]

Sir Henry Mildmay (d. 1664?) sat in the Long Parliament and all the other Parliaments of Charles I's reign for the borough of Maldon, which had been represented earlier by Robert Rich, afterwards Earl of Warwick. Mildmay was Master of the King's Jewel House, and had received many favours from James I and his successor; but during the summer of 1641, after voting against Strafford's attainder (21st April 1641), he changed sides and became a staunch Parliamentarian, being appointed a member of a committee of the Commons as early as 9th September 1641. Later he was appointed one of the King's Judges and attended the trial on 23rd January 1648/9, though he did not go so far as to sign the death-warrant. His grandfather, Sir Walter Mildmay, had made a large fortune under Henry VIII as Commissioner for the Surrender of the Monasteries, and had many years later founded Emmanuel College, the citadel of Puritanism in Cambridge. Sir Henry sat on the Bench with Warwick at the Chelmsford Assizes of 1645, where the nineteen witches were sent to the gallows.[3] Whether this Essex man's sudden desertion of the Royalist cause was in any part due to his witch beliefs it is impossible, for lack of data, to decide.

Sir John Barrington sat for New Town, Hampshire, and Sir Martin Lumley for Essex in the Long Parliament. They were both of them ranged on the Roundhead side in the Civil War.[4] Both of them sat with the Earl of Warwick at the terrible Chelmsford Assizes of 1645. Their convictions on the subject of witchcraft, therefore, can scarcely be doubted.

[1] Whitelock, *Memorials*, vol. iii, p. 128 (Oxford, 1853).
[2] For other examples of Whitelock's credulity see op. cit., vol. iii, pp. 456, 465; vol. iv, p. 51, &c.
[3] Ewen, *Witch Hunting and Witch Trials*, p. 231 (London, 1929).
[4] *Victoria County History of Essex*, vol. ii, pp. 230–1 (London, 1907). For Lumley, see T. Wright, *History of Essex*, vol. ii, p. 63 (London, 1836).

(g) Sir John Danvers (1588?–1655), after sitting in four Parliaments of Charles I, was returned to the Long Parliament for Malmesbury (10th October 1645) in place of 'Anthony Hungerford esq. disabled to sit'. He was one of the most enthusiastic members of the commission to try the King, being absent only twice from its meetings. He signed the death-warrant and became a member of the Council of State (1649–53). At the trial of Joan Peterson, 'the Witch of Wapping' (1652), he used bribery and corruption in order to secure conviction.[1] It is true that Danvers was completely unscrupulous in his methods of enriching himself and that he may have stood to gain indirectly by Joan Peterson's death. Yet his actions clearly imply that he took belief in witchcraft as a matter of course.

One of the sternest opponents of Charles I was Sir Gilbert Pickering (1613–68) of Titchmarsh, on the borders of Northants and Huntingdonshire, two and a half miles from Thrapston. He represented Northamptonshire in the Long Parliament, showed great activity on the Parliamentary side in the Great Rebellion, and acted—though he did not sign the death-warrant—as one of Charles I's judges. He is described by Walker (*Sufferings of the Clergy*, p. 91) as 'first a presbyterian, then an independent, then a Brownist . . . a most furious, fiery implacable man; was the principal agent in casting out most of the learned clergy'. He sat in the various 'parliaments' of the Protectorate, received a summons to Cromwell's 'House of Lords', and was nominated Chamberlain to Cromwell himself; in which capacity he employed his cousin, John Dryden, the poet, as his secretary. At the Restoration he was one of those excepted by the Commons from the Act of Indemnity, and escaped punishment only through the influence of his brother-in-law, Edward Montague, Earl of Sandwich. Sir Gilbert's family had been deep in witchcraft for three generations. His grandfather of the same name, his father, John Pickering, and his uncle, Henry Pickering, had played no inconsiderable part in the Warboys affair. It was the latter, it will be remembered, who warned old Mrs. Samuel that if she did not confess 'he hoped one day to see her burned at the stake, and he himself would bring fire and wood and the children should blow the coals'. All three gave evidence before the Grand Jury and the 'jury of life and death', and did their utmost to secure the conviction of the three Samuels. Few could have been more

---

[1] Ewen, *Witchcraft and Demonianism*, p. 230 (London, 1933).

concerned in doing so, since Mrs. Throckmorton, the mother of the supposedly bewitched girls, was a sister of the younger Pickerings. The elder Sir Gilbert in the last year of his life (1612) arrested and sent to Northampton jail one Arthur Bill of Raunds, who had been ' floated ' together with his father and mother and had failed to sink, and who was said to have bewitched a woman to death and to have employed three spirits named Grissil, Ball, and Jacke.[1] This happened the year before the birth of the Sir Gilbert now under consideration. In view of his family tradition, it is not surprising to find that in 1646 Titchmarsh was the centre of a district in which many witches were arrested.[2] Thus, for example, Anne Desborough confessed that at Titchmarsh she had received two imps resembling mice, named Tib and Jone—the one to injure men, the other cattle; and that she had abjured God and agreed that at her death the imps—who had visited her every day for thirty years—should have her soul. Few records of the Midland Circuit, to which Northamptonshire belonged, survive. Even so, John Stearne's pamphlet *The Confirmation and Discovery of Witchcraft* shows how the whole immediate neighbourhood of Titchmarsh abounded in men and women who were delated for witchcraft.

The traditional hero of the Great Rebellion, John Hampden (1594–1643), represented Buckinghamshire in the Long Parliament. The early death of his father (1597) left him to an exceptional degree under the influence of his mother, Elizabeth, the second daughter of Sir Henry Cromwell of Hinchinbrook. She survived till 1665, when she had reached the age of ninety.[3] She was seventeen years of age at the time when her step-mother, Lady Cromwell, died by the alleged witchcraft of the Samuels (1592), and was turned eighteen before the Warboys trial (1593) spread the increasing witch-mania far and wide over England. There is no reason for supposing that she herself did not come into personal contact with some at least of these horrors. Her son could hardly fail to have grown to manhood overshadowed by such terrible experiences. As little record of his early life survives, it is impossible to assess the amount of his hostility to the Royal Government that was provoked by its restraint of witch-hunting.

[1] Ewen, *Witchcraft and Demonianism*, pp. 207–8.
[2] Op. cit., pp. 306 sqq.
[3] M. Noble, *Memoirs of the Protectorate-House of Cromwell*, vol. ii, p. 69 (London, 1787).

K

It has been stated that of his sons ' one was a cripple, the other something like a lunatic '.[1] Such afflictions were usually attributed to witchcraft, and might well have intensified his fury against the King.

Not a few circumstances point to Hampden's adherence to the witch-beliefs of his mother. Sir Edward Coke (1552–1634), perhaps the most eminent witch-hunter of his age,[2] has been described as the ' idol of his student days in the Temple '.[3] Again, Davila's *History of the Civil Wars of France*, which was so constantly in his hands that his friends called it ' Mr. Hampden's Vade-Mecum ', is not without its large supply of curious and terrifying narratives suggestive of witchcraft.[4] Yet again, the witch-hunting Earl of Warwick held Hampden in high regard, making him together with eleven others an extensive grant of of land in New England.

But perhaps the clearest sign of Hampden's attitude towards witch-belief is to be found in his appointment to the living of Great Hampden. The rector appointed during Hampden's minority (1609) was the scholarly high-churchman, Egeon Askew.[5] During his incumbency Hampden was in the habit of deserting his parish church for the purpose of hearing Puritan divines in the neighbouring parishes.[6] On the death of Askew (1637) he chose as his successor the Puritan William Spurstowe,

[1] Op. cit., vol. ii, p. 76.
Had John Hampden been born half a century later, when witch-belief was losing its hold on educated people, these arguments would have been inadmissible. It is important to remember that throughout his lifetime witch-belief was on the upgrade. Puritans were far more disturbed about witchcraft in 1643 than they had been in 1594.

[2] As Attorney-General Coke had played a leading part in framing the Jacobean Witchcraft Statute of 1604. Several of the most important books in defence of witchcraft were dedicated to him. His *Institutes of the Laws of England*, pt. iii, ch. vi, insist at considerable length upon the heinousness of witchcraft.

[3] H. R. Williamson, *John Hampden*, p. 177 (London, 1933).

[4] Danvila, *Historie of the Civil Warres of France*, William Aylesbury's tr. (London, 1647–8), vol. i, pp. 363–4, vol. ii, pp. 891, 988, &c.

[5] Wood describes him as ' a person as well read in the fathers, commentators, and schoolmen, as any man of his age in the university ' (*Athenæ Oxonienses*, ed. Bliss, vol. i, p. 756). His ecclesiastical colour may be deduced from his *Brotherly Reconcilement* (London, 1605), *passim*, e.g., p. 244, ' If our great gnat-strainers weighed this well . . . they would not for the crosse in Baptisme leave the fountain of living water, and become such enemies to the cross of Christ Jesus. The use whereof, if it be Antichristian and Papal (as they pretend) then was the great Emperour *Constantine* a Papist, then were all the Ancients Papistes, who used it so often. . . .'

[6] H. R. Williamson, *John Hampden* (London, 1933), p. 183.

whose views on the interference of demoniac agencies in human affairs are readily discoverable from his Σατανα Νοηματα ; *or the Wiles of Satan* (London, 1666) :—

> Surely we need no Hermit's Visions [he wrote (p. 31)] to inform us that the air is full of malignant Spirits, and the earth of their snares to entrap the inhabitants of it. *St Paul* points out to us their number as well as their power when he saith, that *we wrastle not with flesh and blood* . . .

The Fall of Satan, he insists (p. 15), was far from leaving him powerless :—

> He hath still the nature though not the perfection of an Angel, and though he be inferiour to them, whose equal originally he was in all kind of endowments, yet still he retains so great a superiority over the Elementary, Sensitive and Intellectual part of the world, as that he is not only dreaded for his power which he puts forth in wonderful effects; but is also adored for his wisdom and knowledge as a God, by many nations in it.

He compares (p. 75) corrupt opinions to changelings and cites the woman of Endor [1] as an example of those who ' use of witchery '.

It was to Hampden that Spurstowe [2] owed his introduction into public life. Had his benefactor entertained any doubts about the seriousness of witchcraft he would scarcely have singled out such a divine for the instruction Sunday by Sunday of himself, his servants, and parishioners. Still less would he have chosen him (1641) as chaplain to the regiment of ' Greencoats ' which he raised to fight against the King.

One of the most energetic opponents of the Royalist Government was Francis Rous (1579–1659), who represented Truro in the Long Parliament. In 1626 he had issued a fierce reply to Richard Montagu's *Appello Caesarem* entitled *Testis Veritatis.* During the Commonwealth he again represented Truro in the ' Parliament ' of 1654. His anxiety for the extirpation of witches is shown by the fact that it was under his patronage that Dr. Nathaniel Homes published his book, *Daemonologie or the Character of the Crying Evils of the Present Times . . . in which . . . are handled the Doctrine of Devils* (London, 1650), which lays particular

---

[1] I. Sam. xxviii, 7 sqq.
[2] For the careers of Spurstowe and Askew see A. E. Ebblewhite, *The Parish Registers of Great Hampden*, pp. 76, 110, 174, &c. (London, 1888).

stress on the reality of the covenant between witches and the Devil.[1]

> The Covenant that these men may be in with the Devil is two-fold, according to the manner of it. First, *Expresse*, to this effect (as hath been confessed by many that have so Covenanted) the Witch or Sorcerer on his part binds himself by a solemne vow . . . And to *seale* this Covenant he presently gives the Devil, either his hand-writing, or some drops of his blood etc.

The grim little volume is dedicated

> ' To the Right Worshipful and much honoured Friend Francis Rous . . . Sir, your Piety, your Learning, your Patronage to both, have encouraged me to bequeath this Peece to you. Though I cannot merit you a Maecaenas to me, the truth may to it. . . .

Rous is of especial interest owing to his close connexion with the acknowledged leader of the Long Parliament, John Pym (1548-1643), who represented Tavistock. Before he was six years old [2] Pym's father died, and his mother became the second wife of Sir Anthony Rous of Halton St. Dominic, Cornwall, the father by his first wife of Francis Rous. Francis thus occupied the place of an elder brother, whom Pym followed at an interval of six years to Broadgates Hall, Oxford (1599), and to the Middle Temple (1602). That Pym's speeches in Parliament on the sub-ject of religion should frequently seem reminiscent of the utterances of Francis Rous is under the circumstances hardly surprising; and it is difficult to suppose that he was not from an early age indoctrinated with the elder man's concern about witchcraft. After the dissolution of the Parliament of 1626 (15th June), in which he had taken part in the attempt to impeach the reputed witch-patron [3] Buckingham, Pym's interest in witchcraft must have been stirred by a sensational trial at Taunton, a few miles from his ancestral home at Brymore. In August two persons, Edmund Bull and Joan Greedy, were tried at the assizes for bewitching one Edward Dinham.[4]

---

[1] Francis Rous had for chaplain Joseph Glanvill, the great writer in defence of witch-beliefs, author of *Sadducismus Triumphatus* (London, 1681), and many works of the same kind. Anthony A. Wood, *Athenae Oxonienses*, ed. Philip Bliss, vol. iii, p. 1244 (London, 1817).

[2] Probably before he was two years old. See S. Reed Brett, *John Pym*, p. xviii (London, 1940).

[3] F. W. Fairholt, *Poems and Songs relating to George Villiers, Duke of Buckingham* (London, Percy Soc., 1850).

[4] British Museum Add. MS. 36, 674, f. 189. T. Wright, *Narratives of Sorcery and Magic*, vol. ii, pp. 139–43 (London, 1851). C. L'E. Ewen, *Witchcraft and Demonianism*, p. 452.

The bewitched man was possibly a member of the old Somerset family of the Dinhams of Corton Dinham and Buckland-Dinham, the elder branch of which had become extinct more than a century earlier. Apart from this possibility there are other reasons for supposing that Pym was not uninterested in the case. The evidence given in court aroused widespread alarm. The bewitched man was stated to have fallen frequently into a trance lasting several hours, during which six men were unable to move his head, and then ' they see somewhat to beate uppe & downe in his stomacke and belly, and sometyme they thrust pinnes and nedles thorowe his handes and nostrils, of which he is insensible neither doeth there any blood appeare '. During his trances two voices besides his own were to be heard carrying on a conversation and disputing over the ownership of his soul. So great was the concern aroused by this evidence that it induced Richard Bernard to undertake the study of works on witchcraft and to publish (London, 1627) his *Guide to Grandjury men*, to which allusion has been made in an earlier chapter.

> Since your Lordships sate at Taunton the last Summer Assizes [wrote Bernard in his dedication to the judges] I have . . . given myself to the reading of many approved relations touching the arraignment and condemnation of Witches: as also treatises of learned men, concerning the devilish Art of Witchcraft, adding withal not a few things, which otherwise I have learned and observed. The occasion offered and the reasons drawing me to this studie, were the strange fits then, and yet continuing upon some judged to be bewitched by those which were then also condemned and executed for the same: My upright meaning in my painstaking with Bull mistaken, a rumour spread, as if I favoured witches, or were of Master Scot's erronious opinions, that witches were silly deceived Melancholics &c.

In his dedication to the ecclesiastical authorities of the Diocese Bernard wrote:—

> The sin of witchcraft and the diabolicall practice thereof, is *omnium scelerum atrocissimum,* and in such as have the knowledge of God, the greatest apostacie from the faith, they renouncing God, and giving themselves by a covenant to the Divell.

It is probable that Bernard, who had long been vicar of Batcombe in Somerset, was personally acquainted with Pym. For Pym was, it should be remembered, a dependent of the family of Rich, and Sir Nathaniel Rich was his closest and most confidential collaborator in parliamentary tactics. In the spring of this very year (22nd April 1626) he had chosen Sir Nathaniel as his assistant in managing the impeachment of Buckingham.[1] Another tie connecting Pym with the Taunton case was Sir John Walter (1566–1630), the senior Judge of Assize, before whom the case was tried. Sir John had been member of Parliament in 1620–22 and 1624 for East Looe, which had formerly been represented by Pym's step-father, Sir Anthony Rous,[2] and he had acted with Pym on several important parliamentary occasions, such as the impeachment of Edward Floyd (1st May 1621).[3] Moreover, as an official of the Exchequer, Pym would be brought into contact with Sir John, who was Chief Baron of the Exchequer. Finally, as one of the neighbouring gentry,[4] Pym would be unlikely to be absent from the Assizes, August being a month when the gentry were usually free from business in London and in a position to share in the life of their native county.

All this, however, is largely surmise. The solid evidence of Pym's zeal for the destruction of witches is to be found in his speech against Sir Edward Dering,[5] one of the chief instigators of the petition of the Grand Jury[6] of Kent (25th March 1642, presented 30th April). Here, Pym argues, Dering would have been better employed in his duty of discovering witches than in using witches' methods to induce the jury to sign the petition.

> *Flectere si nequeam* [*sic*] *superos, Acheronta movebo* [he quoted], instead of inquiring upon the Statute of Witchcraft and Conjuration, he useth his conjurations and enchantments upon them, to conjure them to secrecy; falsely persuading them that they will be bound to it by their oath. When all this would not serve, he then applies himself to the bench; and by the enchantments and conjurations used there, prevails so far as to have it there voted and assented to by such as were present.[7]

[1] C. E. Wade, *John Pym*, pp. 68, 72, and 123 (London, 1912).
[2] *Parochial History of Cornwall*, vol. i, p. 301 (Truro, 1867).
[3] S. R. Gardiner, *History of England 1603–42*, vol. iv, p. 121 (London, 1883); C. E. Wade, *John Pym*, p. 35 (London, 1921).
[4] He was lord of the manor of Cutcombe and Woolavington in N.W. Somerset. He also possessed Hawkewell, Langham, and Poole in the same region, as well as Brymore House. See S. Reed Brett, *John Pym*, ch. i (London, 1940).
[5] See *D.N.B.*, ' On 25 March he took a leading part at the Maidstone assizes in getting up a petition from the grand jury in favour of episcopacy and the prayer book. On this he was impeached by the commons. . . .'
[6] S. R. Gardiner, op. cit., vol. x, pp. 179, 181, 194 sqq. (London, new ed., 1891).
[7] J. Forster, *John Pym*, p. 272 (London, 1837). ' This speech ', wrote Forster (p. 269, n. 2), ' appears anonymously in the common parliamentary histories; but in the Journals it is given to Pym.'

(*h*) On the historic occasion in 1629 when the Speaker was held in the Chair, the three resolutions were read, as has already been remarked, by Denzil Holles. He sat for Dorchester in the Long Parliament. When he took the Presbyterian side against the army in 1648 he issued a scathing attack upon Oliver Cromwell and St. John [1] in which he accused the former of witchcraft.

> You will find in it [he says in his epistle dedicatory addressing Cromwell] some representation of the grosser lines of your features, those outward and notorious enormities, that make you remarkable, and your Pictures easy to be known; which cannot be expected here so fully to the life as I could wish. He can only do that whose eye and hand have been with you, in your secret counsels, who have seen you at your meetings, your Sabbaths, when you have laid by your assumed shapes (with which you have cozened the World) and resumed your own; imparting to each other, and both of you to your Fellow-Witches, the bottom of your designs, the Policy of your Actings, the Turns of your Contrivances, all your Falsehoods, Cozenings, Villainies and Cruelties, with your full intentions to ruin the three kingdoms. All I will say to you is no more than what St *Peter* said to *Simon* the Sorcerer *Repent therefore of this your wickedness.*

A modern man reading these words might easily assume that they were spoken figuratively. Such an assumption cannot be maintained. For, in the first place, witchcraft amongst the rigid Presbyterians, to whom Holles belonged, was far too grimly serious a matter lightly to furnish figures of speech. Secondly, Cromwell was commonly believed in Presbyterian circles to have made a compact with the Devil, with whom he was said later to have had a personal conference on the morning of the battle of Worcester [2]—a matter which will receive notice in a later chapter. It may be noticed that Holles urged in Parliament the restoration to the post of Lord Chief Justice of Sir Ranulph Crewe, who had condemned nine witches to the gallows at Leicester on the unsupported evidence of a small boy (July 1616). The royal displeasure which descended upon Crewe when the boy was discovered to have counterfeited diabolical possession has been mentioned in an earlier chapter. [3]

The borough of Honiton, after a long period in which it had sent no members, sent two to the Long Parliament. One of

---

[1] *Memoirs of Denzil, Lord Holles from 1641–1648* (1699) (reprinted in Baron Maseres's *Select Tracts Relating to the Civil Wars*, pt. i, p. 189. London, 1815).

[2] The story is given in Laurence Echard, *History of England*, 3rd ed., pp. 691 sqq. (London, 1720). Echard derived it from the *History of Independency*.

[3] James Thompson, *History of Leicester*, pp. 344–5 (1849); John Nichols, *History and Antiquities of the County of Leicester*, vol. ii, pt. ii, p. 471 (1795–1815).

these was Walter Yonge (1581?–1649), whose son, John Yonge (*b.* 1603), sat in the same Parliament for Plymouth. Walter, who is chiefly remembered for his diaries and the many omens and wonders they record, was an extremely zealous Puritan. He was, consequently, given an important appointment as a victualler for the navy during the Civil War. His concern about witchcraft is made clear by an entry in his diary for the year 1606.[1]

> This year [he wrote] there was a gentlewoman and a near kins-woman to Doctor Holland's wife, Rector of Exon College in Oxford, strangely possessed and bewitched, so that in her fits she cast out of her nose and mouth pins in great abundance, and did divers other things very strange to be reported.

The Somersetshire borough of Ilchester was represented in the Long Parliament by Robert Hunt (*circ.* 1608–79),[2] who took the Protestation of 3rd May 1641 on the 7th of that month,[3] against ' endeavours to subvert the Fundamental Laws . . . the exercise of an Arbitrary and Tyrannical Government . . . many illegal Taxations . . . divers Innovations and Super-stitions . . . brought into the Church &c.' The succeeding decade of his life is obscure; and he is said to have had some dealings with the Royalists, for which he was disabled from sitting in Parliament. However this may have been, it is clear that he was later regarded as a loyal supporter of the Commonwealth. The Protector selected him as Sheriff of Somerset in 1654, and he served as a J.P. continuously from that date. It was as a J.P. that he became famous for his discoveries of witchcraft. In the spring of 1658 he conducted the examination of Jane Brooks of Shepton Mallet, who was accused of bewitching a small boy, and who was subsequently found guilty at the Somerset Lent Sessions and hanged at Chard on 26th March of the same year.[4] On 26th and 30th January and 7th February 1664/5 he received the sensational confession of Elizabeth Style of Bayford, who was

---

[1] *Diary of Walter Yonge Esq.*, edited by George Roberts, p. 12 (London, Camden Soc., 1848). Thomas Holland was a Fellow of Balliol, Regius Professor of Divinity 1589 and Rector of Exeter 1592. The greater part of Yonge's diary has not been published. It remains in MSS. in the British Museum Library. Yonge was a J.P. for Devon for many years and sheriff in 1628. His only published work was *A Manual for a Justice of the Peace, his vade mecum* (London, 1642).

[2] S. W. Bates Harbin, *Members of Parliament for the County of Somerset*, p. 171 (Taunton, 1939).

[3] J. Rushworth, *Historical Collections*, pt. iii, vol. ii, pp. 241, 246.

[4] Ewen, *Witchcraft and Demonianism*, pp. 335, 336, 341–7, 353–4.

found guilty at the subsequent Somerset Lent Sessions at Taunton. Later the same year he conducted the examinations of two other witches. So famous were his exploits that Joseph Glanvill addressed to him one of his earliest defences of belief in witches.[1]

(i) One of the counsel appointed for the impeachment of Archbishop Laud was Roger Hill (1605-57), who sat for Bridport, Dorsetshire, in the Long Parliament. After being named in the commission of judges appointed for the trial of the King (1649) he was made Judge of Assize for Northamptonshire (1656) and a Baron of the Exchequer. His attitude towards witch-beliefs was by no means ambiguous. For at the Kent Lent Sessions of 17th March 1656/7 held at Maidstone he condemned to death one Mary Allen of Gowdhurst for feeding and employing ' an evil spirit in the likeness of a black Dog '.[2]

The Lancashire boroughs of Newton and Wigan were represented in the Long Parliament by William Ashurst and Alexander Rigby respectively—both of them zealous Puritans. Ashurst afterwards represented Lancashire in the Protectorate ' parliament ' of 1654, and Rigby raised forces in Lancashire and did notable services in the field to the Roundhead cause.[3] That they were both deeply involved in the current witch-mania is shown by a letter written by one Peter Winn to Rigby about an alleged witch who had already been examined by Ashurst.[4] It was written on 14th January 1637/8 in terms that are worthy of notice.

> The bearer hereof, Sara Crosse, wife of one Richard Crosse, deceased, being a long tyme servant to my Lord, and beinge, as all the neighbours conceave, and by his owne confession all the tyme of his sickness and at his last departure, most grievously tormented with divers torments, by wichcrafte of one Anne Spencer, a knowen wich, and, as by her examinations, beinge taken before me and Mr Ashurst, doth appeare, who, in regard of my sudden goinge upp to London, the poore woeman's cause hath beene a little neglected, for I would desire you to certify this my letter to the Bench, and withal to doe the poore woeman that favour as to get her a *mittimus* wheare the said Spencer may forthwith be sent to Lancaster, there to remain till she receive her further tryall according to equity and justice.

[1] *Some Philosophical Considerations touching the Being of Witchcraft. In a Letter to Robert Hunt Esq.* (London, 1666, reprinted 1667).
[2] C. L'E. Ewen, *Witch Hunting and Witch Trials*, pp. 108, 249 (London, 1929).
[3] *Victoria County History of Lancashire*, vol. ii, pp. 232-5 (London, 1908).
[4] Historical MSS. Commission, 14th Report, Appendix pt. iv. MSS. of Lord Kenyon, p. 55 (London, 1894).

One of the knights of the shire for the county of Derby in the Long Parliament till his succession to the earldom of Rutland (29th March 1642) was John Manners (1604-79). He was one of the twenty-two peers who remained at Westminster in defiance of the King's summons (January 1642/3) to Oxford. In July 1643 he was sent with Lord Grey on a mission to Edinburgh to ask the assistance of the Scots in fighting against the King. A few months later he took the Covenant. The various motives that induced him to side with Parliament against the King are impossible to assess. One of them may well have been concern about witchcraft. For in the spring of 1618/9 two, and possibly three more, women were hanged for bewitching his kinsfolk the children of Francis Manners (1578-1632), the sixth Earl of Rutland. The eldest son, Henry, was killed, it was stated at the trial, by witchcraft; the second son, Francis, suffered severe torments, and the daughter, Katherine, fell into a severe illness. The case was one of the most sensational that has ever occurred in England.[1] One of the witches, Joan Flower, after her arrest called for bread and butter, and wishing ' it might never go through her if she were guilty ', fell down dead. Joan's daughter, Margaret, confessed that her mother had obtained a glove belonging to Henry, stroked her cat, Rutterkin, with it, dipped it in hot water, and pricked it often, with the result that Henry fell within a week into a painful illness. Similar use of a glove belonging to Francis made him ill. Joan, according to the confession, attempted to bewitch the Earl and Countess by soaking wool from their bed in warm water and blood and afterwards rubbing it on the belly of Rutterkin. Further terrifying evidence was given about Rutterkin and various other imps employed— one like a rat, another like an owl, and another like a little white dog. One attempt to bewitch the Earl and Countess took the form of boiling ' feathers and blood together, using devilish speeches and strange gestures '. After such recent experiences amongst his own kinsfolk, John the eighth Earl might well have been influenced by resentment against a government that went out of its way to protect witches.

(j) Ralph Ashton (or Assheton) of Middleton was Knight

---

[1] *The Wonderful Discoverie of the Witchcrafts of Margaret and Phillip Flower, daughters of Ioan Flower neere Beuer Castle : Executed at Lincoln, March 11, 1618. . . . Together with the seuerall Examinations and Confessions of Anne Baker, Ioan Willimot, and Ellen Greene, Witches in Leicestershire.* Printed at London, 1619. (Reprinted in *Collection of Tracts*, by J. R. Smith, 1838.)

of the Shire for Lancaster in the Long Parliament and afterwards Colonel in command of the Parliamentarian forces in Lancashire.[1] Few people in the whole of England could have been more deeply concerned about witchcraft than he. For at the Lent Sessions at Lancaster in 1633 three men and one woman of his native village had been condemned to death and hanged on the ground that they 'invoked, entertained (*hospitaverunt*) and employed evil spirits, with the intention of wasting Ralph Ashton of Midleton'. One of the witches, abetted by the others, had also 'bewitched Richard, son and heir apparent of Ralph Ashton of Middleton Lancs., at Middleton, who languished until 25th March following, when he died at Middleton'.[2] This case has already been alluded to as one of the very few which resulted in the execution of witches during the period between the accession of Charles I and the Great Rebellion.

Preston was represented in the Long Parliament by Richard Shuttleworth of Gawthorpe Hall, who was strongly Roundhead in his political sympathies.[1] He played a leading part in preparing the way for the famous witch trial at Lancaster in 1634, which but for the vigilance of Charles I would have resulted in the hanging of seventeen witches. It was Shuttleworth, in company with another Justice of the Peace, who listened to the boy Edmund Robinson (10th February 1633/4) as he unfolded his fantastic story of the two greyhounds changing into a horse and a witch; of their carrying him to the feast at Hoarstones; and much more that has already been noticed. Shuttleworth and his companion accepted the whole of the boy's inventions, and ordered about twenty arrests on the strength of them. They also heard with the same unquestioning credulity the first confession of Margaret Johnson about the appearance of the Devil in the form of a man in suit of black tied with silk points, called Mamillion, to whom she sold her soul.[3]

The terror of witchcraft of a later member of the Long Parliament is told by Richard Baxter [4]:—

My dear Friend Mr Hopkins (Father of my Faithful Brother Mr *George Hopkins* Minister at *Eversham*, till ejected, *Aug* 24 1662 and

[1] *Victoria County History of Lancaster*, vol. ii, pp. 232 sqq. (London, 1908).
[2] Ewen, *Witchcraft and Demonianism*, pp. 408–9 (London, 1933).
[3] Ibid., pp. 244, 248.
[4] R. Baxter, *Certainty of the World of Spirits*, pp. 59–60 (London, 1691).
William Hopkins was elected as one of the two members of Parliament for Bewdley in place of the Royalist members, who were 'disabled to sit', on

Grandfather to Dr *Hopkins* lately Preacher at *Laurences*) a chief Magistrate of *Bewdley*, and since a Member of the Long Parliament, oft pained as he thought with Spleen, but not at all Melancholy came to see me at Mr *Hanburyes*, the last time before I was driven out of the County, and as a great secret told me, that he was possest (meaning, I think Bewicht) : I chid him as Fanciful and Melancholy : But he without any show of Melancholy, affirmed, that it was certainly true : I could not stay with him, and never saw him more. But he long continued in pain and that Conceit, and before he dyed, a piece of wood came down into the *rectum intestinum*, which they were fain to pull out with their fingers, His good Wife told me, it was of the length of ones finger : And that he and they were Sure that he never swallowed any such thing. The best Man it seems may thus be afflicted, as Job, by Satan.

(*k*) John Selden (1584–1654), who sat for Oxford University in the Long Parliament, was less concerned about witchcraft, but a strong upholder of the Jacobean Statute. A man of immense and varied learning, he had strongly opposed the Government of Charles I on many points, showing always a pedantic regard for the ancient privileges of Parliament. In politics he occupied a somewhat isolated position, as he was out of sympathy with the prevailing Puritanism of the Civil Wars, and at times, especially towards the end of his life, veered towards Royalism. His *Table Talk*, compiled by his secretary, Richard Milward, in a more sceptical generation represents him as holding the view— also expressed by Thomas Hobbes, another isolated politician— that though the existence of witchcraft was open to question, the punishment of witches was perfectly right and just.

> The law against witches does not prove that there be any; but it punishes the malice of those people that use such means to take away men's lives. If one should profess that by turning his hat thrice, and crying buz, he could take away a man's life, though in truth he could do no such thing, yet this were a just law made by the State, that whosoever should turn his hat thrice, and cry buz, with an intention to take away a man's life, shall be put to death.

§ 6 (*a*) A shovel full of coins taken at random from a sack and assayed was often regarded as revealing the approximate proportion of silver to alloy in the whole sack full. The handful

---

6th January 1647. He died on the 19th and was buried on the 21st July 1647, ' a gracious and able Christian, then Burgesse elected for Parliament for Burrough of Bewdley ' (*Church Register of Ribbesford*). His son, George Hopkins, M.A., New Inn Hall, Oxon. 1648, aged 27, was Minister of all Saints', Evesham, until ejected in 1662. W. R. Williams, *Parliamentary History of the County of Worcester*, p. 167 (Hereford, 1897).

of members of the Long Parliament opposed to the King whose views on witchcraft have just been stated are probably a fair sample of all the others. This assumption is largely confirmed by the action of the Roundhead members in 1645, when they were informed of the mass executions of witches in East Anglia resulting from the methods of Matthew Hopkins. They issued a special Commission of Oyer and Terminer for the trial of more witches; and in spite of the report that confessions were extorted by improper means they associated with the judges certain Puritan divines, Samuel Fairclough and Edmund Calamy, notable for the strength of their convictions about witchcraft.

The thinness of the pretence that the Commission was intended to protect the accused from injustice may be gathered from a passage in Clark's *Life of Fairclough* [1]

> In the year 1645 a great number of persons in the *County* of *Suffolk* were apprehended, as being *guilty* of the damnable and Diabolical sin of *Witchcraft ;* and divers of them had *confessed* themselves guilty thereof; but a report was carried to the Parliament then sitting, as if some busie men had made use of some *ill Arts*, to extort *such confession* from them; thereupon a special Commission of *Oyer and Terminer* was granted for the Trial of those *Witches ;* in which Commission Mr *Fairclough's* name was inserted, with the name of another *Reverend Divine*. . . . This Learned man therefore, before his first sitting upon the *Bench*, did Preach two Sermons to the *Court* in *Bury* Church; wherein he *first* showed, that there was such a sin as that of *Witchcraft*, that is, of mens *dealing and contracting with* familiar Spirits; and did then *confute* all those *arguments*, which either former or later, *Sadducees* and *Atheists* have produced to the *contrary ;* wherein he gave *great* satisfaction to the whole Auditory. . . .

A few remarks about the wickedness of bearing false witness against the accused were of little account in view of the general trend of his sermons, which insisted on the dread reality of witches' pacts and their fearful consequences.

> The effect was [wrote Hutchinson][2] that they went on to execute them in great Numbers: And therefore we may believe, he recommended these Prosecutions as a Piece of Piety and Reformation . . . But the Clergy of our Church opposed them as far as they had Power.

(*b*) The attitude of the Long Parliament towards witchcraft could hardly be more explicitly expressed than it is in the *Act of General Pardon and Oblivion* (24th February 1651/2), at the end

---

[1] Samuel Clark, *Lives of Sundry Eminent Persons*, p. 172 (London, 1683).
[2] Francis Hutchinson, *Historical Essay concerning Witchcraft* (London, 1718).

of the Civil Wars.[1]   It specially excepted from pardon 'all Offences of Invocations, Conjurations, Witchcrafts, Sorceries, Inchantments and Charms; and all Offences of procuring, abetting or comforting the same; and all persons now Attainted or Convicted of the said offences'.

(c) A further illustration of this attitude lies in the fact that the president of the parliamentary commission that sentenced Charles I to death was a prominent believer in witches, though not a member of Parliament.   John Bradshaw (1602–59) is remembered for his overbearing conduct towards Charles I and various Royalists whom he condemned to death; for the rapidity of his rise from comparative obscurity; for the great wealth which he accumulated, and for his subsequent quarrel with Cromwell.   But his prowess as a witch-hunter finds scarcely any mention in modern historians.   He had been appointed Chief Justice of Chester (22nd February 1646/7) and a judge in Wales (18th March 1646/7)—appointments which gave him the opportunity of displaying his attitude towards witchcraft.   The fragmentary records that survive show that an alleged witch was tried before him at Flint on 7th April 1656, and that later the same year (6th October) at Chester he condemned to death for witchcraft three women, who were duly hanged at Boughton nine days later.   Before the trial John's eldest brother, Henry Bradshaw, was one of those appointed to conduct a preliminary examination of the witches.   Two years later another member of the family, Colonel Bradshaw, is recorded as examining another witch prior to her trial at the next Chester Assizes.[2]   Witch-mania was evidently endemic in the Bradshaw family.

The facts collected in this chapter certainly convey the impression that one amongst the many purposes of the Long Parliament was the leading of a reaction against the scepticism of Charles I on the subject of witchcraft.   The measure of its success may be estimated in the following chapter.

---

[1] Firth and Rait, *Acts and Ordinances of the Interregnum.   1642–60*, vol. ii, pp. 569 (London, 1911).
[2] C. L'E. Ewen, *Witchcraft and Demonianism*, pp. 423, 418, 419, 420 (London, 1933).

CHAPTER VIII

THE SECOND PERIOD OF THE GREAT WITCH SCARE
1642–9

§ 1. THE FARTHER the political pendulum is taken in one direction the farther it will swing back in the opposite direction as soon as it is released. In those parts of England where the authority of Charles I disappeared in the Civil War the long-repressed witch-mania burst out again with a violence that has never been experienced either before or since. The Parliamentary cause first consolidated its power in the south and east and in a few isolated districts of the north and west. It then gradually subdued the whole country. As it did so the witch-scare kept in step with the victorious armies and spread over wide districts that had hitherto been spared. The surviving records probably preserve only a tithe of the full tale of limitless credulity and fiendish cruelty that marked the period between the Battle of Edge Hill and the execution of the King.[1] Even so they are an impressive indication of the violence of the passions roused by a government that had so long stood between the witch-hunter and his prey.

(a) Within twelve months of the outbreak of the Rebellion the incident of the Witch of Newbury [2] casts a vivid light upon the mental anatomy of Parliamentarian soldiers. An anonymous pamphlet printed in London immediately after the events it claims to record places the incident about the time of the First Battle of Newbury (20th September 1643) and insists that it was 'credibly related by Gentlemen, Commanders, and Captains of the Earl of Essex his army'.

> A part of the army marching through Newbury, some of the soldiers being scattered by reason of their loitering by the way, in gathering nuts, apples, plums, blackberries, and the like, one of them by chance in clambering up a tree, being pursued by his fellow or

---

[1] Zachary Grey in his edition of *Hudibras*, vol. ii, p. 11 (London, 1744), said, ' I have somewhere seen an Account of betwixt three and four thousands, that suffer'd in the King's Dominions from the Year 1640 to the King's Restoration '.

[2] *A most Certain, Strange, and true Discovery of a Witch. Being taken by some of the Parliament Forces, as she was standing on a small planck board and sayling on it over the River of Newbury*, &c. Printed by John Hammond, 1643.

comrade in waggish merriment, jesting one with another, espied on
the river being there adjacent, a tall lean slender woman, as he
supposed, to his amazement, and great terror, treading of the water
with her feet, with as much ease and firmness as if one should walk or
trample on the earth . . .

Presumably some old woman was crossing the Kennet on a raft;
but so accustomed were the soldiers to the practice of floating
witches and to the belief that water rejected the servants of the
Devil, that the sight of her caused an immediate panic.   The
officers shared equally in the terror of their men, and ' gave order
to lay hold on her and bring her to them straight, the which
some were fearful, but some being more venturous than other some,
boldly went to her and seized on her by the arms, demanding
what she was? but the woman no whit replying any words unto
them, they brought her unto the Commanders, to whom though
mightily she was urged she did reply as little '.   The higher
command decided to put the old woman to death immediately,
and ordered ' a couple of their soldiers that were approved good
marksmen, to charge and shoot her straight, which they prepared
to do, setting her bolt upright against a mudbank or wall '.
The narrative goes on to assure its readers that they were unable
to kill her either by bullet or sword, though one ' set his carbine
close to her breast ' and another ' drew out his sword and man-
fully run at her with all the force his strength had power to make '.
Finally the problem of killing her was solved by a soldier who was
familiar with the practice of ' blooding ' witches.

> One amongst the rest had heard that piercing or drawing blood
> from forth the veins that cross the temples of the head, it would
> prevail against the strongest sorcery . . . the woman hearing this,
> knew that the Devil had left her and her power was gone, wherefore
> she began aloud to cry, and roar, tearing her hair and making
> piteous moan, which in these words expressed "were and is it come
> to pass that I must die indeed?   Why then his Excellency the Earl
> of Essex shall be fortunate and win the field. . . ."

That so fantastic a story should be published is an illustration
of the growing credulity of the reading public under Parliamentary
rule.   The credibility of the narrative—apart from its embroidery
—is fairly high in view of the haunting dread of witchcraft that
rarely left the Puritan of this age.   It is, moreover, partly confirmed by the *Mercurius Civicus* for September 1643 (21st–28th),
which adds the suspicion that the witch was sent to blow up
Essex's powder magazines.   Here, as so often elsewhere, witches

are assumed as a matter of course to side with the Royalists who protected them, and who supposedly used their spells.

(*b*). About the same time as the killing of the old woman near Newbury the credulous vigilance of Parliamentary soldiers showed itself in Wiltshire. According to a narrative [1] written in 1685/6:—

> Alice Elger, widow, dwelling in Westport, became so audaciously noxious to the good inhabitance, there being none but martial law then, it was about 1643; Malmesbury being then in the hands of the Armys ranged against the King; that the Soldiers and some of the lowest of the people did in the mercat place use her very roughly, moved by an instant emergent, so that shee, perhaps to avoid the like, went home and poysoned herself, as was then believed, and was buried in cross way as a felon of herself.

Malmesbury was occupied by the troops of Sir William Waller on 21st March 1643, and abandoned about a month later. It was reoccupied by the Parliamentarians, and again abandoned during the early summer. It was, consequently, during one of these periods of occupation that Alice Elger probably met her death.[2]

Hitherto, so far as can be ascertained, there had been little trace of witch-mania in Wiltshire. With the invasion of Parliamentary troops it took deep root in many parts of the county—most especially in Malmesbury. During the following generation recorded accusations of witchcraft are very frequent.[3] As will be noticed more than once, witch-mania resembled a highly contagious disease. It was carried by the Parliamentary armies to every region in which they gained the mastery.

In an attempt to restore their power after the Royalist successes of 1643, Parliament resolved to buy the help of the Scottish armies, which consisted largely of veterans from the Thirty Years' War. To gain this vital assistance they pledged themselves to take the Solemn League and Covenant. Henceforth the English Puritans were in the most intimate contact with what was probably at this time the most witch-ridden people in Europe.[4] So deeprooted and widespread were the Scottish convictions of the

---

[1] *The Gentleman's Magazine* for 1832, pt. i, p. 408.
[2] Rushworth, *Historical Collections*, pt. iii, vol. ii, p. 263 (London, 1692); *Mercurius Aulicus* for 22nd April and 23rd July 1643.
[3] Ewen, *Witchcraft and Demonianism*, pp. 324-9, 334, 335, 338, 355, 439-46, 453, 458, &c. (London, 1933).
[4] See S. R. Gardiner, *History of the Great Civil War*, vol. i, pp. 226-7, and J. G. Dalyell, *The Darker Superstitions of Scotland* (Edinburgh, 1834).

L

terrible reality of witchcraft that even the scepticism of the eighteenth century was powerless against them. As late as 1730 William Forbes, Professor of Law at Glasgow, wrote in his *Institutes of the Law of Scotland* (p. 32): 'Witchcraft is the black art whereby strange and wonderful things are wrought by a power derived from the devil.' He firmly rejects the prevailing English view that the belief was obsolete (p. 371).

> Nothing seems plainer to me than that there may be and have been witches, and that perhaps such are now actually existing; which I intend, God willing, to clear in a larger work concerning the criminal law.[1]

The effect of close contact with the Scots after the taking of the Solemn League and Covenant was, inevitably, enormously to strengthen the hands of the English witch-hunters.

§ 2 (a) A year after the taking of the Covenant began the most notorious witch-hunting career of the whole of the period—that of Matthew Hopkins. It is not improbable that other onslaughts of like ferocity took place in the regions controlled by Parliament, though they have left only the faintest traces in surviving records. The accounts even of Hopkins's activities are by no means complete. There is ground for supposing that the tale of his victims is much longer than the extant lists of names of those condemned to the gallows.

The career of Matthew Hopkins before his appearance in the full light of history in March 1644/5 is somewhat obscure. He is said to have been the son of a minister at Wenham in Suffolk and to have become 'a lawyer but of little note' at Ipswich. He appears to have found his profession far from remunerative and to have been anxious to seize any opportunity of improving his fortunes. At an unknown date he removed to Manningtree in Essex, and there found his opportunity in the suspicion that a number of witches were practising their arts in the neighbourhood of his house (1644). In a book written two years later [2] in defence of his witch campaigns, he stated that seven or eight witches made a practice of meeting 'close by his house' every sixth week on a Friday night, in order to offer up 'solemn sacrifices' to the Devil. So strong was their antipathy to Hopkins

---

[1] The first Act against witchcraft in Scotland, dated 1563, was made more severe in 1649.

[2] M. Summers, *The Discovery of Witches* (London, 1928). This contains a reprint of Hopkins's *Discovery of Witches* (1647).

that four of them sent a bear from a distance of twenty-five miles to kill him in his garden.

As he seems never to have had the slightest regard for truth, it may be that many of his assertions are deliberate inventions. The chief interest of his book is that it reveals a careful study of King James's *Daemonologie* and other authorities on continental witch-lore. The career of a witch-finder must have made a double appeal to him. As a staunch Puritan he would find in it the pious labour of destroying the works of the Devil; as a penurious lawyer he would welcome it as a possible ladder to fame and fortune. He soon discovered that old women who were kept without sleep for several nights and otherwise mal-treated could be induced to make the most amazing confessions of guilt. By these means he secured the hanging of nineteen at Chelmsford (July 1645) after the trial already mentioned in connexion with the Earl of Warwick and Sir Harbottle Grimston.

(*b*) He was now well launched on his campaign for the puri-fication of England. He is said to have assumed the title of Witch-finder General and to have been given a special com-mission by the Long Parliament.[1] Having cleared his own neighbourhood of witches, he proceeded immediately to do a like service for the county of Norfolk. Here his exploits can be traced only in a few chance statements of contemporary observers. Thus, for example, *A Perfect Diurnal* (21st–28th July 1645) records [2] the recent ' trial of Norfolk witches, about 40 of them and twenty already executed '. Next he went by invitation to Great Yarmouth, where he tracked down some sixteen suspects, of whom at least five were sentenced to death.[3]

(*c*) Next month (August 1645) he and his usual companions, John Stearne and Mary Philips, both of Manningtree, turned their energies to the purification of Suffolk. Here also records are extremely scanty. They nonetheless reveal that at least 124 suspects were arrested and that of these at least sixty-eight were

---

[1] Notestein, *History of Witchcraft in England*, p. 165 (Washington, 1911), doubts this statement, which is made in *Hudibras*, pt. ii, canto 3.

> Hath not this present Parliament
> A Ledger to the Devil sent
> Fully empowered to treat about
> Finding revolted Witches out?

Hopkins is called Witch-finder General in a memoir written in 1725. See *Notes and Queries*, 21st March 1896, p. 223.

[2] Ewen, *Witchcraft and Demonianism*, p. 279 (London, 1933).

[3] H. Manship, *History of Great Yarmouth*, pp. 273-4 (1854).

condemned to death and duly executed. Many others died in prison.[1] The most remarkable of Hopkins's victims on this occasion was an octogenarian clergyman, John Lowes, who had been vicar of Brandeston, near Framlingham, for some fifty years, during which he had more than once been accused of witchcraft.[2] Suspicions of his dealings with the Devil were confirmed when he was ' swum ' in the Castle Ditch at Framlingham and found to float. Hopkins then resorted to his habitual technique of producing a confession by denying his victim sleep, which seems to have been particularly effective in dealing with very old people. Lowes was, consequently, kept awake for several nights by relays of watchers who ' ran him backwards and forwards about the room until he was out of breath. They then rested him a little and ran him again: and this they did till he was weary of life and scarce sensible of what he did or said.' [3]

Hopkins's efforts were not wasted. The old man confessed that he had made a covenant with the Devil; that he had familiars that sucked his blood; and that he had caused the death of many cattle. The most astonishing part of his confession was that he had seen from the sea wall at Langafort (Landguard?) near Harwich a number of ships sail by, and that he had ordered his yellow imp to go and sink a new vessel which was sailing in the middle of the fleet. He then saw the craft he had selected ' in more trouble and danger than the rest, tumbling up and down with the waves, as if the water had been boiled in a pot; and soon after it sank ', the rest of the ships sailing away in safety. He was found guilty at Bury St. Edmunds in company with seventeen others. By the time of his execution (27th August 1645) he had recovered from his treatment and stoutly maintained his innocence. He asked for a priest to read the burial service of the Prayer Book over his remains and, as this request was inadmissible, he recited the Office himself on his way to the gallows.[4]

---

[1] Ewen, *Witchcraft and Demonianism*, p. 281 (London, 1933).

[2] For a full account of Lowes's past see Ewen, *Witchcraft in the Star Chamber*, pp. 44 sqq. (printed for the author, 1938).

[3] *Notes and Queries*, 21st March, 1896, p. 223; Hutchinson, *Historical Essay Concerning Witchcraft*, p. 68 (London, 1718).

[4] Hutchinson, *Historical Essay Concerning Witchcraft*, p. 67, says that Lowes denied his guilt also at his trial. ' I had this from a Person of Credit, who was then in Court and heard his Tryal '. It is characteristic of Puritan credulity that no attempt appears to have been made by the Court to discover whether any ship had been wrecked at the time and place stated in Lowes's compulsory confession.

The most interesting feature of this case is that Lowes was a Royalist, and on that account especially open to suspicion of witchcraft. Hutchinson says of one of Lowes's companions in misfortune, ' I have been told by one that was present in the Court that one poor fellow confessed that he had sent Imps to Prince Rupert '.[1]

(d) Hopkins's work in Suffolk seems to have terminated with the burning of Old Mother Lakeland at the stake [2] at Ipswich on 9th September 1645. During the spring of the following year Stearne—possibly with the assistance of Hopkins—tracked down the witches of Northamptonshire. But scarcity of records of the Assizes of the Midland Circuit forbids any estimate of the numbers who went to the gallows. Before the end of March Hopkins and Stearne were in Huntingdonshire, eagerly supported by the Justices of the Peace and opposed by John Gaule, the vicar of Great Staughton. At least twenty suspects were brought up for examination, and several are known to have been hanged, but there are no data sufficient for any reliable estimate of their total number. Bedfordshire, to which the witch-finders next turned their steps, has left even fewer records of the accused and the condemned. It is doubtful whether Hopkins had a part in the discovery of witches in Cambridgeshire and the Isle of Ely in September 1647. He is said to have died of consumption about this time.

The total number of witches executed as a result of Hopkins's activities cannot be estimated even in the vaguest figures. It certainly amounted to several hundreds. It may have run into thousands. Such a fearful massacre of an appreciable portion of the female population could only have happened in a district saturated through and through with continental witch-beliefs. And this district, it should be remembered, was the home of the Eastern Association, the backbone of the Great Rebellion, but for which the whole movement would probably have collapsed. That the hostility of East Anglia to the King was not unconnected with his protection of witches is a supposition well worthy of serious consideration.

[1] Hutchinson, op. cit., p. 70.
[2] She was burnt alive because her husband was alleged to have been among her victims. See *The Lawes against Witches . . . also the confession of Mother Lakeland* (London, 1645), p. 8: ' Severall other things she did, for all which she was by Law condemned to die, and in particular to be burned to death, because she was the death of her husband, as she confessed. . . .'

That fear of witches had long been the overmastering emotion of these regions is vouched for by John Gaule, vicar of Great Staughton, a witness all the more credible as a believer in witch-craft himself and a contemporary resident. In his *Select Cases of Conscience touching Witches and Witchcraft* (London 1646) he wrote:—

> Every old woman with a wrinkled face, a furred brow, a hairy lip, a gobber tooth, a squint eye, a squeaking voice, or a scolding tongue, having a rugged coat on her back, a skull-cap on her head, a spindle in her hand, and a Dog or Cat by her side, is not only suspected, but pronounced a witch. Every new disease, notable accident, mirable of nature, rarity of art, nay and strange work and just judgement of God; is by them accounted for no other, but an act and effort of witchcraft. And for this the Witch must be sus-pected; and this suspition, though it bee but late, of a few, and those the under sort, yet it is enough to send for Witch-Searchers, or Witch-Seekers (a trade never taken up in England till this) whose lucatory skil and Experience is not much improved above the outward senses (pp. 5–6).

Gaule was a shameless 'Vicar of Bray'. An outspoken Royalist under Charles I, he paid court to the leading Common-wealth men in the later phases of the Civil War, and lived to welcome Charles II in the most fulsome strains at the Restoration.[1] He was, consequently, not the man lightly to oppose the prevailing sentiment of the moment. This fact gives much additional force to his indictment of the witch-finders and to his description of the witch-terror—a description that is shown by abundant evidence to be in no way exaggerated.

§ 3. It is possible that the witch-terror of the Eastern Counties provides the solution of one of the minor problems of the Civil War—viz., the massacre of the women at Naseby after the Parliamentary victory[2] (14th June 1645). The motives adduced by contemporaries to explain this unusual vengeance on non-combatants in a war[3] which was fought with signal humanity are curiously varied and sometimes contradictory. Several Parliamentary partisans allege two motives: (a) that the women

---

[1] G. L. Kittredge, *Notes on Witchcraft*, p. 7 (Worcester, Mass., 1907), cites Gaule as an example of a Puritan who opposed the persecution of witches. Such a citation is quite unconvincing in view of Gaule's career.

[2] A similar massacre of women was made by the Scottish Covenanters after the battle of Philiphaugh (13th September 1645) a few months later (Hume Brown, *History of Scotland*, vol. ii, p. 264). See also Wishart, *Deeds of Montrose*, chaps. vi and xvii, and Patrick Gordon, *A Shorte Abridgment*, p. 160 (Cambridge, 1911).

[3] That is the First Civil War. The later ones were far less humane.

were Irish and (*b*) that they were leading immoral lives. Thus, for example, John Vicars wrote in a contemporary narrative [1]:—

> Prince Rupert also, or rather Prince Robber, had brought into the field many Irish women, inhumane Whores, with Skeans or long Irish knives about them, to cut the throats of our wounded men, and of such prisoners as they pleased, (the wives of the bloody Rebels in Ireland, his Majesties dearly beloved Subjects) to whom our Souldiers would grant no quarter, about a hundred of them were slain on the ground, and most of the rest of the Whores, and Camp-sluts, that attended that wicked Army, were marked in their faces or noses with slashes and cuts, and some cut off; just rewards for such wicked Strumpets.

A substantially similar account with not a few verbal resemblances was written by ' a Gentleman of publique imployment ' during the night after the battle.[2] The signs of literary dependence of the one account upon the other detract something from their value as evidence. Yet they are corroborated in part by a contemporary ' Letter from a Gentleman in Northampton ' [3] who was to all appearances an eye-witness of most of the events he relates. Describing the captured baggage he wrote:—

> there was many of the waggons laden with rich plunder . . . which the Souldiers soon emptied, as they did the Waggons that carried the middle sort of Ammunition Whoores, who were full of money and rich apparell, there being at least 1500 of that tribe, the gentiler sort in Coaches, whereof I only saw 7 Coaches with Horses taken stuffed with that commodity, and the common rabble of common vermin on foot, 500 of them at least being taken and kept with a guard, untill order was taken to dispose of them and their mates, many of these were Irish women of cruel countenances, some of them were cut by our Souldiers when they tooke them. . . .

---

[1] John Vicars: *The Burning-Bush not Consumed, or, The Fourth and Last Part of the Parliamentarie-Chronicle* (London, 1646).

[2] *An Ordinance of the Lords and Commons assembled in Parliament for Thursday next to be a day of Thanksgiving. . . . Together with two exact Relations of the said Victory. The one from . . . Cromwell. . . . The other from a gallant Gentleman of publique imployment. . . .* London, printed for Ed. Husband June the 17, 1645. The latter letter is dated ' Harborough, June 15. two in the morning '.
The allusion to ' long Irish knives ' may be borrowed from Fairfax's account of the prisoners taken at Nantwich the previous year (29th January 1643): ' 120 Women, that followed the Camp; of whom many had long Knives, with which they were said to have done Mischief'. Rushworth, *Historical Collections*, pt. iii, vol. ii, p. 302 (London, 1692). Whitelock (*Memorials*, p. 146, London, 1682) speaks also of ' 100 Irish women who followed the camp '. The verbal resemblance is noteworthy.

[3] *A more exact and perfect Relation of the Great Victory (By Gods providence) obtained by the Parliaments Forces under command of Sir Tho. Fairfax in Naisby Field, on Saturday 14 June 1645. . . . Being a Letter from a Gentleman in Northampton, to his friend in London.* Published by Command . . . 1645.

Here, it will be noticed, the women are not killed on the spot, as in the other accounts. They are held prisoners for some time, till, apparently, orders come from the commanders ' to dispose of them '.

In spite of this and other inconsistencies of a minor character, most modern historians have accepted unquestioningly the view that the women were Irish and immoral, and that these two circumstances provide a completely satisfactory explanation of their slaughter. Among those who accepted such a view were S. R. Gardiner in the last century and John Buchan in recent times.[1] Yet, despite the authority of these great names, it must be recognized that contemporaries were by no means in agreement as to the motives for the massacre. Clarendon, for example, expressly states that some of the women slain were ' the wives of officers of quality ' and is at a loss for any motive except the ' barbarous cruelty ' which, as a Royalist partisan, he attributes (rather unfairly) to the enemy.[2] Moreover, some others who were Parliamentarian in sympathy seem equally at a loss, and, like Clarendon, say nothing either of Irish blood or bad morals. A contemporary letter-writer, ' G.B. a Gentleman in the Army ', satisfies himself with the laconic statement ' many Women slaine that were in their army, and many taken, which are every one wounded '.[3] That all the survivors without exception should be described as ' wounded ' is certainly curious, yet several Parliamentarian eye-witnesses say nothing either of the killing or of the wounding of so many women. Amongst these are Joshua Sprigge (1618–84), who may have witnessed the battle and who gives one of the fullest extant accounts of it ;[4] Rushworth, who was present in his capacity as Fairfax's secretary, was equally silent, though he mentioned in his *Collections* the women at Nantwich the previous

---

[1] John Buchan, *Oliver Cromwell*, pp. 219–20 (London, 1934).

[2] Clarendon, *History of the Rebellion*, bk. ix, p. 554 (Oxford, 1842).

[3] *A More Particular and Exact Relation of the Victory obtained by the Parliaments Forces under the Command of Sir Thomas Fairfax. Wherein Divers things very considerable are mentioned, which before are omitted in the severall Relations formerly published. Being two Letters, the one written by G. B. a Gentleman in the Army. . . .* London, 1645.

J. Mastin, *History and Antiquities of Naseby*, p. 184 (Cambridge, 1792), has a letter from Fairfax to Lenthall with the following postscript: ' Some Irish are among the prisoners as I am informed, I have not time to make enquiry into it, I desire they may be proceeded against according to the ordnance of parliament. . . .' The letter says nothing of women.

[4] Joshua Sprigge, *Anglia Rediviva ; England's Recovery : being the History of the Motions, Actions, and Successes of the Army under the Immediate Conduct of His Excellency Sr Thomas Fairfax, Kt.* (London, 1647).

year; Leighton and Herbert, the Parliamentary Commissioners, who wrote to Speaker Lenthall on the evening of the battle from ' Nazeby where the fight was this Satterday 14 June 1645 ', merely stated, ' The Standard is ours, the Kings Wagon and many Ladies '.[1] These witnesses could hardly fail to be aware of a massacre on so large a scale. It is therefore possible that the omission to mention it was deliberate and due to the lack of any explanation which would reflect credit upon the Parliamentary forces. Had all the victims of the massacre been Irish and immoral, the writers would have possessed a justification more than sufficient for the Puritan public opinion of the day. They wrote presumably before the explanation, which later established itself as the orthodox Puritan one, had had time to reach them.

Such a conclusion is in part confirmed by a totally different tradition as to the reason for the massacre. This variant tradition, which was preserved by John Bridges (1666–1714), the Antiquary,[2] states that the massacre was a reprisal for certain alleged Royalist atrocities in Cornwall.

> The left wing being thus broken and disordered [wrote Bridges] the army retreated towards Leicester; the conquerors fiercely pursuing them, taking in Clipston Field one of the King's coaches with his cabinet of letters, and killing, besides many men, several women of genteeler figure, whose coaches were overturned in their hasty flight. Particularly in the south part of Farndon field, within the gate-place in the road between Naseby and Farndon, the Parliamentary horse galloping along, as Mr Morton was informed by an eye-witness, cut and slashed the women with sarcasm at every stroke, ' Remember Cornwall, you whores'; Sir Ralph Hopton, as they said, having used their women in Cornwall in like manner.

This tradition knows nothing of Irish women, and appears to agree with the view of Clarendon, corroborated by Leighton and Herbert and by Sir Edward Walker,[3] that many of the sufferers were ladies of quality. Yet the motive assigned to the massacre is unconvincing. For there is little evidence to suggest that any considerable number of Cornishmen were fighting in Fairfax's

---

[1] The term ' lady ' was more definitely indicative of high social status in the seventeenth century than it is to-day. It would scarcely be used, in a serious official report, as a description of Irish camp-followers. Its use corroborates Clarendon's statement that the victims were ' the wives of officers of quality '.

[2] John Bridges, *The History and Antiquities of Northamptonshire*, compiled from the MS. Collections by Peter Whalley, vol. i, p. 575 (Oxford, 1791).

[3] Sir Edward Walker (1612–77) (*Historical Discourses*, p. 115, London, 1705) describes the women as ' soldiers wives some of them of quality '.

army, or that Hopton's troops had been guilty of any notable atrocities in their behaviour towards the women of their native shire.

In all the widely differing accounts of this puzzling massacre there is one point upon which there is substantial agreement—viz., that the women were cut about the face, even those whose lives were spared. It is this point that possibly provides the clue. There was no custom so familiar to the witch-hunter of the seventeenth century as that of 'blooding' witches—drawing blood from their faces in order to deprive them of their magic powers.[1] Allusions to it are innumerable in the witch literature of every important country in Europe. It has already been noticed in connexion with the Witch of Newbury. It should be remembered that a considerable part of Fairfax's forces had recently been recruited in those Eastern Shires where the witch-fury had risen to an intensity unequalled in any other age—under the stimulus of Matthew Hopkins; and that Royalists no less than Papists were commonly supposed to practise the forbidden arts as the most ready means of accomplishing the destruction of their enemies. The discovery of a large number of women—many of them probably ' Papists '—in the Royalist army could hardly fail to point to witchcraft. Consequently the first impulse of the soldiery would be to ' blood ' them all in self-protection, to kill those most vehemently suspect, and to reserve the rest for a more leisurely investigation, since they were now deprived of their diabolical power. This reconstruction of the incident reconciles several discrepancies of the various narratives, and gives a well-understood motive to a series of actions that would otherwise seem curiously inconsequent. The silence of contemporary accounts on the matter of the witchcraft motive is explicable on several grounds, not the least being the common belief that the discussion of the Devil's business brought bad luck.[2] Fear of

---

[1] See, for example, George Giffard, *Dialogue Concerning Witches and Witchcraftes*, pp. 4 and 6 (London, 1593). J. Cotta, *The Infallible True and Assured Witch*, pp. 136–7 (London, 1625). R. Barnard, *A Guide to Grand Jurymen*, pp. 191 sqq. (London, 1627). J. Gaule, *Select Cases of Conscience*, p. 144 (London, 1646). J. C. Daylell, *The Darker Superstitions of Scotland* (Edinburgh, 1834). Ewen, *Witchcraft and Demonianism*, pp. 28, 106, &c. (London, 1933); cf. Shakespeare, *Henry the Sixth*, act i, sc. 10. Talbot says to Joan of Arc:—

> I'll have a bout with thee
> Devil or Devil's Dam, I'll conjure thee,
> *Blood will I draw on thee*, thou art a Witch.

[2] Cf. J. G. Frazer, *Taboo and the Perils of the Soul*, pp. 314 sqq.

ridicule from the many sceptics who had come into existence under Charles I may well have been another.[1]

§ 4. Whether this highly speculative explanation of the massacre at Naseby is true or not cannot at present be decided for lack of data. It is clear, however, that the fortunes of the battle resulted in the rapid conquest of the Royalist parts of England and Wales by the Parliamentarians. It is also clear that wherever the victorious armies went witch-terror went with them into regions hitherto immune. Within four years it had spread even to the far North of England, where it received further stimulants from beyond the Border. The proceedings in the counties of Durham and Northumberland in the year 1649/50 are so significant of the change of attitude towards superstition that followed the Parliamentary supremacy as to deserve especial notice. The inhabitants of these northern shires were now so impressed with the witch-menace that they sent to Scotland to hire the services of skilled ' prickers '. These experts acted on the principle, already mentioned by Bernard and many other writers,[2] that those in the service of the Devil could be detected by means of certain insensitive patches on their bodies. Hence their profession consisted chiefly in the adroit use of a long pin. Many of their performances seem to have left no permanent record. Only those that took place at Newcastle have happened to survive in more than fragmentary form.

John Wheeler of London [wrote Ralph Gardiner][3] upon his oath, said, that in, or about the year 1649, and 1650, being at Newcastle, heard that the magistrates had sent two of their Sergeants, namely, Thomas Shevel, and Cuthbert Nicholson, into Scotland, to agree with a Scotch-man, who pretended knowledge to finde out witches, by pricking them with pins, to come to Newcastle, where he should try such who should be brought to him, and to have twenty-shillings a peece, for all he could condemn as witches, and free passage thither and back again.

When the Sergeants had brought the said witch-finder on horse-

___

[1] It should be clearly understood that this explanation of the Naseby incident lies in the realm of pure speculation. No contemporary account of the battle contains one word about witchcraft. But such speculation is justified on three grounds: (i) the absence of any other explanation which takes account of all the evidence; (ii) the analogy of the Witch of Newbury of 1643 and the slaughter of the women after the Battle of Philiphaugh in September 1645, and (iii) the background of witch-terror against which the incident took place.

[2] Bernard, *A Guide to Grand Jurymen*, p. 219 (London, 1627).

[3] Ralph Gardiner, *Englands Grievance Discovered in relation to the Coal Trade*, pp. 114 sqq. (London, 1655, reprinted Newcastle, 1796).

back to town, the magistrates sent their bell-man through the town, ringing his bell, and crying, all people that would bring any complaint against any woman for a witch, they should be sent for, and tryed by the person appointed.

Thirty women were brought into the town-hall, and stript, and then openly had pins thrust into their bodies, and most of them was found guilty, near twenty seven of them by him, and set aside.

The said reputed witch-finder acquainted lieut. Colonel Hobson, that he knew women, whether they were witches or no, by their looks, and when the said person was searching of a personable, and good-like woman, the said colonel replyed, and said, surely this woman is none, and need not be tryed, but the scotch-man said she was, for the town said she was, and therefore he would try her; and presently in sight of all the people, laid her body naked to the waste, with her cloathes over her head, by which fright and shame, all her blood contracted in one part of her body, and then he ran a pin into her thigh, and then suddenly let her coats fall, and then demanded whether she had nothing of his in her body, but did not bleed, but she being amazed, replied little, then he put his hand up her coats, and pulled out the pin, and set her aside as a guilty person, and child of the devil, and fell to try others whom he made guilty,

Lieutenant colonel Hobson, perceiving the alteration of the fore-said woman, by her blood settling down in her right parts, caused that woman to be brought again, and her cloaths to be pulled up to her thigh, and required the Scot to run pin into the same place, and then it gushed out of blood, and the said Scot cleared her, and said, she was not a child of the devil.

So soon as he had done, and received his wages, he went into Northumberland, to try women there, where he got some, three pound a peece, but Henry Ogle Esq., a late member of parliament, laid hold on him, and required bond of him, to answer the sessions, but he got away for Scotland, and it was conceived if he had stayed, he would have made most of the women of the north, witches, for money.

＊   ＊   ＊   ＊   ＊

The said witch-finder was laid hold of in Scotland, cast into prison, indicted arraigned, and condemned for such like villanie, exercised in Scotland; and upon the gallows he confessed that he had been the death of above two hundred and twenty women in England, and Scotland, for gain of twenty shillings a peece, and beseeched forgiveness and was executed.

Anyone unacquainted with the nature of the witch-terror of the period of the Civil War might easily conclude that Ralph Gardiner, in his zeal against the monopolistic tendencies of the inhabitants of Newcastle, was guilty of exaggeration. The story is, however, almost typical of what was going on all over the country at this time. It is moreover corroborated in part by the

Parish Registers of Newcastle. That of St. Andrew,[1] for example, records the names of fifteen women who ' wer executed in the Town mor for Wiches '. Bulstrode Witelocke also makes a passing allusion to these appalling occurrences.[2]

The part played by a Lieutenant-Colonel [3] in supervising the proceedings is significant as yet another example of the part taken by the Parliamentary armies in spreading the witch-terror into those parts of the country that had previously been unaffected by it. Henry Ogle, who put a stop to the ' pricker's ' activities, was himself a strong supporter of Parliament and a believer in witchcraft—a fact which suggests that the witch-mania of the army sometimes excelled that even of the ordinary Puritan.[4]

A study of the death-roll of witches during the Civil War suggests that constitutional questions were by no means the only ones that led men to take up arms against the King. The readiness of the Roundheads to condemn women in hundreds to the gallows on the flimsiest evidence suggests that the disaffected parts of England had long been seething with discontent, and that the discontent arose not merely from the King's religious persuasion, but largely from the leniency towards witches that was inseparably connected with that persuasion. Such a hypothesis is corroborated by the attitude towards witchcraft that persisted throughout the Commonwealth and Protectorate.

[1] J. S. Burn, *History of Parish Registers*, 2nd ed., p. 125. R. E. C. Waters, *Parish Registers*, p. 57 (London, 1887).
[2] Whitelock, *Memorials*, p. 424 (London, 1732).
[3] There are numerous references to Lieut.-Col. Paul Hobson in Firth and Rait, *Acts and Ordinances of the Interregnum* (London, 1911), e.g., vol. ii, pp. 297, 305, 465, 474, and 661.
[4] M. H. Dodds, *History of Northumberland*, vol. xiv, p. 360: ' During the Civil War in the seventeenth century the squire of Eglingham, Henry Ogle, was a strong supporter of the Parliament. According to tradition Oliver Cromwell spent a night at Eglingham Hall as a guest of Henry Ogle in 1651 '. Later on (1652/3) he examined Margaret Stothard. Her fate is unknown, and there is nothing in the examination to suggest that Ogle was in the least degree sceptical about the existence of witchcraft. See E. Mackenzie, *History of Northumberland*, vol. ii, pp. 33–6. Mackenzie is followed by Notestein in dating this case 1682 instead of 1652. See Ewen, *Witchcraft and Demonianism*, p. 323 ft. n.

CHAPTER IX

OLIVER CROMWELL AND WITCHCRAFT

§ 1. OLIVER CROMWELL is the Sphinx of English History; and no Œdipus has arisen in three hundred years to solve the riddle that he has left to posterity. No single estimate has ever been able to take account of all the conflicting facts recorded of him. He was at once a bibulous sporting squireen and a sullen hypochondriac; a humane protagonist of religious toleration and a bloodthirsty fanatic; a reckless revolutionist and a rigid conservative; the hero of many battlefields and yet haunted in his last years by the dread of assassination; a transparently honest countryman and a subtle and unscrupulous schemer who used all other men as cats' paws. Small wonder that such a puzzling dual personality should leave his views of the current demonianism in obscurity. Not one word of the voluminous writings and speeches of the Lord Protector points to his opinions on the subject that was stirring his own faction and many of his closest associates to such appalling miscarriages of justice.

(a) His silence has sometimes been interpreted to mean that he did not believe in the existence of witches. But the *argumentum e silentio* really pulls, in this instance, in the opposite direction. Surrounded on all sides, as he was throughout his life, by furious witch-hunters, he would have had the amplest opportunity for the expression of his scepticism had it existed in any degree. The part played by his grandfather and uncles in securing the conviction of the famous Witches of Warboys has already been mentioned. Further, it should be noticed that the Church of All Saints', Huntingdon, in which Sir Henry Cromwell's annual witch lecture was given, was intimately connected with the early life of the Lord Protector. It was here that his father, Robert Cromwell, was buried (1617), in spite of his residence in the parish of St. John. It was here, too, that his friend and old schoolmaster, Thomas Beard, had his lecturership. Beard's intense convictions about the dread reality of witchcraft have already been illustrated; and a multitude of Cromwell's lifelong associates and friends held convictions scarcely less intense. It would, indeed, be difficult to discover any associate of the Lord Protector who is known to have had serious doubts of the reality of witchcraft. He lived, moreover, almost the whole of his life in the midst of districts notorious for the execution of witches. Had he entertained serious doubts, it is difficult to suppose that so frank and conscientious a man would never have given them utterance.

(b) A stronger argument against Cromwell's belief in witchcraft is that he was an Independent by persuasion, and consequently opposed to the Presbyterians, who were the most convinced of all witch-hunters. It is suggested that as the Independents were less dogmatic and more tolerant than the more orthodox Puritans, they would be less prone to accept Continental theories of witchcraft. There is certainly some reason in this argument; but it cannot safely be pressed very far. For the Independents accepted in substance those doctrinal tenets of Calvin that could be bent with such fatal ease in the direction of belief in the activities of the Devil in human affairs. Moreover, the army, which was largely Independent in sympathy, showed at least as much zeal in the hunting of witches as any other section of the community. Instances of this are frequent in the previous chapter. It should be remembered, too, that though Cromwell was comparatively tolerant in religious matters, his toleration did not extend over a very wide area. He was by no means a stranger to outbursts of fanatical blood-lust—especially when he came into contact with Roman Catholics, whether at Basing House or in many of the towns of Ireland. He had, too, that deep strain of mysticism that is common in men of Welsh blood. The word 'melancholy', which was frequently applied by seventeenth-century writers to persons troubled by strange fancies about witchcraft,[1] was applied by at least two contemporary observers to Cromwell in his younger days.

(c) Thus, for example, Dr. Theodore Mayenne, sometime

[1] For example, Thomas Ady, *A Candle in the Dark*, p. 124 (London, 1655): 'Some indeed have in a melancholly distraction of minde confessed voluntarily, yea and accused themselves to be Witches. . . .' More, *Antidote against Atheism*, bk. iii (London, 1653), uses the word 'melancholy' in this sense repeatedly. The full title of J. Webster's book (1677) is *The Displaying of supposed Witchcraft, wherein is affirmed that there are many sorts of deceivers and impostors, and Divers persons under a passive Delusion of Melancholy and Fancy*. M. Andreas Laurentins: *A Discourse of the Preservation of Sight*, tr. by R. Surphlet (1599), p. 100: 'We may say as much of melancholike persons. Their imagination is troubled . . . by the intercourse and medling of evil angels, which cause them oftentimes to foretell and forge very strange things in their imaginations' (Shakespeare Assoc. Reprint, Oxford, 1938).

physician to James I, enters in his notes under the date September 15th 1628 that he was consulted by ' Mons. Cromwell ' and found him *valde melancholicus*.[1]   Sir Philip Warwick [2] is more explicit.

> After the redition of Oxford [he wrote] I living some time with the Lady Beadle (my wife's sister) near Huntingdon, had occasion to converse with Mr Cromwell's physician, Dr Simcott, who assured me that for many years his patient was a most splenetic man, and had fancies about the cross in that town, and that he called up to him at midnight, and such unseasonable hours, very many times, upon a strong fancy, which made him believe he was dying; and there went a story of him that in the day-time, lying melancholy in his bed, he believed that a spirit appeared to him and told him that he should be the greatest man (not mentioning the word King) in this kingdom. Which his uncle, Sir Thomas Steward, who left him all the little estate Cromwell had, told him it was traitorous to relate.

Though this piece of tradition had doubtless been embroidered in the course of more than half a century and coloured by the writer's strongly Royalist sentiment, it is significant that it both stresses the word 'melancholy' and goes on to interpret it in the usual seventeenth-century sense.

(*d*) In spite of Cromwell's temperament and environment, it has been maintained that he was free from the prevalent superstition, on the ground that he issued a pardon in 1655 to a certain Margaret Gingell who was condemned to death at Salisbury in the April of that year for ' bewitching Ellianor Lyddiard to death ' and for ' bewitching Anne Beedle, so that she is pined and lamed '. [3] The little that is known about this obscure case is, however, insufficient to support the argument.   The circumstances surrounding it are briefly the following.   Before dawn on 11th March 1655, Colonel John Penruddock, a Royalist squire, entered Salisbury at the head of about 180 horsemen, arrested in their beds two judges who had come to the city for the Assizes, and proclaimed Charles II.   The Royalist force then set out by way of Blandford and Yeovil for Cornwall.   They were intercepted by a Roundhead force at South Molton and fifty or sixty of them taken

---

[1] Ellis, *Original Letters illustrative of English History*, 2nd Series, vol. iii, p. 248. Mayenne is quoted by Richard Baxter (*Certainty of the World of Spirits*, p. 121, London, 1691) as writing, ' That Melancholy is the Seat, the Bath, and the Kingdom of the Devil, I well know; and that that Prince of Darkness lurking under the thick Cloudiness of that black Humour, immixeth himself in divers Diseases, and that he exciteth Cruel Troubles (or Storms) in divers Subjects I have by manifold experience found, &c.'

[2] Sir Philip Warwick, *Memoires*, p. 249 (London, 1701).

[3] Thomas Birch, *State Papers of John Thurloe*, vol. iii, p. 366 (London, 1742).

prisoner. The leading Roundheads of Wiltshire then sought to implicate as many as possible of their neighbours in the conspiracy; and some, against whom there was little chance of securing a conviction for treason, were charged with other offences. Such, at least, appears to be the meaning of a letter from Roger Hill, the assistant to the Commonwealth attorney-general, to Secretary Thurloe.[1]

> Such as we have heere, that we intend to proceed against for treason are John Lucas. . . . The rest we shall indict for highway men and horse stealers. The evidence will not set them higher. . . . Some of that crew, whom we find will be good witnesses, we shall forbear to prosecute for the present. The proofs we find very lame, our busynes haveinge not bene soe well prepared for us, as it might have bene; we shall be the more carefull and industrious to make up what is short. . . .

In the midst of a list of prisoners, some charged with treason and others with offences such as highway robbery or horse-stealing, but all really for their connexion with Penruddock's conspiracy, came the name of Margaret Gingell and her charge of witchcraft. It is therefore probable, though not of course certain, that her real offence was complicity in the conspiracy, and that a charge of witchcraft was brought against her as more likely to secure a conviction than a charge of treason. If this is so, Cromwell's pardon may have no bearing upon his beliefs about witchcraft, and may have been due merely to the suspicion that the over-zealous Roundhead magistrates of Wiltshire had secured the condemnation of persons who were innocent of complicity in the conspiracy. It is not even certain that Cromwell, in the midst of all his other work, was personally concerned about the pardon.[2]

§ 2(a) In considering the Lord Protector's attitude towards witchcraft, it is perhaps more to the purpose to notice that three important members of his immediate entourage were active supporters of the prosecution of witches. One of these was Gervase Bennett of Snelston in Derbyshire.[3] He became a member of the Protector's Council, and was numbered among the important Army Committee as well as the Commissioners of

---

[1] Thomas Birch, *State Papers of John Thurloe*, vol. iii, p. 365 (London, 1742).
[2] Inderwick, *The Interregnum*, p. 189 (London, 1891); *Perfect Proceedings in State Affairs*, nos. 287–8.
[3] Lysons, *Magna Britannia*, vol. v, Derbyshire, pp. cliv and 122 (London, 1817); *Cal. of St. P. Dom, 1653–4*, p. 230, &c. (London, 1879). It was from an encounter with Bennett that the Quakers derived their name. Fox, *Journal*, pp. 37–8.

M

Excise and Customs. It is therefore probable that he enjoyed Cromwell's confidence to an exceptional degree. On 18th June, 1650, he sat as Justice of the Peace to receive information upon oath against a certain widow of Ilkestone in Derbyshire named Ann Wagg, who was accused of witchcraft. The evidence he admitted shows his convictions in such a clear light that a few specimens deserve quotation. The village baker deposed that he was on his way to church on the Lord's Day with his wife and servant-maid when Ann Wagg met them. She 'stood in the way & frowned on the said maide but uttered noe Words & presently the Mayd fell sick & was not able to goe a Stones Cast'. The baker and his wife were so disturbed by this ominous event that they kept the girl with them all the following night

> & about nine of the Clock in the night the Mayd cryed out Master Mr but this Infor and his wife being both awake could not answer her untill Something went out of the Maydes bed and the this Infor gott of his bed and the Maid said see you not this Catt, looke where she goes & this Infor could not stir till the Catt was gone & then this Infor went to the Mayd & then shee cryed out of her throate & there her Winde was stopt. And then the Mayd haveinge formerly heard that the putting the tongues into the fire the Woman if she was a witch Could not goe, She did put the tongues into the fire & and said Anne [1] did not goe till they were taken forth againe.

The baker added that the minister's wife had recently been ill, and the minister, suspecting that Ann Wagg was the cause, 'fetcht her downe and his Wife drew blood on her '.

A husbandman informed the Justice that when a neighbour had refused to provide Ann Wagg with milk, she had gone away grumbling, and next morning the neighbour found his calf dead. A village woman testified that her refusal to sell some whey to Ann Wagg was followed by the sudden illness of her child. A few weeks later her refusal to sell some butter to Ann Wagg was followed by the sudden death of her child during the night. Another village woman said that her daughter before she died had accused Ann Wagg of bewitching her. Another attributed the death of her child also to the same witch.[2]

No record remains of the fate of Ann Wagg. But, as many

---

[1] It was apparently assumed that Ann Wagg was present in the form of the cat.

[2] The evidence of the various informants is given in full in J. C. Cox, *Three Centuries of Derbyshire Annals*, vol. ii, pp. 89 sqq. (London, 1890).

witches were condemned at this time on far less evidence, it is not improbable that she ended her days on the gallows. That Gervase Bennet could accept and sign such evidence leaves little doubt that his credulity on the subject of witchcraft had few limits.

(*b*) Another witch-hunting member of the Lord Protector's immediate entourage was Sir John Danvers, whose part in the trial of Joan Peterson, the Witch of Wapping, has already been mentioned. Danvers rose high in Cromwell's favour as a result of the zeal he displayed on the Commission for the King's trial. He signed the death-warrant, and was appointed the following month to a seat on the Council of State, which he retained till the Council's dissolution in 1653.

The true origins of the trial of Joan Peterson are probably given in an anonymous pamphlet published shortly after her execution.[1] According to this pamphlet certain disinherited relatives of Lady Mary Powell were determined to be revenged on one Anne Levingstone, who had benefited richly under the provisions of Lady Mary Powell's will. They went, consequently, to Joan Peterson and offered her large rewards as an inducement to swear that Anne Levingstone had murdered Lady Mary Powell. On Joan Peterson's repeated refusals to have anything to do with the conspiracy, they decided that she must either be put to death or else terrified into helping them, as she already knew too much about their schemes. The readiest method of accomplishing their purpose was a charge of witchcraft. For Joan was famous for her skill in curing the diseases of man and beast.

Sir John Danvers himself is accused of being a party to the conspiracy. Whether this is so or not, it is clear that he exerted himself to the utmost to secure Peterson's condemnation. For her trial he came and sat on the Bench which he had not before occupied for several years; and he seems to have acquiesced in the unfair practices of the prosecutors. In view of this the evidence accepted by the court is of especial interest—all the more so as the trial took place in London in the Lord Protector's immediate neighbourhood. According to a contemporary pamphlet written presumably by someone who had been present at the

---

[1] *A Declaration in Answer to several lying Pamphlets concerning the Witch of Wapping . . . showing the Bloudy Plot and wicked conspiracy* . . . London. Printed in the year 1652.

trial,[1] a certain Christopher Wilson had refused to pay Joan a debt for her medical services. Whereupon she had shouted angrily, ' You had been better you had given me my money for you shall be ten times worse than ever you were.' Wilson immediately afterwards ' fell into very strange fits, and for twelve hours together would rage and rave like a mad man, and afterwards for twelve hours more would slabber out his tongue, and walk up and down like a meer changeling. . . .' Even more terrifying was the story of two women who were watching over a sick child.

> About midnight they espied (to their thinking) a great black cat come to the cradles side, and rock the cradle, whereupon one of the women took up the fire-fork to strike at it, and it immediately vanished, about an hour after the cat came again to the cradle side, whereupon the other woman kicked at it, but it presently vanished, and that leg she kicked with began to swell and be very sore, whereupon they were both afraid, and calling up the master of the house they took their leave.

On their way home they met a baker, who told them that he had seen a great black cat ' that had so frighted him that his hair stood an end ', and that ' he thought in his conscience the Peterson had bewitched the aforesaid child, for (qd the Baker) I met the witch a little before going down to the Island '.

A maid servant of Peterson's told of a conversation between her mistress and a squirrel which lasted ' a great part of the night '. When asked about the subject of this strange talk she replied that ' she heard her conference very perfectly, but she was so be-witched by it, that she could not remember one word '. This evidence was confirmed by a report that Joan Peterson's son, a boy of seven or eight years old, had told his school-fellows that his mother had a squirrel ' that taught her what she should do '. A neighbour who had been sitting by his fire talking to Peterson late one evening told how ' he perceived as it were a black dog, who went directly to *Peterson*, and put his head under her arm-pits, whereat the man was so astonished, that he ran out of the house as if he had been frighted out of his wits '. In view of all this evidence, and much more like it, Joan's execution at Tyburn a few days later (11th April 1652) is hardly surprising.

---

[1] ' The Witch of Wapping or An Exact and Perfect Relation, of the Life and Devilish Practises of Joan Peterson, that dwelt in *Spruce Island* near Wapping; who was condemned for practising Witch-craft and sentenced to be Hanged at *Tyburn*, on *Munday* the 11th of *April*, 1652. . . . London. Printed for Th. Spring 1652.'

(*c*) Another of the closest associates of Cromwell during the Protectorate was Roger Boyle (1621–79), Baron Broghill and first Earl of Orrery. Though at first an opponent, he was won over by the bold personal intervention of Cromwell,[1] who offered him a general's command in Ireland (1649). After serving with the utmost zeal in that country and in Scotland, he was included in a special council which the Protector was in the habit of consulting upon matters of prime importance, and nominated to the so-called House of Lords (1657). It was chiefly at his instance that Parliament recommended Cromwell to adopt the title of King.[2] After the death of Oliver he was conspicuous for his efforts to consolidate the Government of Richard.

Broghill's dread of witchcraft is amply attested by Richard Baxter, whom he supplied with important material for his *Certainty of the World of Spirits* (London, 1691). Thus, for example, on the French story of the Demon of Mascon Baxter wrote (p. 18) :—

1. I will begin with that most convincing Instance, which you may have read in a Book, called, *The Devil of Mascon.*[3]

Above twenty Years ago, the new Earl of *Orery*, then Lord *Broghil*, a person of well-known Understanding, and not inclined to weak Credulity, told me of much of what is written in that Book, and more; and said that he was familiar with Mr Perreaud, a Reverend Worthy Protestant Minister, in whose house all was done and had his son for his servant in his Chamber for many years; and from Mr Perreaud had the Narrative. Not long after Dr *Peter Moulin*, Prebend of *Canterbury* and Son to the famous *Peter Moulin* printed the Book, as having it from his Father, who had it of Mr Perreaud: And Mr Robert *Boyle*, Brother of the Earl of *Orery*, a Man famous for Learning, Honesty and Charity, and far also from weak Credulity, prefixeth an Epistle to it, owning it an undoubted Truth, being acquainted with the Author, Mr *Perreaud*, as his Brother was. All these three worthy Persons (the E. of *Orery*, Mr *Boyle*, and Dr *Pet. Moulin*) through God's Mercy are yet living . . . (p. 20) The said Earl of *Orery*, told me of many effects

[1] S. R. Gardiner, *History of the Commonwealth and Protectorate 1649–56*, vol. i, p. 95 (London, 1903).
Morrice, *Memoirs of the Earl of Orrery*, p. 11 (1742).
[2] Ludlow, *Memoirs*, p. 247; Whitelock, *Memorials*, p. 656.
[3] Francis Perreaud, *Relation of the chief Things which an Unclean Spirit did and said in his House at Mascon*, &c. Out of the French by Pet. du Moulin; together, with a letter of Robert Boyle Esq., to the said Pet. du Moulin (Oxford, 1658). The French original was printed at Geneva (1st ed., 1653; 2nd, 1656). The English translation went through several editions; and a Welsh one was published in London in 1681. The author, François Perrault or Perreaud (1572–1657), was Calvinist Pastor of Thoiry.

of Witchcraft and Devils (Men carried about) near him in *Ireland*, which I shall not particularly recite, though many Witnesses were named.

Later (pp. 57, 58) Baxter includes a couple of bloodcurdling stories derived from Broghill, who was obviously greatly concerned about witchcraft.[1]

(*d*) The legend that John Milton was one of the Protector's most intimate friends and mentors has long disappeared even from school text-books. Nevertheless the fact remains that in his office as ' Secretary for Foreign Tongues ' he was the mouthpiece of Cromwellian governments in their foreign affairs and their ablest defender before the bar of European public opinion. His continued support of Richard Cromwell suggests a close tie with the Protectoral family. For this reason, and still more because of his pre-eminence amongst the writers of his day, the question has often been asked what was Milton's attitude towards belief in witchcraft? Though brought up in Presbyterian tenets, he was in later life by no means a typical Puritan, as his Arian views and his advocacy of easy divorce and of polygamy show. Were his views about witchcraft the typical Puritan ones? Now that his works have been published in their entirety in a definitive [2] edition the question is a fairly easy one to answer. A number of his writings show that he accepted the current beliefs of the witch-hunters of his day. Thus, for example, in his *Tetrachordon* he enumerates ' witchery ' among the inducements to a marriage which would justify a divorce.[3] In his *Prolusiones* he alludes to the

---

[1] For the witch-beliefs of Cromwell's Chaplain, Peter Sterry, see Sterry's *Discourse of the Freedom of the Will* (London, 1675), p. 111. ' The *second state* into which the Soul passeth, is the Fall. This is the second Scene, which opens itself in the soul, a Scene of Trouble and Tumult, of Darkness and Storms, of Witchcrafts, Devils, Death and Wrath; of Privations and Contrarieties, which make the Vanity more full, which heighten, set off, *enlarge* the Harmony and Unity.'

See also his Sermon before the Commons, *The Spirit Convincing of Sinne*, pp. 7, 23 (London, 1646); also ' *The Comings Forth of Christ*, A Sermon preached before Parliament, 1 Nov. 1649 ' (London, 1650), pp. 7, 30, 33, 34, 37–8.

[2] *The Columbia Edition of the Works of John Milton* (New York, Columbia University Press, 1937–40).

[3] *Tetrachordon. Expositions upon the four chief places in Scripture, which treat of marriage, or nullities of marriage.* ' (What God hath joined, let no man put asunder.) But heare the Christian prudence lies to consider what God hath joyn'd; shall we say that God hath joyn'd error, fraud, unfitnesse, wrath, contention, perpetual lonlinesse, perpetuall discord; what ever lust, or wine, or witchery, threate, or enticement, avarice or ambition hath joyn'd together, faithfull with unfaithfull, Christian with anti-christian, hate with hate, or hate with love, shall we say this is God's joyning? ' *Columbia Edition of Works*, vol. iv, p. 151.

feasts prepared by the Devil for a witches' sabbat.[1] In his *Pro Populo Anglicano Defensio* he treats of Saul's experiences with the woman of Endor (I Samuel xxviii. 7-25), whom he calls a witch, though she is not so called in the Biblical narrative.[2] In his *Apology against a Pamphlet* he alludes to the belief that a witch had to take something belonging to her intended victim in order to be able to exercise her powers against him.[3] In *The Doctrine and Discipline of Divorce* he argues that one may not do evil that good may come, and cites as an example the classical ' Sorceresse Medea '.[4] In his *Brief History of Moscovia* he records how witches were said to have warned Shusky against anyone named Michalovitch, and how their prophecy was at last fulfilled. For in spite of Shusky's efforts to exterminate persons of that name he was at last succeeded by a Michalovitch.[5] Amongst the ' *Outlines for Tragedies* ' left behind among Milton's papers was one much on the

---

[1] ' Videtis apparatus nostros, quaeso vos, quibus palato sunt commessamini. Verum hariolor dicturos vos, epulas hasce, veluti nocturnae illae dapes quae à Daemone veneficis apparantur, nullo condiri sale, vereorque ne discedatis jejuniores quam venistis.' *Columbia Edition of Works*, vol. xii, p. 238.

' You perceive our preparations. I beseech you, you who have an appetite to fill up full. But I prophesy that you are about to say that these dishes, like the nocturnal feasts which are prepared by the devil for witches, are not seasoned with salt; and I fear you may go away more hungry than you came.'

[2] *Joannis Miltoni Angli Pro Populo Anglicano Defensio contra Claudii Anonymi, aliàs Salmasii Defensionem Regiam.*

Salmasius had quoted the prophet Samuel in support of the view (I Samuel viii, 10–18) that a king had a right to exercise an arbitrary rule. Milton replied: ' Noli Prophetam Dei falsò insimulare; quem tu dum juris regii isto loco doctorem habere putas, non verum nobis affers Samuelem; sed, ut venefica illa, inanem umbram evocas; qumvis et illum ab inferis Samuelem non adeò mendacem fuisse credam, quin illud quod tu jus regium vocas, potiùs tyrannicum dicturus fuisset.' *Columbia Edition of Works*, vol. vii, p. 95.

' Neither bring a false accusation against a prophet of God; for by supposing that in this passage he expounds the right of kings, you bring not before us the right Samuel, but call up an empty shade, as did the witch. Though for my part I verily believe that even that Samuel from Hell would not have been such a liar as not to call your right of kings rather the extravagance of tyranny.'

[3] *An Apology Against a Pamphlet call'd A Modest Confutation of the Animadversions upon the Remonstrant against Smectymnus.*

' Why were we not thus wise at our parting from Rome? Ah like a crafty adulteresse she forgot not all her smooth looks and inticing words at her parting; yet keep these letters, these tokens, and these few ornaments; I am not all so greedy of what is mine, let them preserve with you a memory of what I am? No, but of what I once was, once fair and lovely in your eyes. Thus did those tender hearted reformers suffer themselves to be overcome with harlot's language. She like a witch, but with a contrary policy did not take away something of theirs that she might still have power to bewitch them, but for the same intent left something of her own behind her.' *Columbia Edition of Works*, vol. iii, pt. i, pp. 335–6.

[4] *Columbia Edition of Works*, vol. iii, pt. ii, p. 464.

[5] *Columbia Edition of Works*, vol. x, pp. 360–1.

lines of the witchcraft plays of the early seventeenth century.[1] The Scottish usurper Natholocus, hearing of a conspiracy, ' sends a witch to know the event. The witch tells the messenger that he shall slay Natholocus. He detests it but in his journie home changes his mind & performs it.' Other passages might be adduced to show that Milton was not behind his Puritan contemporaries in his convictions about witchcraft.[2]

These four examples—Gervase Bennet, Sir John Danvers, Lord Broghill, and John Milton—serve to show that the Protector reposed his confidence in witch-hunters of no small credulity. To these might be added his favourite chaplain, Dr. John Owen.[3] His confidant Bulstrode Whitelock has already been mentioned in another connexion. There is no evidence that he ever sought to persuade them to change their opinions or that he himself was not in hearty agreement with them.

§ 3. Cromwell, despite all his efforts to cover up the rule of the sword, was a military despot supported by a devoted army. From the year 1652—if not for many years earlier—till his death he was in command of greater arbitrary power than any other ruler of Great Britain either before or since his time. Had he disbelieved in the possibility of witchcraft, the trials and executions of witches would soon have become impossible. Had he seriously doubted the reality of pacts with the Devil, his doubts would certainly have been reflected in a general slackening of witch prosecutions. It has often been argued that such a slackening is perceivable during the period of his undisputed sway [4] (1652–8). The investigation of records during the past twenty years has made this argument extremely doubtful. Thus, for example, the imperfect records of the Home Circuit show that during this period at least forty persons were indicted for witchcraft in the Eastern Counties covered by this Circuit, and that at least ten,

---

[1] *Columbia Edition of Works*, vol. xviii, p. 245. Other examples are *Pro Se Defensio*, vol. ix, pp. 123–5; iii, 345, 268. It should be remembered that *Comus* lines 513 sqq. were written when men's minds were filled with resentment at the liberation of the Lancashire Witches in 1634. It is possible that they were written with a didactic aim for those who were sceptical about the reality of witchcraft. Compare *Lycidas*, lines 100 sqq.

[2] His *De Doctrinâ Christianâ* appears to derive much from the works of Robert Fludd, the Rosicrucian, and from the Jewish Cabbala—both sources of 'witch-lore. On Fludd see John Webster, *The Displaying of Supposed Witchcraft*, pp. 319–20 (London, 1677).

[3] *The Works of John Owen*, ed. W. H. Gould, vol. iii, pp. 57, 141–2, &c. (London, 1852).

[4] G. L. Kittredge, *Notes on Witchcraft*, p. 7 (Worcester, Mass., 1907).

and more probably thirteen or fourteen, were executed.[1] These figures are lower than those for the period of the First Civil War; but the wonder is that after Hopkins's measures of wholesale extermination any possible suspects were left alive in the Eastern Counties. That such suspects were still being hunted down hardly suggests that the witch terror was being discouraged by those in authority—especially when it is recognized that the figures of those indicted compare most unfavourably with those of any period of equal length during the reigns of either Charles I (up to the Civil War) or Charles II.

Even if it were granted that Cromwell was too preoccupied with pressing affairs of State to take note of the Assizes of the Home Circuit, it can scarcely be conceded that he was blind to the events in the Capital which took place within a mile or two of his own residence. Had any serious doubt of the reality of witchcraft entered his mind, he would surely have made use of his virtually unlimited power to prevent indictments for this dread offence at the Middlesex Sessions. There is nothing to suggest that he ever did so. On the contrary, the imperfect records that have survived for the period 1652–8 suggest that indictments for witchcraft were at least as frequent as they had ever been in any earlier period. Thus, for example, in the year 1652 at least three women were tried at the Middlesex Sessions for witchcraft. Of these one was hanged, one was acquitted, and the fate of the third, one Temperance Fosset of Whitechapel, is unrecorded. In the following year at least two women were tried. One was acquitted, and the other found guilty and hanged. In 1656 one woman was tried and acquitted and another, a certain Ellen Lynley, was committed for witchcraft, her fate being unrecorded. In 1657 at least two women were tried and acquitted.[2]

These were by no means the only indictments for witchcraft in London during Cromwell's period of supremacy. Casual allusions in contemporary literature convey the impression that

---

[1] Ewen, *Witch Hunting and Witch Trials*, p. 108 (London, 1929). Godfrey Davies, *The Early Stuarts 1603–60* makes the astonishing statement that there was 'an almost total cessation, [of executions for witchcraft] during the Commonwealth and Protectorate', p. 368 (London, 1937). Pollock and Maitland (*History of English Law*, p. 556) take the true view that the 'days of the Commonwealth were the worst days for witches in England'.

On Scottish witch-hunting at this time see M. Coate, *Social Life in Stuart England* (London, 1924), p. 163.

[2] For details see Ewen, *Witchcraft and Demonianism*, pp. 434–5 (London, 1933); Notestein, *History of Witchcraft in England*, p. 410, places the trial of Grace Box in 1654. The date should be 1656.

there were a great many more. For instance, *A True and Perfect List of the Names of the Prisoners in Newgate* (1652) shows (p. 5) that a certain Susan Simpson was tried at the Old Bailey in February 1652 on a charge of bewitching a child; and *Mr. William Lilly's History of his Life* (2nd ed., pp. 73–5, 115, 116) shows that he was involved in a witchcraft charge in 1654.

Over the country as a whole indictments for witchcraft have never been so widespread before or since the period of Cromwell's supremacy. Hardly a county in England or Wales was without at least one during the six years in question. Many shires of the West which never before had indictments that have left any record now had them for the first time. Thus there is little in the proceedings of the courts anywhere in England to suggest that Cromwell either did, or attempted to do, anything to curb the zeal of witch-hunters.

§ 4. Another possible clue to the Lord Protector's attitude might be sought in the Press of the period when it was subject to his complete control. By an Act of the Rump (20th September 1649) it was ordered that 'no book or pamphlet treatise, sheet or sheet of news' should be published without a licence.[1] Six years later the Council was even more stringent. It ordered (28th August 1655) the appointment of commissioners to put in force the Act against unlicensed printing, and at the same time directed that no newspaper should be allowed to appear without a licence from the Secretary of State.[2] If, therefore, the Lord Protector had any misgivings about pamphlets, which had an enormous effect in propagating witch-mania, it might well be expected that such pamphlets would cease during the period of his supremacy. In fact no such cessation occurred. On the contrary, a perusal of the *Catalogue of the Thomason Tracts* (London, 1908) for the years 1652–8 suggests that the output of terrifying pamphlets on witchcraft, diabolism, and kindred subjects was larger during this period than it was in any period of the same length either before or since, not excluding even the great output during the first five years of the Civil War. Moreover, apart from mere pamphlets, the Commonwealth witnessed the publication or republication of many of the weightiest volumes on witchcraft that have ever been produced in this country.

[1] S. R. Gardiner, *History of the Commonwealth and Protectorate*, vol. i, pp. 173–4 (London, 1903).
[2] Op. cit., bk. iii.

(*a*) It was in London in 1653 that Henry More (1614–87) published his *Antidote against Atheism*, in which he used witchcraft and magic as one of the weightiest of all his arguments for the existence of God. His collection of terrifying stories of witches and diabolical apparitions is one of the largest and most curious in all literature.[1] No story seemed too extravagant for More to accept and to defend with an impressive array of ingenuity and erudition. With the utmost gravity he referred to a certain ' Old Strangridge ' of Cambridge, who ' was carried over Shelford Steeple upon a black Hogge and tore his breeches upon the weather-cock '. He dealt at length with the contemporary case of Ann Bodenham, who was hanged at Salisbury the year his book was published (1653), and was at pains to argue that all the accusations against her were fully credible—including the making of magic circles and the raising of Beelzebub, Tormentor, Satan, and Lucifer to do her bidding, the observance of events in a distant house by means of a magic glass, and the existence of ' the Red Book, half wrote over with blood, being a catalogue of those that had sealed to the Devil ' that was now ' in Hampshire '.[1]

So far from being suppressed by the censorship, More's book was reissued within two years (1655) in a new edition ' corrected and enlarged: With an Appendix thereunto annexed '. Though More as a Platonist differed widely from Cromwell in his religious views, he was not regarded with disfavour. For he was offered the Mastership of Christ's College, Cambridge, of which he was a Fellow, the year after his book appeared (1654) ; and other preferments were pressed upon him.

(*b*) A learned defender of witch-hunting to whom the Lord Protector showed more signal favour was Meric Casaubon (1599–1671). In *A Treatise Concerning Enthusiasm* (London, 1656, p. 118) he touched lightly upon the subject, reserving a fuller treatment for his *True and Faithful Relation of what passed for many yeers Between Dr John Dee and Some Spirits*, which was published (1659) the year after Cromwell's death. In the preface to this latter book he admits that

> this Licentious Age will afford many . . . who . . . when they hear of so many Spirits as are here mentioned, and so many strange Apparitions . . . will be ready to laugh at any other that give credit to such things . . . Were we to argue the case by Scripture, the business would soon be at an end ; there being no controverted

[1] Op. cit., bk. iii, ch. vii.

point among men, that I know of, that can receive a more Ample, Full, Clear and speedy determination, than this business of *Spirits*, and *Witches*, and *Apparitions* may if the Word of God might be Judge.

Granted that there have been impostures and mistakes in the history of witchcraft, he argues, the same thing is true also of medical science, but that does not induce one to dispense with medical aid in case of illness.   The general consensus of men in all ages supports a belief in the reality of witchcraft.

I do very much wonder that any man being a Scholar, and not strongly prepossessed, that doth not believe in *Spirits* &c. can say that he ever read the books of Tryals and Confessions of Witches and Wizards, such I mean, as have been written by learned and judicious men.   Such as, for example, I account *Nichol. Remigius* [1] his *Demonolatria* . . . grounded especially upon the Confessions and Condemnations of no less than 900 men and women in *Lorraine* within the compass of a few years.   That he was a learned man, I think no body will deny that hath read him; and that he was no very credulous and superstitious man (though a Papist) that also is most certain: and I have wondered at his liberty many times.   I know not how it is now in those places; but by what I have read and heard of the doings of Witches and Sorcerers in *Geneva* and *Savoy* in former times (I could say somewhat of myself, how my life was preserved there very strangely,[2] but my witnesses are not, and I will not bring their credit into question for such a businesse) I am of opinion That he that should have maintained that there was no such thing as Witches and Spirits, etc. would have been thought by most either mad or brain-sick (so frequent and visible were the effects to sober eyes) or a Witch himself.

(*c*) Though Casaubon differed from Cromwell both in politics and religion, the Lord Protector viewed him with the utmost favour.   As early as 1649 he invited him to come and 'confer about matters of moment'.   Cromwell's purpose was to induce him to 'write a history of the late war, desiring withal that nothing but matters of fact should be impartially set down'. When Meric declined with the candid excuse that 'he would be forced to make such reflections as would be ungrateful, if not injurious, to his lordship', Cromwell persisted in his request, and made out an order 'that upon the first demand three or four hundred pounds should be delivered to him by a London bookseller without acknowledging the benefactor'.   But Meric, who had made a wealthy marriage in 1651, did not avail himself of this

---

[1] Nicolas Remi (1554–1600) was *procureur général* to Duke Henry II of Lorraine.   His *Daemonolatreia* was published at Lyons 1595 . . . 4⁰.   It is quoted in Ch. III, § 4 (*b*).
    [2] Meric Casaubon was born at Geneva (1599).

munificence. Finally, he received a message to the effect that ' if he would do as requested, the lieutenant general would restore him all his father's books, which were then in the royal library, having been purchased by King James, and would give him a patent for £300 a year, to be paid so long as the youngest son of Dr. Casaubon should live '. Such an urgent desire that posterity should see the Civil War with the eyes of a notorious paladin of witch-beliefs hardly argues scepticism on Cromwell's part.[1]

Another opponent who was marked out for favour by the Lord Protector was Sir Matthew Hale (1609–76). Though he had been subjected to a thoroughly Puritan education, Hale had shown some Royalist sympathies during the Civil War. In spite of these Cromwell chose him as a Justice of the Common Pleas in 1654. It is scarcely possible that he could have been unaware of the strength of Hale's convictions about the terrific reality of witchcraft. For the new Justice was an outspoken man; and so strong were his convictions that, even after the Restoration had struck a severe blow to the witch-hunters' cause, he managed to secure the conviction and execution of several witches in various parts of England. At Bury St. Edmunds in March 1664/5, at the trial of Rose Cullender and Amy Duny, he allowed such experiments to be made in court and uttered such a charge as could only lead to a conviction by an East Anglian jury of the day.[2]

> That there were such creatures as witches he made no doubt at all; for, first, the Scriptures had affirmed so much. Secondly the wisdom of all nations had provided laws against such persons, which is an argument of their confidence of such a crime. . . .

[1] Menasseh ben Israel, with whom Cromwell negotiated for the re-admission of the Jews to England, was a propagandist for witch-beliefs of virtually unlimited credulity. His book, נשמת חיים (on the immortality of the soul) (Amsterdam, 1651), is written in unpointed Hebrew. But its contents may be fairly deduced from the Latin summary of its contents:

> Lib. iii. cap. 14. *Per sensus probatur, daemones esse ; imprimis cum experientia teste vivos obsident.* . . . *Item quomodo multorum morborum causa sit diabolus.* Cap. xvi. *De spiritibus incubis et succubis, varia exempla ex Zoare, et quomodo illud fiat.* Cap. xviii. *Qua arte fascinentur sponsi, ut cum sponsa congredi nequeant ; varia veterum exempla.* Cap. xix. *De novem Idolatriae speciebus, praecipue incantatione.* Cap. xxiv. *An Magi mutare se possint in animalium formas.* Cap. xxvi. *Quid sit, sagas, hariolos et mortuos consulere.* Cap. xxix. *Ostenditur, quomodo per nomina impurorum spirituum multa miranda patrentur. Eius rei multa insignia exempla.*

Cromwell granted Menasseh ben Israel an annual pension of £100. A. M. Hyamson, *History of the Jews in England*, p. 210 (London, 1908).
[2] *A Tryal of Witches at the Assizes held at Bury St. Edmunds . . . before Sir Matthew Hale* (1682).

A year later, at Lancaster, Hale [1] sentenced to death Isabel Rigby for bewitching two of her neighbours at Hindley (March 1666). Had Cromwell entertained any doubts about the reality of witchcraft he would scarcely have raised (1654) such a witch-hunter to the judicial bench. Whether by design or accident, Cromwell is found repeatedly to single out notorious witch-hunters—even those politically opposed to him—for especial favour and advancement.

§ 5. If the Lord Protector ever made even the faintest attempt in word or deed to curb the witch-mania, contemporaries were unaware of it. Thomas Ady in *A Candle in the Dark* (London, 1655) made an attempt to diminish the prevailing credulity by casting doubt upon the authorship of the *Daemonologie* (p. 140). 'Whether this Work was either composed by King *James*, or by the Bishop,[2] may well be suspected, or rather,' he suggests, ' by some *Scotish* man, blinded by *Scotish* Mist, who desired to set forth his own Tenents for the upholding of Popish errours.' If Ady were prepared to go these lengths in his attempt to discredit the witch-mania, he would doubtless have insinuated, had there been the slightest suspicion of such a thing, that the Lord Protector was opposed to witch-hunting.

He does nothing of the kind. On the contrary, he deplores in forcible language the vast increase in credulity that had marked the last few years (pp. 114–15) :—

> And people are now so infected with this damnable Heresie, of ascribing to the power of Witches, that seldom hath a man the hand of God against him in his estate, or health, or body, or any way, but presently he cryeth out of some poor innocent Neighbour, that he or she hath bewitched him; for, saith he, such an old man or woman came lately to my door, and desired some relief, and I denied it, and God forgive me my heart did rise against her at that time, my mind gave me she looked like a Witch, and presently my Child, my Wife, my Self, my Horse, my Cow, my Sheep, my Sow, my Hogge, my Dogge, my Cat, or somewhat was thus and thus handled, in such a strange manner, as I dare swear she is a Witch, or else how should those things be, or come to pass? seldom goeth any man or woman to a Physician for cure of any disease, but one question they ask a Physician is, Sir, do you think this Party is in ill handling, or under an ill tongue? or more plainly, Sir, do you not think the Party

---

[1] Ewen, *Witchcraft and Demonianism*, p. 411 (London, 1933). The other judge on this occasion was Sir Richard Rainsford, Baron of the Exchequer. Hale, as his superior, would probably try the more important criminal cases.

[2] The Bishop of Winchester.

is bewitched? and to this man an ignorant Physician will answer, Yes, verily; the reason is, *Ignorantiae pallium maleficium et incantatio,* a cloak for the Physicians ignorance, when he cannot find the nature of the Disease, he saith, the Party is bewitched.[1]

During Cromwell's period of supremacy many of the Anglican clergy of Charles I's reign had been ejected from their livings.[2] In their place were Puritan ministers largely under the control of the Government. If, therefore, the Lord Protector had disapproved of witch-hunting, he could have used them as an indirect means of influencing public opinion. It is clear that he never attempted to do so; for the Puritan ministers, according to Ady, took the lead [3] in intensifying the witch-mania (p. 126):—

> It is, and hath been, the manner of these latter Ages [he wrote] for a Minister to go to such, and instead of instructing them . . . they urge them to lying Confessions . . . let but any man that is wise, and free from prejudice, go and hear but the Confessions that are so commonly alleged, and he may see with what catching, and cavelling, what thwarting and lying, what flat and plain Knavery these confessions are wrung from poor innocent people, and what monstrous additions and multiplications are afterwards invented to make the matter seem true, which yet is most damnably false.

This description of the methods used by ministers to wring confessions from suspects is abundantly corroborated elsewhere.

The tradition that Cromwell himself on the morning of the battle of Worcester ' had a conference personally with the Devil,

---

[1] Francis Osborn (1593–1659), a supporter of the Cromwellian régime, makes a similar comment on the frequency of witch executions in his *Advice to a Son* (1656) '. . . and *Witches so abound,* as seems by their frequent Executions, which makes me think the strongest Fascination is incircled within the *ignorance* of the Judges, *malice* of the Witnesses, or stupidity of the poor Parties accused ' (pt. i, v, § 28).

[2] Professor Whiting (*Studies in English Puritanism from the Restoration to the Revolution 1660–88,* p. 9, London, 1931) estimates the number of parish priests ejected at about 3,500 out of a total under 11,000. Those not ejected were probably Puritans already before the Rebellion.

[3] Even William Lilly, the almanack-maker, had his life jeopardized by two Cromwellian ministers. *William Lilly's History of his Life and Times* (London, 1715), pp. 73–4: ' In 1655 I was indicted at *Hicks's Hall* by a half-witted young Woman. . . . The Cause of the Indictment was, For that I had given Judgment upon stollen Goods, and received 2s. 6d.—And this was said to be contrary to an Act in King *James's* Time made. . . . This mad woman was put upon this Action against me by two Ministers, who had framed for her a very ingenious Speech, which she could speak without book . . . I spoke for myself . . . that the Study of Astrology was lawful, and not contradicted by any Scripture; that I neither had nor ever did, use any, Charms, Sorceries or Inchantments related in the Bill of Indictment, &c.'

with whom he made a contract ' [1] may have been created after his death. But it was probably founded upon the current gossip of his day. The Presbyterians, who disliked him as a ' sectary ', would be prone to accuse him, as they did their other enemies, of covenanting with the Devil. It is chiefly of interest as one of the many instances of the boundless credulity that affected even the most highly placed officials of Commonwealth England.[2]

§ 6. The view that Cromwell differed from his relatives, friends, comrades in arms, and co-religionists on the subject of witchcraft rests on nebulous foundations. The whole atmosphere in which he lived from the cradle to the grave, no less than the things done during the period of his supremacy, makes it almost impossible. In the circumstances the burden of proof should fairly rest upon those who assert his scepticism in the matter of witchcraft. Cromwell was not made of the same stuff as typical revolutionaries. He smarted under no great personal wrong. He was fairly prosperous in his possessions and genial amongst his numerous friends. His family life was a singularly happy one. He was not grasping or covetous. He was not ambitious. He was profoundly conservative in his outlook. Why, then, did he push the quarrel with his King to such an extremity of implacable vengeance as to shock all Europe and to ruin ultimately the cause for which he had fought? The answer lies clearly in his religious convictions; and that these convictions were affronted by Charles I's protection of witches is in a high degree probable, although no word of his can be quoted to this effect. That he did not pass his whole life in a frenzy of terror about witches, as did many of his Presbyterian opponents, may readily be admitted. But that he took witch-belief as a matter of course and without question is the conclusion most consonant with the evidence available.

[1] The story is given in full in Laurence Echard, *History of England*, 3rd ed., pp. 691 sqq. (London, 1720). Echard derived it from the *History of Independency*. W. C. Abbott, *Writings and Speeches of Oliver Cromwell*, vol. ii, p. 458 (Harvard Univ. Press, 1939).

[2] For examples see F. A. Inderwick, *The Interregnum*, pp. 130 sqq. (London, 1891). It was during the Protectorate that Richard Baxter received many letters describing examples of witchcraft. R. Baxter's *Certainty of the World of Spirits*, pp. 22–38 and 128–46, &c. (London, 1691).

CHAPTER X

CONCLUSION

§ 1. THE WITCH-TERROR did not suddenly disappear with the Restoration, because the Restoration restored so little. In an age when the ownership of land meant the possession of power, Royalists, who had sold their estates under the Commonwealth in order to pay their fines, did not recover them; and the Puritans who had bought them remained in possession after the Restoration.[1] Thus Puritanism was reinforced amongst the landed families at the expense of High Anglicanism. At the same time a large number of Puritan ministers who had been intruded into livings during the Rebellion conformed to the rites of the Anglican Church[2] and, thus, increased for a time the Puritan tendencies amongst the Anglican clergy. Moreover, a large number of officials of the Commonwealth and Protectorate continued to hold office under the restored Stuarts. Amongst them were several judges, or barristers subsequently promoted to the Bench, such as John Arthur,[3] who condemned Julian Cox for witchcraft at Taunton in 1663; Sir Matthew Hale,[4] who passed sentence upon Amy Duny and Rose Cullender at Bury St. Edmunds[5] in

[1] H. E. Chesney, 'The Transference of Lands in England 1640–60'. (In *Transactions of the Royal Historical Society*, 4th Series, vol. xv, 1932, pp. 181 sqq.)

[2] The number of Puritan ministers who vacated their livings on St. Bartholomew's Day 1662 has been variously estimated. See C. E. Whiting, *Studies in English Puritanism*, pp. 9 sqq. (London, 1931). But there is little doubt that the great majority conformed. Thus, for example, in Monmouthshire eighty-eight Royalist priests were ejected from their livings during the Rebellion, and only five of them were reinstated at the Restoration. The number of ministers ejected in 1662 was only eleven. It therefore appears that about seventy-two of them conformed. See W. N. Johns, *Historical Traditions and Facts Relating to the County of Monmouth* (Newport, 1885). Substantially similar figures survive for the Diocese of Exeter. For the County of Essex see H. Smith, *The Ecclesiastical History of Essex under the Long Parliament and Commonwealth* (Colchester, 1932).

[3] Arthur had been a member of Cromwell's ' Parliament ' of 1656 and had been made a law serjeant in 1658.

[4] Hale had always been a Puritan. He had been made Justice of Common Pleas by Oliver Cromwell in 1654 and had been a member of Cromwell's ' Parliament ' of the same year.

[5] *A Tryal of Witches at the Assizes held at Bury St Edmonds for the County of Suffolk on the Tenth day of March 1664, before Sir Matthew Hale Kt., &c.*, 1682.

181

1664/5; Sir Richard Rainsford,[1] who tried Anne Tilling and Judith Witchell at Salisbury in 1671/2, and Sir Thomas Raymond,[2] who condemned Temperance Lloyd at Exeter [3] as late as August 1682.

Thus witch-mania died hard. Nevertheless with the revival of Stuart Royalism [4] and the notable decline of Calvinism it rapidly relaxed its hold upon the more educated classes. The figures for the Home Circuit are significant.[5] Between 1658 and 1667 twenty-three persons were indicted for witchcraft and one of them hanged. Between 1668 and 1677 twelve persons were indicted and none was hanged—nor, indeed, were any ever hanged henceforth for witchcraft. No witchcraft trial took place in Middlesex after 1670.[6] Judges with Royalist traditions gradually overcame the superstitions that had taken such deep roots during the era of the Great Rebellion. Francis North,[7] Sir John Reresby, John Kelyng,[8] the much-maligned Sir George Jefferies, Edward Herbert, and Sir John Powell constantly saved those accused of witchcraft by exposing the deceptions of their accusers much as Charles I's judges had done. Above all, Sir John Holt,[9] whose early life had been a scandal to the Puritans, is known to have secured an acquittal in no fewer than eleven witch trials. At the same time Justices of the Peace grew more chary of sending accused witches to the Assize Courts. Also the Puritans who had become Anglican clergy in 1660 gradually diminished, and their witch-beliefs with them. Such beliefs became more and more derided and their defenders increasingly on the defensive. At

---

[1] Rainsford had been Recorder of Northampton under the Protectorate since 1653.

[2] Raymond was son of Robert Raymond of Bowers-Giffard in Essex. He was called to the Bar during the Protectorate (11th February 1656).

[3] For details see *Life of Sir Francis North* (1742), p. 130.

[4] F. Hutchinson, *Historical Essay concerning Witchcraft* (London, 1718): 'About that Time [1679], one condemned at Ely, but reprieved by King *Charles II* and afterwards the Fellow that pretended to have been bewitched, was hanged at *Chelmsford* in *Essex*, and confess'd that he had counterfeited his Fits and Vomitings, as I have been informed'.

[5] C. L'E. Ewen, *Witch Hunting and Witch Trials*, p. 99 (London, 1929).

[6] W. Notestein, *Witchcraft in England 1558–1718*, p. 278 (Washington, 1911).

[7] Roger North, *Life of the Rt. Hon. Francis North, Baron of Guilford* (London, 1742).

[8] Kelyng had been a devoted Royalist during the Great Rebellion. Clarendon described him to Charles II as 'a person of eminent learning, eminent suffering, never wore his gown after the Rebellion, but was always in gaol'. He himself on his being made a judge in 1663 speaks of his 'twenty years' silence' (*Fasti Oxonienses*, vol. i, p. 404; *Keble*, p. 526).

[9] Notestein, op. cit.. p. 320: 'Without doubt Chief Justice Holt did more than any other man in English history to end the prosecution of witches'.

the beginning of the seventeenth century educated men believed in witchcraft and the ignorant were inclined to doubt. Before the end of the century educated men doubted and few besides the ignorant believed. Thus, for example, Joseph Glanvill in his *Philosophical Considerations touching the Being of Witches and Witchcraft* (London, 1667, 1st ed. 1666) admits that '*Men*, otherwise *witty* and *ingenious*, are fall'n into the conceit that there's *no such thing* as a *Witch* or *Apparition*, but that these are the *creatures* of *Melancholy* and *Superstition*, foster'd by *ignorance* and *design*. . . .' In his preface to another edition—that of 1668—Glanvill wrote: 'There is one *Argument* against me which is not to be dealt with, viz., a *mighty confidence* grounded upon *nothing*, that *swaggers* and *huffs* and swears that there are no WITCHES'. A dozen years later, in his Preface to the Second Part of *Sadducismus Triumphatus* (London, 1681), he wrote:

> Of all Relations of Fact, there are none like to give a Man such trouble and disreputation, as those that relate to Witchcraft and Apparitions, which so great a party of men (in this age especially) do so railly and laugh at, and without more ado, are resolved to explode and despise, as meer Winter Tales·and Old Wives Fables.

It is probable that the last execution in England for witchcraft took place at Exeter in March 1684/5,[1] though it is possible, but highly improbable, that there were executions for this offence at Northampton in 1705 and at Huntingdon in 1716.[2] The last persons committed for witchcraft were Jane Clerk of Great Wigston in Leicestershire, together with her son and daughter. At the Summer Sessions in Leicester in September 1717 the Grand Jury threw out the bills against them.

Though witch-hunting in the later Stuart period was clearly a lost cause, it found men of considerable energy and ability, such as Meric Casaubon, George Sinclair, Joseph Glanvil, Henry Hallywell, and Richard Baxter,[3] ready to wield their doughty

---

[1] The witch was Alicia Molland, condemned to death by Sir Creswell Levinz. Ewen, *Witchcraft and Demonianism*, pp. 129 and 444 (London, 1933). Sir Creswell (1627–1701) was admitted a sizar at Trinity College, Cambridge, in 1648, and later entered Gray's Inn. What part he took during the Commonwealth and Protectorate is unknown. He acted for the prosecution in the alleged 'Popish Plot' of 1679. He was made a judge in 1681, but discharged—for what reason is unknown—by James II in 1686.

[2] On this see W. Notestein, *A History of Witchcraft in England 1558–1718*, pp. 375 sqq. (Washington, 1911).

[3] For these see the Bibliography. Henry Hallywell (1640–1703) had been a Fellow of Christ's College, Cambridge. He was Rector of Slaugham (1679–92) and Prebendary of Chichester (1690–1703).

pens in its defence. Their opponents, who had the future on their side, were markedly inferior in originality and literary skill. Two only are worthy of notice, John Wagstaffe and John Webster.

(a) *The Question of Witchcraft Debated* first appeared in 1669, and was reissued in a second and enlarged edition, to meet the opposition [1] it had aroused, in 1671. The author, John Wagstaffe (1633–77), of Oriel College, Oxford, was described by a contemporary as ' a little crooked man, and of despicable presence '. He is said to have injured his health by the ' continued bibbing of strong and high-tasted liquors ' and to have died ' in a manner distracted '. Much of his book follows the beaten track in showing that the Bible ' hath been falsely translated in those places which speak of Witchcraft ' and ' that the Opinion of Witches hath had its foundation in Heathen Fables '. Most stories of witches, the argument continues, are ' founded partly in the juggling delusions of confederated impostors, and partly again in the errors or rediculous mistakes of vulgar rumours: Just as in the. city of *London,* hath been confidently reported to be attempted by a Fire-ball, when a poor Link-boy knocking of his Link, had left part of its flames blazing in a door ' (1st ed., p. 62).

Finally Wagstaffe appeals (1st ed., p. 79) to humanity :—

> We stand in need of another *Hercules Liberator,* who as the former freed the World from humane Sacrifices, should in like manner travel from Country to Country, and by his all-commanding Authority, free it from this evil and base custome of torturing people to confess themselves Witches, and burning them after extorted Confessions. Surely the blood of men ought not to be so cheap, nor so easily to be shed, by such who under the Name of God, do gratifie exorbitant passion and selfish ends; for without question, under this side Heaven, there is nothing so sacred as the life of man. . . .

(b) *The Displaying of Supposed Witchcraft, Wherein is affirmed that there are many sorts of Deceivers and Impostors* appeared in 1677 in the form of a folio of some 350 pages. Its author, John Webster (1610–82) (not to be confused with the dramatist of the same names), had been everything by turns and nothing long— Anglican parson, schoolmaster, chaplain to a Roundhead army, and famous preacher. Later he recoiled from Puritanism and had his property seized by the Protectorate Government (1657). He then devoted himself to the study of metallurgy, and later to medicine. Like Wagstaffe, he refutes the Scriptural arguments in

---

[1] It was assailed by Meric Casaubon in the second part of *Credulity and Incredulity* (1670) and by ' R. T.' in *The Opinion of Witchcraft Vindicated* (1670).

favour of witch-belief and stresses the likelihood of imposture. But, unlike Wagstaffe, he admits belief in stories of apparitions, and gives so many gruesome examples that the total effect of his volume as an antidote to superstition is rather dubious.[1]

(c) Two notable men of this period have sometime been cited [2] as examples of witch-believers who, contrary to the general rule, were anti-Puritans and Royalists. They are Robert Boyle (1627–91), the famous scientist, and George Hickes (1642–1715), the Non-juror. Boyle is scarcely a sound example. True, he believed in witchcraft. He subscribed publicly to the truth of the stories of the ' demon of Mascon ' published by François Perreaud, the Calvinist pastor of Thoiry (Geneva, 1653). But can he be fairly described as especially anti-Calvinist or Royalist? Much of his early education was entrusted to a native of Geneva named Marcombes, who became his friend and confidant. During his continental travels (1638–44) he spent nearly two years at Geneva, and from about the time of that visit he always dated his religious ' conversion '. During the greater part of his adult life he was governor of the Corporation for the Spread of the Gospel in New England. On his return from his travels in 1644, at the height of the First Civil War, he showed few signs of Royalism and, later, acquiesced comfortably in the Commonwealth and Protectorate. His letters to his sister, Lady Ranelagh, show him busily immersed in his chemical experiments at the time of the execution of Charles I. After the Restoration he expressed disapproval of the Penal Laws against nonconformists. It would surely be an over-statement to describe such a man ás an enthusiastic Royalist or anti-Puritan.

George Hickes may be a sounder example of an exception to the general rule. Both his conduct and his utterances show him to have been a consistent high churchman and Royalist throughout his life.[3] At school at Northallerton in Yorkshire during the Protectorate he was taught strongly Royalist views. At St. John's College, Oxford (1659), he fell foul of the Puritan President Thankful Owen. Finally he became a Non-juror, sacrificing his

---

[1] Kittredge, *Witchcraft in Old and New England*, pp. 343 sqq. (Cambridge, Mass., 1929). Webster does not completely deny the existence of witches. He only denies the more extravagant statements about their powers.

[2] Kittredge, *ibid.*, pp. 336 sqq. (Cambridge, Mass., 1929).

[3] His elder brother, John Hickes (1633–85), was a nonconformist divine. He was executed at Taunton for participation in Monmouth's Rebellion. See *English Historical Review*, October 1887, pp. 752–4.

rich ecclesiastical preferments to his loyalty to the legitimate Stuart line. His alleged views on witchcraft are to be found in a short work with a long title: ' *Ravillac Redivivus*, being a Narrative of the late Tryal of Mr James Mitchell a Conventicle-Preacher, who was executed the 18th of January last, for an attempt which was made on the Sacred Person of the Archbishop of St Andrew's. To which is Annexed, An Account of the Tryall of that most wicked *Pharisee* Major Thomas Weir, who was Executed for Adultery, Incest and Bestiality. In which are many Observable Passages, especially relating to the present affairs of *Church* and *State* ' (London, 1678).

In this the author writes (p. 64) of Jane, the sister of the notorious Major Weir:—

> The sum of *Jane* his Sisters Libel is reducible to these two Heads. First to a charge of Incest, which she committed with her Brother; and Secondly, to the charge of Sorcery, and Witchcraft, but most especially in consulting Witches, Necromancers and Devils; and yet more particularly for keeping and conversing with a Familiar Spirit, while she liv'd at *Dalkeith*, which she us'd to spin extraordinary quantities of Yarn for her, in a shorter time than three or four Women could have done the same. All which she judicially confessed in the Face of the court.

Of Major Weir it states (p. 66) :—

> Thus far I have given you a *juridical* Account of the detestable crimes of this Hypocritical and Monstrous Man; I now proceed to acquaint you with other particulars, no less surprising than the former; which upon strict enquiry I have reason to believe to be true, as those that are juridically prov'd.

There follows a description of Weir's magic staff to which the writer adds:—

> *Apollonius Thyanaeus* had such a Magical Staff as this, which I believe was a Sacramental Symbol which the Devil gave to the Major, and the Court had some such apprehensions of it, for it was ordered by the Judges to be burnt with his body.

The book is generally supposed to have been written by Hicks at the request of the Duke of Lauderdale, to whom he was chaplain, in Scotland, though, curiously enough, it does not bear his name on the title-page or elsewhere.[1] It is merely

---

[1] Wood states that he suppressed his name from fear of Whig vengeance. *Athenae Oxonienses*, ed. Bliss (London, 1820), p. 566: ' he wrote and publish'd a book called *Ravillac Redivivus*, which occasion'd him (by some menaces given out) to disguise himself under a feigned name and character, to secure himself from the murderous Scottish whiggs '.

described as ' a Letter from a Scottish *to an* English *Gentleman* '. ' Scottish Gentleman ' is a curious pseudonym for Hickes, who was not a Scot. Nonetheless—assuming that he really was the author—was he writing his own personal views, or merely acting as amanuensis to Lauderdale? [1] (The chaplain was the usual amanuensis for a busy nobleman.) If the former alternative be true, then Hickes presents the rare—almost unique—example [2] of a Royalist high churchman who believed in witchcraft—and that at a time when witch-belief amongst educated men was rapidly waning. A sermon, *The Spirit of Enthusiasm Exorcised* (London, 1680), touches the fringe of witch-belief (pp. 18–19); so also does a letter of Hickes to Samuel Pepys (19th June 1700) dealing with Second Sight, elves, &c.

(*d*) The literature of Queen Anne's reign leaves no doubt that witchcraft had become a standing joke amongst educated people. To give one example out of many—Sir Richard Steele wrote in the *Tatler* (no. 21, 28th May 1709) :—

> Three young ladies of our town were indicted for witchcraft. One by spirits locked in a bottle and magic herbs drew hundreds of men to her; the second cut off by night the limbs of dead bodies and muttering words buried them; the third moulded pieces of dough into the shapes of men women and children and then heated them. They had nothing to say in their own defence but downright denying the facts, which is like to avail very little when they come upon their trials . . . The parson will believe nothing of all this; so that the whole town cries out: ' Shame! that one of his cast should be such an atheist.'

Nine years later *The Historical Essay concerning Witchcraft* (1718) of Francis Hutchinson [3] (1660–1739), perpetual curate of St. James's, Bury St. Edmunds, finally placed the rejection of witch-

---

[1] Lauderdale had been the rising hope of the Scottish Presbyterians during the Great Rebellion. He was a Hebrew scholar versed in rabbinical lore (Hearne, *Collections*, 1886, vol. i, p. 268). Thus he had the characteristics which were usually accompanied by a strong belief in witchcraft.

[2] Isaac Barrow (1630–77), the mathematician, another Royalist, used witchcraft, after the manner of the Cambridge Platonists, as an argument against atheism, though he admits that witch-beliefs are subject to much fraud and delusion.

[3] He was made Bishop of Down and Connor in 1721.

He argues in his Preface that witch-beliefs were still widespread amongst the common people, who were much influenced by books in defence of these beliefs (p. xiv): ' These Books and Narratives are in Tradesmen's Shops and Farmers' Houses, and are read with great Eagerness, and are continually levening the Minds of the Youth, who delight in such Subjects; and considering what sore Evils these Notions bring when they prevail, I hope no Man will think but they must still be combated, oppos'd and kept down '.

beliefs upon the solid basis of historical research and critical analysis. Within twenty years of its publication an Act of Parliament (9 Geo. II, 1736) made it no longer possible to condemn persons to the gallows for witchcraft.

(*e*) This Act repeals the Acts of James I and of Mary I of Scotland, and further enacts that

> no Prosecution, Suit or Proceeding, shall be commenced or carried on against any person or Persons for Witchcraft, Sorcery, Inchantment, or Conjuration, or for charging another with any such offence, in any Court whatsoever in *Great Britain*
>
> IV. And for the more effectual preventing and punishing any pretences to such arts and powers as are before-mentioned, whereby ignorant persons are frequently deluded and defrauded; be it further enacted . . . that if any person shall . . . pretend to exercise or use any kind of Witchcraft, Sorcery, Inchantment, or Conjuration, or undertake to tell fortunes, or pretend from his or her skill or knowledge in any occult or crafty science to discover where or in what manner any Goods or Chattels, supposed to have been stolen or lost, may be found; every person so offending . . . shall for every such offence suffer imprisonment by the space of one whole year . . . and once in every quarter of the said year, in the market Town of the proper County, upon the market day, there stand openly on the Pillory for the space of one hour . . .

The Act met with little opposition from the literate classes, except for an anonymous pamphleteer, who published *The Witch of Endor ; or a Plea for the Divine Administration by the Agency of Good and Evil Spirits* (London, 1736).

§ 2 (*a*) But the witch-mania of the seventeenth-century Puritan, which had been so widely spread by the armies of the Great Rebellion, did not fail to leave an almost indelible mark upon the mass of illiterate people. Attacks by violent mobs upon reputed witches were a common feature of English life even as late as the Victorian era. A typical example for the middle of the eighteenth century (22nd April 1751) is related in some detail in the *Gentleman's Magazine*. The landlord of an inn at Tring in Hertfordshire

> giving out that he was bewitched by one Osborne and his wife, harmless people above 70, had it cried at several market towns that they were to be tried by ducking that day, which occasioned a vast concourse. The parish officers having removed the old couple from the Workhouse into the Church for security, the mob missing them, broke the Workhouse windows, pulled down the pales, and demolished part of the house; and, seizing the governor threatened to drown him and fire the town, having straw in their hands for the purpose.

The poor wretches were at length, for public safety, delivered up, stript stark naked by the mob, their thumbs tied to their toes, then dragged two miles, and thrown into a muddy stream. After much ducking and ill-usage, the old woman was thrown, quite naked on the bank, almost choaked with mud, and expired in a few minutes, being kick'd and beat with sticks even after she was dead; and the Man lies dangerously ill of his bruises.

The Coroner's inquest found about thirty of the mob guilty of wilful murder; and one of them, Thomas Colley, a chimney-sweep, was afterwards executed for murder and hung in chains.

In the records of mob violence against witches that have come down to us from comparatively recent times the technique of the Parliamentarian witch-finders of the Great Rebellion is regularly maintained—' swimming ', ' blooding ', and weighing her against the Bible. It is noticeable also that such violent outbursts are far more frequent in the south-east, which was the home of seven-teenth-century Puritanism, than in the traditionally Royalist parts of the country. Examples for the later eighteenth century so notable as to be recorded in the *Gentleman's Magazine* are as follows :—[1]

In 1759:—

One *Susanna Hannokes*, an elderly woman of *Wingrove* near *Aylesbury*, was accused by a neighbour of bewitching her spinning wheel, so that she could not make it go round, and offered to make an oath before a magistrate; on which the husband, in order to justify his wife, insisted on her being tried by the church bible, and that the accuser should be present: Accordingly she was conducted to the parish church, where she was stript of all her cloaths to her shift and under-coat, and weighed against the bible; when to the no small mortification of her accuser, she out-weighed it, and was honourably acquitted of the charge.

The following year at ' the General Quarter Sessions for *Leicester* two persons concerned in ducking for witches all the poor old women in *Glen* and *Burton Overy*, were sentenced to stand in the pillory twice, and to lie in jail one month '.

Two years later it is recorded that

A number of people surrounded the house of *John Pritchers*, of *West Langdon* in *Kent*, and under the notion of her bewitching one *Ladd*, a boy about 13 years old, dragged out his wife by violence, and compelled her to go to the said *Ladd's* father's house, about a mile from her own, where they forced her into the room where the boy

[1] The references are *Gentleman's Magazine*, 1759, p. 93; 1760, p. 346; 1762, p. 596; 1769, p. 506; 1776, p. 332; 1785, pt. ii, p. 658.

was, scratched her arms and face in a most cruel manner, to draw blood, as they said, of the witch, and then threatened to swim her; but some people of condition interposing the poor woman's life was happily preserved; and the persons concerned in carrying on the imposture, particularly one *Beard*, and *Ladd's* wife, being carried before a magistrate, and compelled to make satisfaction to the unhappy injured woman, the mob dispersed, and the country that was every where in tumult is again quieted. The boy pretended to void needles and pins from his body, and his father and mother upheld the deceit, and collected large sums of money of those whose compassion was excited by so melancholy a situation.

In 1769:—

Wm Adams of Granchester, and his wife, having being indicted at the quarter sessions for Cambridge, for the ill treatment of Phoebe Haly of Caldicot, a supposed witch, severally pleaded guilty, and having first agreed to pay the poor woman five guineas, the court fined the man 13*s*. 4*d*. and dismissed them both with a severe reprimand.

In 1776:—

A woman at Earls-hilton, in Leicestershire, being some time since seized with an uncommon disorder, her friends took it into their heads that she was bewitched by a poor old creature in the neighbourhood who could scarce crawl. To this miserable object the deseased, her husband and son, (a soldier) went, on the 20th past, and threatened to destroy her if she would not instantly suffer blood to be drawn from her body, bless the woman, and remove her disorder. Hesitating a little, the son drew his sword, and pointing it to her breast, swore that he would plunge it into her heart if she did not immediately comply, which being consented to, they all returned home seemingly satisfied. But the patient nor being relieved on the day of this article, they raised a mob, seized the old woman, dragged her to a pond, cruelly plunged her into the water, and were proceeding to practise the barbarous experiments upon her that were usual in times of ignorance and superstition, when fortunately for her, she was rescued from their hands by the humanity of the neighbouring gentlemen.

Nine years later comes the following item of news (1785):—

About the latter end of last month, a poor woman of Mear's Ashby Northamptonshire, being suspected of witchcraft, voluntarily offered herself for trial. The vulgar notion is, that a witch, if thrown into the water will *swim ;* but this poor woman, being thrown into a pond, sank instantly and was with difficulty saved. On which the cry was, *No witch ! No witch !*

(*b*) It is probable that the Methodist movement gave an impetus to mob violence against witches in the latter part of the eighteenth century and helped witch-beliefs to survive so late into the following century. For the movement was responsible for a great revival and extension of Calvinism amongst the less-educated classes. Also, John Wesley himself—almost alone in his day amongst men of his high intellectual and cultural level—repeatedly and emphatically affirmed his belief in the stern reality of witchcraft. He was connected through both father and mother with the Puritans of the seventeenth century; and many of his utterances suggest a Puritan born a century too late:—[1]

> It is true likewise, [he wrote] that the English in general, and indeed most of the men of learning in Europe, have given up all accounts of witches and apparitions as mere old wives' fables. I am sorry for it, and I willingly take this opportunity of entering my solemn protest against this violent compliment which so many that believe in the Bible pay to those who do not believe it. I owe them no such service. I take knowledge that these are at the bottom of the outcry which has been raised, and with such insolence spread throughout the nation, in direct opposition not only to the Bible, but to the suffrages of the wisest and best men of all ages and nations. They well know (whether Christians know it or not) that the giving up of witchcraft is in effect giving up the Bible.

In one of his letters he wrote: ' I have no doubt of the substance both of Glanvil's and Cotton Mather's narratives.' [2]

It would be extremely difficult to find educated Englishmen of this period who would have agreed with Wesley's downright profession of belief in witchcraft. The words of Sir William Blackstone (1723–80) in his *Commentaries* (iv, 60, Oxford 1775) have often been quoted :—

> To deny the possibility, nay, actual existence, of witchcraft and sorcery is at once flatly to contradict the revealed word of God . . . and the thing itself is a truth to which every nation in the world hath in its turn borne testimony.

But this is a much milder expression of opinion. It is concerned with witchcraft in older times and, as such, is akin to Dr. Johnson's

---

[1] W. E. H. Lecky, *History of England in the Eighteenth Century*, vol. ii, p. 593, 2nd ed. (London, 1879). See *John Wesley's Journal*, vol. iii, pp. 411 sqq. for the year 1770 (Everyman's Library).

Contrast the article on ' Witchcraft' in the First Edition of *Encyclopædia Britannica*, vol. iii (London, 1773), where it is stated that it is ' a kind of sorcery, especially in women, in which it is ridiculously supposed that an old woman by entering into contract with the devil, is enabled, in many instances to change the course of nature. . . . In times of ignorance and superstition, many severe laws were made against witches. . . .'

[2] Wesley, however, was far from being a Calvinist, though his theological position changed from time to time.

view, expressed in reply to Andrew Crosbie's suggestion that
'an Act of Parliament put an end to witchcraft'.

> No, sir, witchcraft had ceased; and therefore an Act of Parlia-
> ment was passed to prevent persecution for what was not witch-
> craft.   Why it ceased we cannot tell, as we cannot tell the reason
> of many other things.[1]

To find anything really on a par with Wesley's robust credulity
at this period it is necessary to go to a much more obscure person—
viz., Edmund Jones, a Monmouthshire Independent minister who
had come under the influence of the Methodist Revival,[2] and who
published in 1779 *A Geographical, Historical, and Religious Account
of the Parish of Aberystruth, in the County of Monmouth.*[3]   Jones was
familiar with the leading witchcraft writers of the seventeenth
century, and gives many examples of 'spirits of hell' appearing
in his native parish of Aberystruth, in which he, like his father
and mother, underwent the experience of 'conversion'.   Amongst
the many apparitions narrated, one that he personally saw is
curiously suggestive of a coven or a witches' sabbat.

> If any think [he wrote (pp. 75–6)] I am too credulous in these
> relations, and speak of things of which I myself have had no ex-
> perience, I must let them know they are mistaken; for when a very
> young boy, going with my aunt, Elizabeth Roger, my mother's
> sister, in the day time, somewhat early in the morning, but after
> sun rising, from Havodavel towards my father's house, at Pen y
> Llwyn, at the end of the upper field of Kae yr Keven,[4] by the way-
> side which we were passing, I saw the likeness of a sheepfold with a
> door towards the south, and over the door, instead of a lintel, the
> resemblance of a dried branch of a tree, I think of a hazel tree;
> and within the fold a company of many people; some sitting down,
> and some going in and coming out, bowing their heads as they passed
> under the branch.   It seemed to me as if they had been lately
> dancing, and that there was a musician amongst them.   Among the
> rest, over against the door, I well remember the resemblance of a
> fair woman with a high crown hat, and a red jacket, who made a

---

[1] James Boswell, *Journal of a Tour to the Hebrides*, Monday, 16th August
(1st ed., 1785).

[2] He revised Dr. Gillias's *Memoirs of the Life of the Rev. G. Whitfield* (London,
1772, &c.).   His revised edition was published in 1812.

[3] Published at Trevecka (i.e., Trefecca).   Trefecca House was the residence
of Howel Harris (1713–73), one of the founders of Calvinistic Methodism,
and also of the Countess of Huntingdon, who made Tredustan Court, in the
neighbourhood, a college for teachers of 'the connection'.   Aberystruth is
Blaina, which was in the large parish of Llanwenarth, near Abergavenny.

[4] 'Cae yr cefn' would mean in Welsh 'field of the ridge'.   But, may not
'Keven' be a corruption of 'Coven'?   If so, the place would be a traditional
site of a witches' sabbat.

better appearance than the rest, and whom I think they seemed to honour: I have still a pretty clear idea of her white face and well formed countenance. The men wore white cravats; and I always think they were the perfect resemblance of persons who lived in the world before my time; for there is a resemblance of their form and countenances still remaining in my mind.

After his death another collection of his was published at Newport, Monmouthshire, in 1813, under the title, *A Relation of Apparitions of Spirits, in the County of Monmouth, and the Principality of Wales : with other notable relations from England : together with observations about them, and instructions from them : designed to confute and prevent the infidelity of denying the being and Apparition of Spirits ; which tends to Irreligion and Atheism.*[1]

Of the origin and purpose of the book, he says in the Preface :—

> I have this to say, as it appears in diverse places in the ensuing Treatise, that my conversation about these things was with religious persons, many of them Ministers of the Gospel, from whom I had these accounts.[2]

In the course of his relations he regrets the passing of the Witch-craft Act of 1736.

> Had His Majesty King George the II read the history of Witch-craft, and known as much as we do in some parts of Wales, he would not have called upon his Parliament to determine that there are no such thing as Witches, and his parliament would hardly have com-plimented him therein. (p. 25.)

His story of Lewis Thomas, the father of Thomas Lewis, 'the famous preacher of the Gospel of *Lanharan* in Glamorganshire' has something of the authentic seventeenth-century flavour about it. One night he and his wife, who had lately quarrelled with a couple of gipsies,

> heard like a bowl rowling above stairs, from the upper end of the chamber to the middle of the room—stopping awhile—then rowling down to the foot of the stairs; upon which Lewis Thomas said to his wife ' I believe the old Gipsy is come to give thee a visit.' Next morning when she arose, she saw, on the floor the print of a bare foot without a toe,—dipped in soot and gone from the foot of the stairs

[1] He had already published *A Relation of Ghosts and Apparitions, which Commonly Appear in the Principality of Wales* (Bristol, 1767).

[2] The third edition of *Encyclopædia Britannica* (vol. xviii, Edinburgh, 1797) in its article on ' Witchcraft ' says, rather optimistically: ' It would be ridiculous to attempt a serious refutation of the existence of witches; and at present, luckily, the task is unnecessary. In this country at least, the dis-couragement long given to all suspicion of witchcraft, and the repeal of the statutes against the crime, have very much weakened, though perhaps they have not entirely eradicated, the persuasion '.

towards the door.   The next day they went to the churn, the cream soon began to froth as if it was turning to butter, but it did not though they churned much; they at length poured it into a vessel, where, after it had stayed some time, came a thick slimy cream above, and underneath it was water coloured with a little milk.   They boiled the cream—having a notion that it would torment the Witch, and they were no more disturbed that way.

This was no Apparition, but the malicious trick of an old Witch in compact with the Devil.   The fashionable incredulity is to deny the being of Witches.   I am not certain whether they deny that there ever were such persons in the world or that there were none at present.   If they deny that there ever were such things as Witches, the Scripture of truth is against them (pp. 17–18).

The whole book is of especial interest as one of the last of the long series produced by Puritan witch-hunters ever since the accession of Queen Elizabeth.   Wales, which appears to have been comparatively free from witch-terrors in earlier times, became one of the last strongholds of witch-belief after the coming of the Methodists.

One more strenuous assertion of the reality of witchcraft appeared as late as 1821, the occasion being the repeal of the Irish Statute of 1587, which had been allowed to linger on into the nineteenth century.   It took the form of a tractate by an anonymous writer, suggested by internal evidence to have belonged to the Anglican Evangelical movement, which was one of the offshoots of the Methodist revival.   Its title is a good index to its contents: *Antipas ; a Solemn Appeal to the Right Reverend the Archbishops and Bishops . . . with reference to several bills passed, or passing through the Imperial Parliament ; especially that concerning Witchcraft and Sorcery* (London, 1821).   The first and larger portion of the work is addressed to the prelates and argues that Acts of Parliament in relief of dissenters have resulted in the growth of ' Popery and Infidelity '.

There is [it proceeds (p. 17)] another and more desperate enemy still, the parent and instigator of the other two, against whose extra-ordinary machinations the defenders of the faith will be called to contend, even against the ' Ruler of the Darkness of this World '; he has another instrument of assault (the most dangerous because the least suspected) which a Christian soldier must be prepared to resist, not by weapons of modern philosophy, or modern history, but by putting on the whole armour of God.

' This instrument, my Lords, is SORCERY or WITCH-CRAFT.'   There follows a long catena of the familiar witchcraft passages of Scripture from Exodus xxii. 18 to Revelation xviii. 23 (pp. 18–25). From the Bishops the writer turns to the House of Lords, who had recently passed the Bill repealing the Act against Witchcraft for Ireland. An account of the proceedings is quoted from *The New Times :* ' This bill was read a third time, and passed. Lord —— observed that midnight was a most appropriate time to pass such a measure (*laughter*) '. Such a flippant attitude the writer profoundly deprecates (p. 36) :—

> As the word of God, which cannot lie, declares witchcraft to be one of his instruments of delusion, and calls ' the well-favoured harlot THE MISTRESS OF WITCHCRAFTS that selleth nations'; —as the *divine* law punished that sin with death, and nations addicted to it with destruction; such offences, I must deem not unworthy of the notice of *human* legislators, and no matter of MIDNIGHT MERRIMENT in a Christian senate.

Curiously enough, this tractate appeared only nine years before the publication of Sir Walter Scott's *Letters on Demonology and Witchcraft* (1830), about which the author remarks :—

> Even the present fashion of the world seems to be ill suited for studies of this fantastic nature; and the most ordinary mechanic has learning sufficient to laugh at the figments which in former times were believed by persons far advanced in the deepest knowledge of the age.

That Scott overrated the scepticism of the mass of the people there can be no doubt. The frequency of popular outbursts of witch-mania in many parts of Great Britain showed few signs of decrease for several generations after his time.

(*c*) (i) To what extent the Methodist movement may have tended to perpetuate witch-mania amongst the common people it is impossible to say. It is, however, noticeable that those parts of England in which the movement took deepest root—viz., Somerset, Devon, and Cornwall—have been distinguished during the past hundred years for the vitality of their popular witch-beliefs. Out of the many recorded examples a few are worth noticing. A resident at Bridgwater in Somerset [1] wrote in 1853 :—

> I was lately informed by a member of my congregation that two children living near his house were bewitched. I made enquiries into the matter, and found that witchcraft is by far less uncommon than I had imagined . . . A cottager who does not live five minutes walk from my house, found his pig seized with a strange and

---

[1] *Notes and Queries*, 1st Series, vol. vii, pp. 613–14, 25th June 1853.

unaccountable disorder. He . . . immediately went to a white witch (a gentleman who drives a flourishing trade in this neighbourhood). He received his directions and went home and implicitly followed them . . . lancing each foot and both ears of the pig, he allowed the blood to run into a piece of common dowlas.[1] Then taking two large pins he pierced the dowlas in opposite directions . . . entered his cottage . . . placed the bloody rag upon the fire . . . and reading a few verses of the Bible, waited till the dowlas was burned . . . Some time ago a lane in this town began to be looked upon with a mysterious awe, for every evening a strange white rabbit would appear . . . and . . . disappear . . . At last a large party of bold-hearted men . . . were successful enough to find the white rabbit in a garden . . . one of these caught the white rabbit by the ears.

The rabbit on being kicked immediately disappeared.

The old woman whom all suspected, was laid up in her bed for three days afterwards, unable to walk about: all in consequence of the kick she had received in the shape of a white rabbit.

The Ilfracombe Gazette for 6th May 1893 made the following report:—

At the Yeovil Borough Petty Sessions on Tuesday Frederick Terrell, a 'bus driver, was bound over in his own recognisance of £10 to keep the peace for six months for having threatened Harriett Carew on March 24th. The defendant had gone to the complainant, accused her of being an ' old witch ' and asked her to take a spell off his sister. He said he would beat her brains out and throw her over a wall if she would come out of her house. He also accused her of staying up all night and burning stuff with which to bewitch people. Since then people had called ' witch ' after her in the streets.

Cases of witch-belief in Devonshire are frequently to be found in the newspapers. *The Standard* for 16th February 1888 gives a typical example:—

A case of alleged witchcraft came before the Totnes magistrates, yesterday. A cab proprietor named Heard summoned his son for threatening his life, and accusing him of bewitching his (the son's) daughter. In his defence the son said his father had bewitched his daughter, the result being that she had suffered for months with chronic disease in the arms. He took her to several Plymouth doctors, and spent over £50 in endeavouring to have her cured. She next went into a hospital, where it was advised that the arm should be amputated. He refused to allow this, and took her to a ' white witch ' at Newton, who said she was overlooked by her grandfather. The ' white witch ', however, soon cured her.

[1] A strong calico or a coarse kind of linen named after the town of Daoulas in Brittany.

The Standard for 18th October 1877 reports a case containing some similar features :—

The case of the North Devon White Witch came before the Earl of Devon and other magistrates at Exeter yesterday. The name of the so-called witch is John Harper . . . The proceeding leading to his being brought before the magistrates arose in consequence of the death of the wife of a cattle doctor. A medical man . . . pronouncing her case hopeless, her husband went a journey of twelve miles to see a white witch. He . . . enquired as to the day, the hour and the planet under which she was born. From a box he produced some rods with the names of the planets written on parchment attached, and, placing them one at a time in the woman's hands, directed her to strike a piece of metal which he produced, and as she complied with her directions spoke some words in a low tone. He also . . . gave her a powder . . . She . . . died a day or two afterwards. When asked what his charges were the witch said twenty-five shillings, and that sum was paid him . . . Some persons spoke as to the cures effected by Harper in some cases after medical men had given up all hopes . . . It was denied that he said there must be three persons of one faith before he could do any good.

A resident in Exeter in 1898 wrote [1] as follows about local witch-beliefs :—

Two women of the lower classes were quarrelling violently the other evening in Heavitree, a suburb of Exeter. One yelled to the other, ' You wretch, you always keep a black and a white pig, so that you can witch us; you ought to be scragged ! ' The one so addressed, it seems, has lived in her cottage some twenty years. She has during this period always kept a couple of pigs, one of each colour; and her neighbours consider she does this so that she may enjoy the very questionable powers of witchcraft. No butcher in the neighbourhood will buy her pigs, as, if he were known to do so, he would certainly lose the local custom on which he relies.

To come to Devonshire witch-lore of a more recent date—*The Times* for 15th September 1926 contains an account of the defence of a man, summoned at Newton Abbot for deserting his wife. He stated that he could not endure the ' witchcraft ' business which she practised. She told fortunes and spoke to people about witchcraft. Also, when their boy was ill, she accused him of having put something on the rug to make him so. She also put salt round his chair. One day, when he had left his watch at home, his wife accused him of having placed it near her photograph to ' work ' on her.

Witch-beliefs in Cornwall appear to have been at least as

[1] *Notes and Queries*, 9th Series, vol. ii, pp. 466–7, 10th December 1898.

widespread and tenacious as those of Devon.   The following notes [1] were written in Cornwall in 1855:—

The belief in witchcraft holds its ground very firmly, and of all superstitions it will probably be the last to die out . . .   The notion that mysterious compacts are formed between evil spirits and wicked men has become almost obsolete.   In the present day such a bargain is rarely suspected, and there are few found hardy enough to avow themselves parties to so unholy a transaction.   One instance occurs to my memory of a poor unhappy fellow who pretended . . . to have sold himself to the devil . . . He was not, however, actively vicious . . . except . . . when the depth of his potations had not left him enough to pay his reckoning.   He was then accustomed to hold his hat up the chimney, and demand money, which was promptly showered down into it.   The coin so obtained the landlord invariably refused with a shudder, and was glad to get quit of him on those terms.   The faculty of witchcraft is held to be hereditary, and it is not the least cruel of the effects of this horrible creed that many really good-natured souls have on this account been kept aloof by their neighbours, and rendered miserable by being ever the object of unkind suspicions.   When communication with such persons cannot be avoided, their ill-will is deprecated by a slavish deference.   If met on the highway, care is taken to pass them on the right hand . . . Witches are supposed to have the power of changing their shape and resuming it again at will . . .   The most common results of the witches malice, or, as it is termed, *the ill-wish*, are misfortunes in business, diseases of an obstinate and deadly character in the family, or among cattle. . . .

An examination of these and many other recorded examples suggests that they are survivals of the witch-beliefs of the seventeenth century rather than products of the Methodist revival, though that revival may very well have tended to increase their vitality.   Such a conclusion is confirmed by a consideration of other areas of Britain where witch-beliefs have been most in evidence during the past century.   Thus, for example, Scotland, the land where witch-mania reached the highest intensity in the seventeenth century, remains relatively so to-day.   Out of a superabundance of examples a very few must suffice.

(ii) *The Morayshire Advertiser* for June 1862 contains the following paragraph:—

A farmer's wife in Kellas grew seriously ill the other day, and her imagination having struck her that she was bewitched, the sister of the far-famed Willox was consequently sent for, who came upwards of forty miles to visit the unfortunate woman.   She, being a believer in this superstitious idea, administered the following cure:—A large

---

[1] *Notes and Queries*, 1st Series, vol. xi, p. 497, 30th June 1855.

male cat was caught, and a fire kindled in the kail yard. The cat was then tied by the hind legs, and hung over the fire, and in this way burned to death.

In a report on the state of the prisons in Scotland for 1878 the following record appears in connexion with the county prison at Dingwall.[1]

> W.G. aged 24. I live near Tain and am a fisherman. I am in prison for assaulting a woman named M.M. She is about 60. I had assaulted her because she was 'bewitching' everything I had. She prevented me from catching fish, and caused my boat to be upset. The other men said they should have no chance of catching any herrings while I was with them, and they would not let me go out with them. M.M. is known by all the neighbourhood to be a *witch*. She has been a hundred times milking the cows in the shape of a hare, though I never saw her do so myself. People believe, in my neighbourhood, that if anyone gets blood from a witch she can do them no more harm, and that is the reason why I cut M. with my penknife; but I held the knife so that it might go into her as short a way as possible. All I wanted was to get blood. I was not the first person who wanted to draw blood from her. Those that advised me to cut her told me that if I did not she would drown me, and the rest who were in the boat with me, as sure as any man was ever drowned. It is hard to think I should be put in prison, for the Bible orders us to punish witches, and there is not a man on the jury who does not know M. to be a witch.

(iii) In England in the sixteenth and seventeenth centuries, it should be remembered, far more witches were put to death in Essex [2] than in any other shire. It is, consequently, a fact of some significance that records of witch-belief in modern times are peculiarly frequent here. A few examples out of many must suffice.

The *Daily News* for 22nd June 1880 contains the following report:—

> At the Dunmow Petty Sessions yesterday, Charles and Peter Brewster, father and son, two labouring men, were charged with misbehaving themselves towards Susan Sharpe, wife of an army pensioner living at High Easter, in a manner likely to lead to a breach of the peace. The evidence showed that defendants were under the impression that complainant was a witch, and they wanted to put her to the test by throwing her into a pond to see whether she would sink or float. They affirmed she had bewitched the younger defendant and his wife; the furniture in the house was dis-

---

[1] *Notes and Queries*, 5th Series, vol. x, p. 205.
[2] E. Smith, 'Witchcraft and Superstition' in *Memorials of Old Essex*, ed. A. Clifton Kelway, pp. 247 sqq. (London, 1908).

turbed, their domestic animals died, their bed rocked like a swinging boat, and shadows appeared in their bedroom; on one occasion there were three in bed to witness the shadowy apparition, and they strongly asserted that the ' shape ' was that of the complainant. The elder defendant had visited certain reputed ' cunning ' men and women in the villages around with a view to baffle the witch's evil designs, but without effect; ' all sorts of things ' had been tried, but they could get no peace, and the reports they set abroad caused quite an excitement in the locality. The Chairman (the Rev. E. F. Gepp) said such things as they had done might have led to a serious riot some years ago. They were bound over to keep the peace for six months.

It need scarcely be remarked that several features of this case are strangely reminiscent of things that happened in this region in the time of Matthew Hopkins.

The following extract from the *East London Advertiser* for 1st August 1903 indicates the survival of an older type of Essex witchcraft :—

> A Bishops Stortford barber was cutting the hair of a customer from a neighbouring village [1] on Tuesday, when he was requested to save a piece of hair from the nape of the neck. The barber ascertained that the man imagined someone in the village had done him an injury, and to have revenge he intended to cast a spell upon him. The hair from the nape of the heck, the lips, the armpits, the pairings of the nails, and other ingredients, mixed with water, were to be corked up in a bottle and placed on the fire at night. Desiring sickness to fall upon his enemy, his wish would be accomplished as the bottle burst, which would be as near midnight as possible.

Other parts of East Anglia and the neighbouring counties are almost as rich as Essex in examples of modern witch-mania, which form a link between almost contemporary events and the era of the Great Rebellion. It is true that other parts of Britain where the Parliamentarian cause found comparatively little support have provided examples of witch-belief in recent times—such as parts of Wales, Worcestershire, Warwickshire, Dorset, and Northumberland. But here their incidence appears to be less frequent and the beliefs themselves more vague and nebulous.

§ 3. The fury aroused amongst the common people in comparatively modern times by the suspicion of witchcraft is not without its relevance for the era of the Great Rebellion. It points to a far greater fury in an age when even stronger beliefs

---

[1] Bishops Stortford is on the Hertfordshire side of the border; but the context implies that the customer's village was in Essex.

in witchcraft were shared by most persons of authority and influence. It raises again the question whether Charles I's restraint of witch prosecutions infuriated a very considerable portion of his subjects, who had few other reasons for discontent, and drove them into the Parliamentarian camp.

The difficulty of arriving at a decisive answer lies in the tantalizing shortage of contemporary evidence. The output per annum of written or printed documents for the early Stuart period was far smaller than that of the succeeding periods, and fewer of them have survived. Nor is this the only difficulty. Many contemporary writers showed a curious reticence about witchcraft.[1] It has already been noted, for example, that Gilbert Burnet (1643–1715), in his *Life of Sir Matthew Hale* (1682), passes over in complete silence what are, perhaps, the most important features of the great judge's career—viz., his strongly expressed convictions about witchcraft and his sentences on some of the last witches to be put to death in this country. A similar reticence seems to have afflicted far more recent writers. Thus the *Dictionary of National Biography* devotes more than fifteen columns to the life of Richard Baxter but makes no mention of his many defences of witch-beliefs or of his *Certainty of the World of Spirits*, a work of outstanding importance, as the last of its kind to be published in England. Another difficulty is the inaccessibility of the material. There are, possibly, rich mines of material in the Record Office or in private hands which it has not yet been possible to exploit. Furthermore, most modern writers upon witchcraft have been more interested in its nature and alleged phenomena than in the effect of the superstition upon the course of English history.

In spite of these many impediments, certain tentative conclusions, though they go farther than the evidence warrants, may be stated. In the first place, it is clear that the Calvinists were, as far as evidence survives, invariably believers in the reality of witchcraft, and that the Royalists by the time of the Great Rebellion were, almost without exception, averse from the prose-

---

[1] At the trial of Alexander Sussums of Melford in 1645, it was stated that his mother and aunt had been hanged, and his grandmother burned, for witchcraft (C. L'Estrange Ewen, *Witchcraft and Demonianism*, p. 298). Yet no record of the trial or execution of any of these appears to exist. At the trial of Elizabeth Man of Wickham the same year it was stated that her mother had been hanged for a witch (op. cit., p. 292). The trial and execution of the mother appears to have left no trace.

cution of witches. Hence the Rebellion was, viewed from one standpoint, a struggle between the destroyers and the defenders of reputed witches.

Secondly, it is clear that by the time of the Great Rebellion the inhabitants of large and important regions of England had been indoctrinated with a witch-terror that rose to an all-absorbing obsession. Men of consequence pointed to almost all the common misfortunes—sickness or death of man or beast, storm and tempest, drought or floods, and failure of crops—as the work of witches, to be averted only by their destruction. With such instructors the multitude could scarcely fail to regard a government that protected witches as an intolerable menace to everything they valued, whether in this world or the next.[1] Hence many who did not necessarily share the religious, social, or constitutional motives of the Parliamentarians would be terrified into supporting them. Moreover, the repellant features of a Puritan ascendancy would be outweighed, to their terror-stricken view, by the alternative—destruction of body and soul by the emissaries of Satan. At the same time many would be attracted to Puritanism, not only as the one defence against a government that befriended witches, but as the one school of religious thought which faced, instead of minimizing or deriding, the reality of the black art. Thus when the balance stood even as between King and Parliament, witch-belief may well have been the make-weight that brought it down heavily on the Parliamentary side, and decided the fate of the royal cause and many other causes that were bound up with it. But for the strength of witch-belief the stream of English history from the seventeenth century to the present day might—for good or ill—have run through different channels and carried with it a different type of government, a different social structure, and even a somewhat different civilization. All this is, of course, merely a provisional hypothesis based on the scanty evidence as yet available and detailed in this volume. Vastly more evidence is required before

---

[1] There is, possibly, a hint of this view in Hobbes, *Leviathan*, ch. ii (1651): ' For as for witches ', he wrote, ' I think not that their witchcraft is any real power. . . . And for fairies and walking ghosts, the opinion of them has, I think, been on purpose, either taught or not confuted. . . . If this superstitious fear of spirits were taken away, and with it, prognostics from dreams, false prophecies, and many other things depending thereon, by which crafty ambitious persons abuse the simple people, men would be much more fitted than they are for civil obedience.'

its truth or falsity can be finally proved. It is quite conceivable that further research may result in its repudiation. Meanwhile it should be remembered that not once nor twice in the story of scientific research an hypothesis has done yeoman service before perishing at the hands of those whom it had itself refocillated.

BIBLIOGRAPHY

Works of the first importance for the study of English Witchcraft are marked with a double asterisk (**). Others of especial importance are given a single asterisk (*).

Abbotsford Club Miscellany, vol. i. (Edinburgh, 1837.)
Adams, W. H. D. *Witch, Warlock, and Magician*. (London, 1889.)
*Ady, T. *A Candle in the Dark*. (London, 1655, 2nd ed. 1661.)
Alse Gooderidge, The Most Wonderful and True Story of. (London, 1597.)
Amos, Andrew, *The Great Oyer of Poisoning, the Trial of the Earl of Somerset*. (London, 1846.)
Anonymous, *The Devil seen at St. Albans*. (1648.) A Satire.
Aquinas, St. Thomas. *Summa Theologica*. Pars Prima, l–lxiv, cx–cxiv. Prima Secundae, lxxv–lxxx, Secunda Secundae, xciv, xcv. (1274. Reprinted Paris, 1880.)
Archæologia, Index.
Arnot, Hugo. *Criminal Trials*. (Edinburgh, 1785.)
Arraignment and Trial of Jennet Preston, of Gisborne in Craven in the Countie of York. (London, 1612.)
Ashton, J. *The Devil in Britain and America*. (London, 1896.)
Aubrey, J. *Remains of Gentilism and Judaism*. (Ed. J. Britten, Folklore Soc. Publ., iv, 1881.)
—— *Miscellanies*. (1696 new ed., London, 1784.)
Baddeley, R. *The Boy of Bilson*. (London, 1622.)
Baines, Edward. *History of the County Palatine and Duchy of Lancaster*. (London, 1836.)
Baissac, Jules. *Les Grands Jours de la Sorcellerie*. (Paris, 1890.)
Bannatyne Club. *Memoirs of Sir James Melville*. (Edinburgh, 1827.)
—— *Historie and Life of King James the Sext*. (Edinburgh, 1825.)
—— *Diary of John Nicoll*. (Edinburgh, 1836.)
—— *Spottiswode's History of the Church of Scotland*. (Edinburgh, 1847–50.)
*Baxter, Richard. *Certainty of the World of Spirits*. (London, 1691.)
Beaumont, John. *Historical Treatise of Spirits*. (London, 1705.)
*Bernard, Richard. *Guide to Grand Jurymen*. (London, 1627; 1629; 1630.)
Berwickshire Naturalists Club, vol. xi. (Alnwick, 1887.)
Bezold, F. von. 'Jean Bodin als Okkultist und seine Démonomanie.' (In *Historische Zeitschrift*, Band 105, pp. 1 sqq., 1910.)
Bibliotheca Diabolica. (1874.)
Black, G. F. *A Calendar of Cases of Witchcraft in Scotland 1510–1727*. (New York, 1938.)
Black, G. F. *Scottish Antiquary*, vol. ix. (Edinburgh, 1895.)
Black, George F. *A List of Works Relating to Lycanthropy*. (New York Public Library, 1920.)
Blackwood's Edinburgh Magazine. (Edinburgh, 1817.) *Passim*.
Boas, R. P. and L. S. *Cotton Mather, Keeper of the Puritan Conscience*. (New York, 1928.)
Bodin, Jean. *De la Démonomanie des Sorciers*. (Paris, 1580; Rouen, 1604.)
An edition was published in Latin at Basle in 1581: *De Magorum Demonomania*.
—— *Le Fléau des Demons et Sorciers*. (Nyort, 1616.)
Boguet, Henri. *Discours des Sorciers*. (Lyons, 1608.)
Booker, J. *The Bloody Almanack*. (1643.)

Bourignon, Antoinette. *La Parole de Dieu.* (Amsterdam, 1683.)
—— *La Vie Exterieur.* (Amsterdam, 1683.)
Bovett, Richard. *Pandæmonium.* (London, 1684.)
Bower, Edmund. *Dr. Lambe Revived.* (London, 1653.)
Brand, John. *Popular Antiquities of Great Britain,* ed. W. C. Hazlitt, vol. iii. (London, 1870.)
Bragge, F. *The Witch of Walkerne.* (London, 1712.)
Brigges, Agnes. *The discovery of a late counterfeyted possession by the devyl in two maydens.* (1574.)
Bromhall, Thomas. *Treatise of Spectres.* (London, 1658.)
Browne, Sir Thomas. *Religio Medici.* (1642.)
Burkitt. *The Religion of the Manichees.* (Cambridge, 1925.)
Burns, Begg. *Proceedings of the Society of Antiquaries of Scotland.* New Series, vol. x. (Edinburgh.)
Burr, G. L. *Narratives of Witchcraft Cases.* (New York, 1914.)
—— 'New England's Place in the History of Witchcraft.' (*Proceedings of the American Antiquarian Society,* October 1911.)
Burton, J. H. *Criminal Trials in Scotland,* 2 vols. (London, 1852.)
—— *History of Scotland,* vol. iv, pp. 72, 320; vol. vii, pp. 114 sqq. (Edinburgh, 1873.)
Burton, Robert. *The Anatomy of Melancholy.* (London, 1621; 1624; 1632; 1638.)
Byloff, F. *Das Verbrechen der Zauberei—crimen magiae.* (Graz., 1902.)
Caillet, A. L. *Manuel Bibliographique des Sciences Psychiques où Occultes,* &c. 3 vols. (Paris, 1913.)
Calef, Robert. *More Wonders of the Invisible World.* (Salem, 1861.)
Calendar of State Papers, Domestic, 1584. (London, 1865.)
Calmet, A. *Traité sur les Apparitions des Esprits et sur les Vampires,* 2 vols. (Paris, 1751.)
Cambridge History of English Literature, vol. vii, ch. xvi, *The Witch Controversy Pamphleteers,* by H. V. Routh. (Cambridge, 1911.)
Campbell, John Gregorson. *Superstitions of the Highlands.* (Glasgow, 1902.)
Carpzov, Benedict. *Practicae novae . . . rerum criminalium.* (Leipzig, 1635.)
Casaubon, Meric. *A Treatise Concerning Enthusiasm.* (London, 1665.)
—— *Credulity and Incredulity.* (London, 1668; 2nd pt., 1670.)
—— *A True and Faithful Relation of what passed for many yeers Between Dr. Dee and Some Spirits.* (London, 1859.)
Chambers, Robert. *Domestic Annals of Scotland.* (Edinburgh, 1861.)
Chetham Society, *Moore Rental.* (Manchester, 1847.)
—— *Potts, Discoverie of Witchcraft.* (Manchester, 1858.)
Clarke, Samuel. *Lives of Two and Twenty English Divines.* (London, 1660.)
—— *Lives of Sundry Eminent Persons in this Later Age,* pp. 172 sqq. (London, 1683.)
Coate, M. *Social Life in Stuart England,* p. 163. (London, 1924.)
Coke, Sir Ed. *Institute,* pt. iii, ch. 6.
Collection of Modern Relations of Matter of Fact Concerning Witches, Witchcraft. (London, 1693.)
Collection of Rare and Curious Tracts relating to Witchcraft. (London, 1838.)
Collin de Plancy. *Dictionnaire Infernale,* 4 vols. (Paris, 1825–26.)
Cook, John. *Charles I, his Case,* p. 27. (London, 1649.)
Cooper, Margaret. *A True and Most Dreadful Discourse of a Woman possessed with the Devill.* (1584; reprinted 1886.)
*Cooper, Thomas. *The Mystery of Witchcraft.* (London, 1617.)
—— *Pleasant Treatise of Witches.* (London, 1673.)
*Cotta, J. *Triall of Witch-craft.* (London, 1616.)
*—— *Infallible True and Assured Witch.* (London, 1625.)
County Folklore, vol. iii: *Orkney.* (London, 1901.)
Crawfurd, Raymond. *The King's Evil.* (Oxford, 1911.)

Crouch, Nathaniel. See ' R.B.'
Cudworth, Ralph. *The True Intellectual System of the Universe.* (1678.)
Cunningham, Allan. *Traditional Tales of the English and Scottish Peasantry.* (London, 1874.)
Cutts, E. L. ' Curious Extracts from a MS. Diary of the Time of James II and William and Mary.' In *Transactions of the Essex Archæological Society,* vol. i, pp. 117 sqq. (Colchester, 1858.)
Dalton, M. *The Country Justice.* (London, 1618; latest ed., 1746.)
Dalyell, J. G. *The Darker Superstitions of Scotland.* (Edinburgh, 1834.)
Danaeu, Lambert. *De Veneficiis.* (Cologne, 1575.) Published originally in French at Geneva in 1564, and subsequently translated into Latin, English and German.
Darrell, John. *A Brief Relation of the Possession of W. Sommers.* (1598.)
—— *A Narrative of the Grievous Vexation by the Devil of Seven Persons in Lancashire.* (1600.)
d'Autun, Jacques. *L'incrédulité sçavante et la crédulité ignorante.* (1674.)
Davenport, J. *The Witches of Huntingdon.* (London, 1646.)
Davies, J. Ceredig. *Welsh Folklore.* (Aberystwith, 1911.)
Defoe, D. *A System of Magic or a History of the Black Art.* (London, 1727, published anonymously.)
De la Martinière. *Voyage des Pais Septentrionaux.* (Paris, 1682.)
Delassus, Jules. *Les Incubes et les Succubes.* (Paris, 1897.)
De Lancre, Pierre. *L'Incredulité et Mescreance du Sortilege.* (Paris, 1622.)
—— *Tableau de l'Inconstance des mauvais Anges.* (Paris, 1613.)
Delrio, M. A. *Disquisitionum Magicarum Libri Sex.* (Louvain, 1599.)
Denham Tracts. (London, 1895.)
Detection of Damnable Drifts. (1579.)
De Valle de Moura. *Liber de Incantationibus seu Ensalmis.* (Evora, 1620.)
Diefenbach, G. *Hexenwahn vor und nach der Glaubenspaltung.* (Frankfort, 1886.)
Divels Delusions, The. (London, 1649.)
Doctor Lamb's Darling : or Strange and Terrible News from Salisbury. (London, 1653.)
Doctor Lamb Revived, or Witchcraft condemn'd in Anne Bodenham. (London, 1653.)
Doughty, H. N. *Blackwood's Magazine,* March 1898.
Echard, L. *History of England,* 3rd ed. (London, 1720.)
Elich, Philip Ludwig. *Daemonomagia, sive de demonis cacurgia.* (Frankfort, 1607.)
Elven, Henry van. *La Tradition,* vol. v. (Paris, 1895.)
Ennemoser, Joseph. *History of Magic.* English trans., 2 vols. (London, 1854.)
**Ewen, C. L'Estrange. *Witch Hunting and Witch Trials.* (London, 1929.)
—— **Witchcraft and Demonianism.* (London, 1933.)
—— *Witchcraft and the Star Chamber.* (Printed for the Author, 1938.)
—— *Witchcraft in the Norfolk Circuit.* (1939.)
—— ' Robert Radcliffe, fifth Earl of Sussex: Witchcraft Accusations.' In *Transactions of the Essex Archæological Soc.,* vol. xxii, pp. 232 sqq. (Colchester, 1940.)
Examination of Certain Witches at Chelmsford. Philobiblion Society, vol. viii. (London, 1863-4.)
Examination of A. Baker, Joane Willimot, and Ellen Greene. (London, 1619.)
Examination of Joane Williford, Joan Cariden, and Jane Hott. (London, 1645.) Reprinted in *Collection of Rare and Curious Tracts.* (London, 1838.)
Examination of John Walsh. (London, 1566.)
*Fairfax, Edward. *Demonologia,* ed. W. Grainge. (Harrogate, 1882.) This was originally published in 1622 under the title: *A Discourse of Witchcraft as it was acted in the Family of Mr. Edward Fairfax, &c.* It was reprinted in the Philobiblion Soc. Miscellanies, vol. v. (1858-9.)
Farnsworth, R. *Witchcraft lashed out from the Religious Seed and Israel of God.* (1655.)

Ferguson, J. *Bibliographical Notes on the Witchcraft Literature of Scotland.* (Edinburgh, 1897.)

*Filmer, Sir Robert. *An Advertisement to the Jurymen of England touching Witches.* (1653.)

Flower, *The Wonderful Discoverie of the Witchcrafts of Margaret and Philip.* (London, 1619.)

Fludd, R. *Dr. Fludd's answer to M. Foster.* (1631; 1638.)

Forbes, William. *Institutes of the Law of Scotland.* (Edinburgh, 1722–30.)

Foster, Tryall of Ann. (Northampton, 1881.)

Fountainhall, Lord. *Decisions.* (Edinburgh, 1759.)

Foxe, John. *History of the Acts and Monuments of the Church.* (1st ed., 1563; 2nd, 1570; 3rd, 1576; 4th, 1583; 5th, 1596); ed. Josiah Pratt (London, 1877), vol. ii, 95, 121; iii, 131, 850; iv, 656; v, 129, &c., &c.

Frazer, J. G. *Balder the Beautiful,* vols. i and ii. (London, 1913.)

Full Tryals of Notorious Witches at Worcester. (London, n.d.)

Gage, Thomas. *The English-American his Travail by Sea and Land,* pp. 167 sqq. (London, 1648.)

Gardiner, Ralph. *England's Grievance,* &c. (London, 1655.)

Gardiner, S. R. *History of England from the Accession of James I,* vol. vii. (London, 1891.)

Gaule, J. *Select Cases of Conscience.* (London, 1646.)

—— *Occult Philosophie.* (n.d.)

—— *The Mag-Astro-Mancer.* (London, 1652.)

Gee, John. *The Foot out of the Snare.* (London, 1624.)

Gemmill, W. N. *The Salem Witch Trials.* (Chicago, 1924.)

Gentleman's Magazine.

Gentleman's Magazine Library : English Topography, vol. iv, p. 88; vol. viii, p. 113.

—— Popular Superstitions: Index.

Gerish, William Blyth. *Relation of Mary Hall of Gadsden.* (1912.)

—— *The Divel's Delusions.* Bishops Stortford. (1914.)

—— *The Severall Practices of Johane Harrison.* (1909.)

—— *Witchcraft Cases from the Hertfordshire Records 1589–1670.* (1920.)

Gibbons, A. *Ely Episcopal Records.* (Lincoln, 1891.)

Giffard, George. *A Dialogue concerning Witches and Witchcraftes.* (London, 1593; 1603; Shakespeare Assoc., Oxford, 1931.)

—— *Discourse of the Subtle Practices of Devils.* (1587.)

Gilbert, W. 'Witchcraft in Essex.' (*Transactions of the Essex Archæological Soc.,* vol. xi, New Series, 1911, pp. 211 sqq.)

Giraldus Cambrensis. *Opera* (Rolls Series), vol. v, p. 106.

*Glanvil, Joseph. *Sadducismus Triumphatus.* (London, 1689.)

Godwin, William. *Lives of the Necromancers.* (London, 1834.)

Goldsmid, E. *Confessions of Witches under Torture.* (Edinburgh, 1886.)

Goodcole, Henry. *Wonderfull Discoverie of Elizabeth Sawyer.* (London, 1621.)

Goulart, S. *Thrésor des histories admirables.* (1610.)

Grainge, W. See 'Fairfax'.

Grässe, J. G. T. *Bibliotheca Magica et Pneumatica.* (Leipzig, 1843.)

Green, S. A. *Groton in Witchcraft Times.* (Cambridge, Mass., 1883.)

Greve, J. (An Arminian preacher of Arnheim, Holland.) *Tribunal Reformatum.* (1622.)

Grillandus, Paul. *Tractatus duo de Sortilegiis et Lamiis.* (Frankfort, 1592.)

Grillot de Givry. *Witchcraft, Magic and Alchemy.* (London, 1931.)

Guazzo, F. M. *Compendium Maleficarum.* (Milan, 1608.)

Hale, John. *A Modest Enquiry,* ed. Burr. (New York, 1914.)

*Hale, Sir Matthew. *Collection of Modern Relations.* (London, 1693.)

Hallywell, Henry. *Melampronoea ; or a Discourse on the Polity and Kingdom of Darkness.* (London, 1681.)

Hansen, J. *Quellen und Untersuchungen zur Geschichte des Hexenwahns.* (Bonn, 1901.)
Harflete, H. *Vox Caelorum, Predictions Defended.* (1646.)
Harou, Alfred. *La Tradition,* vol. vi. (Paris, 1892.)
H(arrison), R(obert). *Of Ghostes and Spirites walking by Night.* (1572. Ed. for Shakespeare Assoc., 1929.)
*Harsnett, Samuel. *A discovery of the Fraudulent Practices of J. Darrell.* (1599.)
*——— *A Declaration of the Egregious Popish Impostures.* (1603; re-issued 1604, 1605.)
Hartwell, Abraham. *A True Discourse upon the Matter of Martha Brossier of Romorantin.* Translated out of French. (London, 1599.)
Hector, William. *Judicial Records of Renfrewshire.* (Paisley, 1876.)
Heywood, Thomas. Γυναικειον, *or nine Books of Various History concerning Women.* (London, 1624.)
——— *The Hierarchy of Blessed Angels.* (London, 1635.)
Heywood and Broome, Richard. *The Late Lancashire Witches.* (1634.)
Hibbert, Samuel. *Description of the Shetland Isles.* (Edinburgh, 1922.)
Highland Papers, vol. iii, *Witchcraft in Bute.* (Edinburgh, 1920.)
Historical MSS. Comm. Reports, vol. i, 122, vi, 104, vii, 111, 145.
Hole, Christina. *Witchcraft in England.* (London, 1945.)
Holland, H. *A Treatise against Witchcraft.* (Cambridge, 1590.)
——— *Spiritual Preservatives against the Pestilence.* (1593.)
Hollingshed (or Holingshed), Raphael. *Chronicles.* (London, 1587.)
Hollingsworth, A. G. *History of Stowmarket.* (Ipswich, 1844.)
Homes, N. *Daemonologie and Theologie.* (1650.)
*Hopkins, Matthew. *Discovery of Witches.* (London, 1647, ed. M. Summers, 1928.)
Horneck, Anthony. Appendix to Glanvil's *Sadducismus Triumphatus.* (London, 1681.)
Horst, K. *Dämonologie oder Geschichte des Glaubens an Zauberei.* (Frankfort, 1818.)
Howell, J. *Familiar Letters.* (Ed. Joseph Jacobs, 2 vols., London, 1890–2.)
**Hutchinson, Francis. *Historical Essay concerning Witchcraft.* (London, 1718.)
Hutchinson, John. *History of the Province of Massachuset's Bay.* (1828.)
Inch, Trial of Isobel. (Ardrossan,? 1855.)
Ives, G. *A History of Penal Methods,* ch. ii, ' The Witch Trials '. (1914.)
Jaggard, W. *Folklore, Superstition and Witchcraft in Shakespeare. A Bibliography.* (1896.)
*James I. *Daemonologie.* (Edinburgh, 1597; 2nd ed., London, 1603; reprinted 1924.)
Jones, Edmund. *A Relation of Apparitions of Spirits in the County of Monmouth and Principality of Wales.* (Newport, 1813.)
Jonson, Ben. *The Devil is an Ass.* (First acted, 1616.)
——— *The Masque of the Queenes.* (1609.)
Jordan, Edward. *A brief discourse of the disease called the Suffocation of the Mother.* (1603.)
Journal of Anatomy, vols. xiii and xxv. (London, 1879, 1891.)
Journal d'un bourgeois de Paris. Panthéon Littéraire. (Paris, 1838.)
Justiciary Court, Edinburgh, Records of the Proceedings of. (Edinburgh, 1905.)
Kampschulte, F. W. *Johann Calvin seine Kirche und Sein Staat in Genf,* vol. i. (Leipzig, 1869.)
Kittredge, G. L. *English Witchcraft and James I.* (New York, 1912.)
*——— *Witchcraft in Old and New England.* (Cambridge, Mass., 1929.)
Kopp, H. *Die Alchemie in älterer und neuerer Zeit,* 2 vols. (Heidelberg, 1886.)
Ladame, P. *Procès criminel de la dernière sorcière brûlée à Genève 1652.* (Paris, 1888.)
——— *Les Mandragores à Genève au xvi me et xvii me siècles.* (1892.)

Längin, G. *Religion und Hexenprozesse.* (Leipzig, 1888.)
Lamont, John. *Diary.* Maitland Club. (Edinburgh, 1830.)
Lavater, Lewes. *Of Ghosts and Spirites Walking by Nyght* (1572), ed. Wilson and Yardley. (Oxford, 1929.) The first ed. was published at Zürich in 1569 in German. French ed. (Geneva and Paris, 1571); Latin trans. (Zürich, 1570.)
Law, Robert. *Memorialls.* (Ed. Sharpe, Edinburgh, 1818.)
Law, T. G. 'Devil-Hunting in Elizabethan England' (in *The Nineteenth Century,* March 1894).
Lawes against Witches and Coniuration and some brief Notes and Observations for the Discovery of Witches. Being very useful for these Times, wherein the Devil reignes and prevailes over the Soules of poor Creatures, in drawing them to that crying Sin of Witchcraft. . . . Published by Authority. (London, 1645.)
**Lea, H. C. *Materials towards a History of Witchcraft,* 3 vols. (Philadelphia, 1939.)
—— *History of the Inquisition in the Middle Ages,* 3 vols. (1888.)
—— *History of the Inquisition in Spain,* 4 vols. (New York, 1906–7.)
*Lecky, W. H. *History of Rationalism in England,* vol. i, new ed. (London, 1912.)
—— *History of England in the Eighteenth Century,* 3rd ed., vol. i, pp. 266–7; iii, p. 504.
Legge, F. 'Witchcraft in Scotland' (in *Scottish Review,* vol. xviii, October 1891).
Legué, G. *Urbain Grandier et les possédées de Loudon.* (Paris, 1884.)
Lemoine, Jules. *La Tradition,* vol. vi. (Paris, 1892.)
Lilburn, John. *Innocency and Truth Justified against the aspersions of W. Prinn.* (1646.)
Lilly, William. *Christian Astrology Modestly Treated in three books.* (1647.)
—— *Monarchy or No Monarchy in England.* (1651.)
—— *An Easie Method whereby to Judge the Effects depending on Eclipses.* (1652.)
—— *Anima Astrologiae or a Guide for the Astrologers.* (1676.)
Lynn Linton, Mrs. *Witch Stories.* (London, 1861 and 1883.)
Mackenzie, Sir George. *Laws and Customs of Scotland.* (Edinburgh, 1699.)
Madden, R. R. *Phantasmata or Illusions and Fanaticisms,* 2 vols. (London, 1857.)
Maitland Club Miscellany, vol. ii. (Glasgow, 1840.)
Maitland, S. R. *Puritan Thaumaturgy.*
Mason, J. *Anatomie of Sorcery.* (1612.)
Massé, Pierre. *De l'imposture et tromperie des diables, devins, enchanteurs, &c.* (Paris, 1579.)
Masson. *La Sorcellerie au xvii Siècle.* (Paris, 1904.)
Mather, Cotton. *Discourse on the Wonders of the Invisible World.* (Boston, 1693.)
—— *Memorable Providences relating to Witchcraft and Possession.* (Boston, 1689.)
Mather, Increase. *Remarkable Providences.* (London, 1890.)
Maury, Alfred. *La Magie et L'Astrologie,* 3 ed. (Paris, 1864.)
Meyer, Carl. *Der Aberglaube des Mittelalters und der nächst folgenden Jahrhunderte.* (Basel, 1884.)
Michaelis, Sebastian. *Admirable Historie of the Possession and Conversion of a Penitent Woman.* (London, 1613.)
—— *A Discourse of Spirits.* (London, 1613.) Trans. from French (Paris, 1587).
Michelet, J. *La Sorcière.* (Paris, 1862.)
Middlesex County Records. *Index.*
Moore, G. H. *Bibliographical Notes on Witchcraft.* (1888.)
*More, Henry. *Antidote against Atheism.* (London, 1653.)
Murray, M. A. *The Witch-Cult in Western Europe.* (Oxford, 1921.) Contains a useful bibliography.
—— *The God of the Witches.* (London, 1933.)
—— 'Witchcraft' (in *Encycl. Britannica,* 14th ed.) (London, 1929.)

Murray, T. D. *Jeanne d'Arc.* (London, 1902.)
Narrative of the Sufferings of a Young Girle. (Edinburgh, 1698.)
Nashe, Thomas. *The Terrors of the Night.* (1594.) *Nashe's Works,* ed. McKerrow, R.B., 5 vols. (1904–10.)
Negelin, J. von. *Weltgeschichte des Aberglaubens.* (Berlin, 1931.)
Nicolai, Heinrich. *De Magicis Actionibus.* (Dantzig, 1649.)
Nider, J. *Formicarius.* (Douai, 1602.)
Nodé, Pierre. *Déclamation contre l'Erreur exécrable des Maléficiers Sorcieres,* &c. (Paris, 1578.)
North Riding Record Society, vol. iii. *Index.*
Notes and Queries, 2nd Series, vol. vii, p. 147 (1859); vol. ix, pp. 11, 266 (1860); 6th Series, vol. xii, p. 259; 10th Series, vol. ii, pp. 265, 491, &c., &c.
**Notestein, Wallace. *History of Witchcraft in England.* (Washington, 1911.)
Nynauld, J. de. *De la Lycanthropie, transformation et extase des Sorciers, avec la réfutation des argumens de Bodin.* (Paris, 1615.)
Owen, Ch. *The Scene of Delusions.* (London, 1712.)
Parker Society. *Index.*
Pastor, L. von. *History of the Popes from the Close of the Middle Ages.* Eng. trans., vol. v, pp. 347 sqq. (London, 1898.) (On the Bull of 1484.)
Paulus, N. *Hexenwahn und Hexenprozess in 16te Jahrhundert.* (Freiburg I.B., 1910.)
Pearson, Karl. *Chances of Death.* (London, 1897.)
Peck, Francis. *Desiderata Curiosa,* vol. ii, Lib. xii. (London, 1735.)
*Perkins, W. *Discourse on the Damned Art of Witchcraft.* (Cambridge University Press, 1608; 10, 29.)
Perreauld, François. *The Devill of Mascon.* Trans. by Du Moulin (1658) of *Démonologie.* (1653.)
Peterson, Tryall of Mrs. Joan. (London, 1652.) Thomason Tracts.
Petto, Samuel. *A faithful Narrative.* (London, 1693.)
Philipps, Fabian. *King Charles the First no Man of Blood but a Martyr for his People.* (1649.)
Pike, L. O. *History of Crime in England.* (London, 1873–6.)
Pinkerton, John. *Voyages.* (London, 1808–14.)
Pitcairn, Robert. *Criminal Trials.* (Edinburgh, 1833.)
Pittenweem, A true and full Relation of the Witches of. (Edinburgh, 1704.)
Pitts, J. L. *Witchcraft and Devil Lore in the Channel Islands.* (Guernsey, 1886.)
Pleasant Treatise of Witches. (London, 1673.)
*Potts, Thomas. *Discoverie of Witches.* (London, 1613.) Reprinted by Chetham Society. (Manchester, 1845.) Ed. G. B. Harrison. (1929.)
Pressey, W. J. ' The Records of the Archdeaconries of Essex and Colchester.' (*Transactions of the Essex Archæological Soc.,* vol. xix, New Series, 1930, pp. 1 sqq.)
Preston, John (Master of Emmanuel College, Cambridge). *Sermon before his Majesty* (i.e., James I), p. 33. (London, 1630.)
Quibell, J. E. *Hierakonpolis,* vol. ii. (London, 1902.)
Ravaisson, François. *Archives de la Bastille.* (Paris, 1873.)
R.B. *The Kingdom of Darkness.* (London, 1706.) R.B. stands for Richard Burton, a pseudonym of Nathaniel Crouch, the publisher.
Records of the Justiciary Court of Edinburgh. (Edinburgh, 1905.)
Reinach, S. *Orpheus.* (1910.)
—— *Cults, Myths, and Religions.* (Trans. 1912.)
Remigius, Nicholas. *Demonolatria.* (Colon. Agripp, 1596; 1st ed., Lyons, 1595; Hamburg, 1693.)
Reresby, Sir John. *Memoirs and Travels.* (London, 1813.)
Reyburn, H. Y. *John Calvin,* p. 129. (London, 1914.)
Ricardus, A. *De praestigiis et incantationibus daemonum.* (Basel, 1568.)
*Roberts, Alexander. *Treatise of Witchcraft.* (London, 1618.)

Römer, W. *Der Hexenbulle des Papster Innocenz viii.* (Schaffhausen, 1889.)
Roset, Michel. *Les Chroniques de Genève,* ed. H. Fazy, pp. 306–8. (Geneva, 1894.)
Roskoff, G. *Geschichte der Teufels.* (Leipzig, 1869.)
Ross, William. *Aberdour and Inchcolme.* (Edinburgh, 1885.)
Rymer, Thomas. *Foedera.* (London, 1704.)
Sadducismus Debellatus. (London, 1698.)
St. Osees, A true and just Recorde of all the Witches taken at. (London, 1582.)
Sandys, George. *Relation of a Journey.* (London, 1632.)
Saunders, W. H. B. *Legends and Traditions of Huntingdonshire.* (1886.)
Sawyer, Wonderful Discoverie of Elizabeth. (1621.)
Scheltema, J. *Geschiednis der Hecksenprocessen.* (Haarlem, 1828.)
Scheible, J. *Kleine Wunder-Schauplatz.* (1855.)
*Scot, Reginald. *Discoverie of Witchcraft.* (London, 1584; 1651; 1665.) Reprinted, 1886; ed. M. Summers, 1930.
Scots Magazine. (Edinburgh, 1772 and 1814.)
Scott, Sir Walter. *Demonology and Witchcraft.* Murray's Family Library, 1829–47. Reprinted London, 1883.
Scottish Antiquary, vol. ix. (Edinburgh, 1891.)
Scottish Historical Society, vol. xxv. (Edinburgh, 1896.)
Sedgewick, William. *The Spirituall Madman.* (1648.)
Selden, John. *Table-Talk.* Ed. R. Milward, 1689; ed. S. H. Reynolds. (Oxford, 1892.)
Sergeant, P. W. *Witches and Warlocks.* (1936.)
Severo, S. *El Nigromantico.* (Granada, 1670.)
Seymour, St. J. D. *Irish Witchcraft and Demonology.* (Dublin, 1913.)
Sharpe, Charles Kirkpatrick. *Historical Account of Witchcraft in Scotland.* (London, 1884.)
Shaw, Elinor and Mary Phillips. (Northampton, 1866.)
Sinclair, George. *The Hydrostaticks.* (Edinburgh, 1672.)
*—— *Satan's Invisible World Discovered.* (Edinburgh, 1685.)
Sinclair, John. *Statistical Account of Scotland,* vol. xviii. (Edinburgh, 1796.)
Sinistrari de Ameno, L. M. *Demoniality.* (Paris, 1879.)
Smith, Charlotte Fell. *John Dee (1527–1608).* (London, 1909.)
Smith, Edward. 'Witchcraft and Superstition' (in *Memorials of Old Essex,* ed. Clifton Kelway). (London, 1908.)
Society of Antiquaries of Scotland. New Series, vol. x. (Edinburgh.)
*Soldan, W. G. and Heppe, U. *Geschichte der Hexenprozesse,* 3rd ed. by Max Bauer. (Munich, 1912.)
Spalding Club Miscellany. (Aberdeen, 1841.)
Spee, Friedrich von. *Cautio Criminalis.* (Rinteln, 1631; Cologne and Frankfort, 1632.)
Spence, Lewis. *An Encyclopædia of Occultism.* (London, 1920.)
Spottiswode, John. *History of the Church of Scotland.* (Edinburgh, 1847–50.)
Spottiswoode Miscellany. (Edinburgh, 1844–5.)
*Sprenger, J., and Institoris, H. *Malleus Maleficarum.* (1489; Lyons, 1669.) German trans. (Berlin, 1906); English trans., 1928.
Stearne, John. *Confirmation and Discovery of Witchcraft.* (London, 1648.)
Steinhausen, G. *Quellen und Studien zur Geschichte der Hexenprozesse.* (1898.)
Stewart, W. G. *Popular Superstitions of the Highlanders.* (Edinburgh, 1823.)
Stoeber, A. *Zur Geschichte des Volksaberglauben im Anfänge des 16 Jahrhunderts.* 2nd ed. (Basle, 1875.)
Strange Relation of a Young Woman possesst with a Devill. By name Joyce Dovey, dwelling at Bewdley near Worcester. (London, 1647.)
*Summers, Montague. *The Geography of Witchcraft.* (London, 1927.)
*—— *History of Witchcraft.* (London, 1927.) Contains a useful bibliography.
*—— *A Popular History of Witchcraft.* (London, 1937.)
Surtees Society, vol. xl. (Durham, 1861.)

Tandler, Tobias. *De Spectris, de Fascinio et Incantatione.*
Tanner. *Theologica Scholastica.* 4 vols. (Ingolstadt, 1626.)
Taylor, John. *Tracts relating to Northamptonshire.* (Northampton, 1866.) .
—— *The Witchcraft Delusion in Colonial Connecticut.* (New York n. d.)
Thomas, N. W. 'Witchcraft' in *Encycl. Britannica.* 11th ed. (Cambridge, 1911.)
Thorpe, Benjamin. *Monumenta Ecclesiastica.* (? London, 1840.)
Torreblanca, F. *Daemonologia sive de Magiae naturali doemonica licita et illicita.*
    (Mainz, 1623.)
*True and Exact Relation of the Severall Informations Examinations and Confessions of
    the late Witches, arraigned and executed in the County of Essex.* (London, 1645.)
True and Faithfull Relation of what passed between Dr. Dee and some spirits. (London,
    1659.) Preface by Meric Casaubon.
True and iust Recorde of all the Witches taken at St. Oses. By W. W. (London,
    1582.)
Tryalls of Four Notorious Witches at Worcester. (London, n. d.)
Tuke, H. *History of Insanity in the British Isles.* (London, 1882.)
Tylor, E. B. *Primitive Culture.* (New ed. London, 1920.)
Vetter. *Relations between England and Zurich during the Reformation.* (London,
    1904.)
Vicars, T. *The Madnesse of Astrologers.* (1624.)
*Wagstaffe, J. *Question of Witchcraft.* (London, 1669; 2nd ed., 1671.)
Walker, John. *Sufferings of the Clergy of England,* p. 299. (London, 1714.)
Walsh, Examination of John. (London, 1566.)
Warboys, The most strange Discovery of the Three Witches of. (1593.)
Warren, H. *Magic and Astrology vindicated from false aspersions.* (1651.)
Waterhouse, E. *An Humble Apologie for Learning and Learned Men.* (1653.)
*Webster, J. *Displaying of Supposed Witchcraft.* (London, 1677.)
Weyer, J. (Wierus). *De Praestigiis daemonun et incantationibus et veneficiis.* (Basle,
    1563, 1564; 3rd ed., 1566; 4th ed., 158.)
—— *De Lamiis.* (Basle, 1577, 1582. German trans. Frankfort, 1586.)
—— *Opera Omnia.* (Amsterdam, 1660.)
Whitaker, T. D. *History of Whalley.* (London, 1818.)
White, A. D. *History of the Warfare of Science with Theology.* 2 vols. (New
    York, 1896.)
Whitelock, B. *Memorials.* (1682; 2nd ed., 1732.) *Index.*
Whiting, C. E. *Studies in English Puritanism from the Restoration to the Revolution
    1660–88.* (London, 1931.)
Williams, Charles. *Witchcraft.* (London, 1941.)
Williams, Howard. *The Superstitions of Witchcraft.* (London, 1865.)
Wilson, Arthur. *Life and Reign of James I,* pp. 107–12.
Winsor, J. 'The Literature of Witchcraft in New England.' (*Proceedings
    of the American Antiquarian Soc.,* 1895.)
Witch of Wapping, The. Thomason Tracts. (London, 1652.)
Witchcraft, Collection of Rare and Curious Tracts on. (Edinburgh, 1820.)
Witches of Northamptonshire. (London, 1612.)
Wittman, A. *Die Gestalt der Hexe in der deutschen Sage.* (Bruchsal, 1933.)
Wonderfull Discoverie of Elizabeth Sawyer. (London, 1621.)
Wonderful Discoverie of the Witchcrafts of Margaret and Philip Flower. (London,
    1619.)
*Wonderfull News from the North, or a True Relation of the Sad and Grievous Torments,
    inflicted upon the Bodies of three Children of Mr. George Muschamp, late of the
    County of Northumberland, by Witchcraft.* (London, 1650.)
*Wright, T. *Narratives of Sorcery and Magic.* 2 vols. (London, 1852.)
York Castle Depositions. (Surtees Society.)
Yve-Plessis, R. *Essai d'une Bibliographie française méthodique et raisonné de la
    Sorcellerie.* (Paris, 1901.)
Zockler. 'Hexen und Hexenprozesse' in Hauck's *Realencyklopädie für
    protestantische Theologie und Kirche.* (Leipzig, 1900.)

INDEX